DEFENDING TRINITY COLLEGE DUBLIN, EASTER 1916

The general had so wished to do this, and was so sorry he had not managed to do it that it seemed to him as if it had really happened. Perhaps it might really have been so? Could one possibly make out amid all that confusion what did or did not happen?

—Tolstoy, *War and Peace*

Defending Trinity College Dublin, Easter 1916

Anzacs and the Rising

Rory Sweetman

FOUR COURTS PRESS

Set in 10.5pt on 13.5pt CaslonPro by
Carrigboy Typesetting Services for
FOUR COURTS PRESS LTD
7 Malpas Street, Dublin 8, Ireland
www.fourcourtspress.ie
and in North America for
FOUR COURTS PRESS
c/o IPG, 814 N Franklin St, Chicago, IL 60622.

A catalogue record for this title is available
from the British Library.

ISBN 978-1-84682-784-6

Trinity College Dublin
Association & Trust

Printed in England,
by TJ International, Padstow, Cornwall.

In memory of my father, Patrick Gerard Sweetman (1919–2001), his brothers, Jimmy, Tommy and Matt, and his sisters, Mary, Peggy, Liz, Nora, Eileen, Josie, Kitty and Christine.

Contents

LIST OF ILLUSTRATIONS 9
ACKNOWLEDGMENTS 11
ABBREVIATIONS 13
FOREWORD 15
INTRODUCTION 17
1. Remembering and forgetting 21
2. 'That English fort in Ireland' 30
3. 'Duty well fulfilled' 36
4. From the uttermost ends of the Earth 55
5. Whatiffery 76
6. Epilogue 82
APPENDICES: letters and reports 97
DRAMATIS PERSONAE 142
BIBLIOGRAPHY 147
INDEX 159

Illustrations

(between pages 64 and 65)

1. Map of Trinity College (1913).
2. The official party at the OTC review.
3. General Maxwell inspecting the OTC.
4. Major R.W. Tate speaking at the cup presentation ceremony.
5. Prime Minister Asquith leaving Richmond Barracks.
6. Professor John Joly.
7. Captain Ernest Alton.
8. Corporal John Godwin Garland.
9. Map showing the OTC headquarters and parade ground.
10. British troops in Parliament (Front) Square during Easter Week.
11. 'The morning wash – Troops in Trinity College'.
12. 'The British Lion and his cubs aroused'.
13. Anzacs crossing College Green after the Rising ended.
14. 'These Anzacs assisted in quelling the Dublin disturbances'.
15. The ruins of Wynn's Hotel.
16. The north-eastern corner of Trinity College's grounds.
17. A map showing the dispositions of the crown and rebel forces.
18. The ruins of the GPO from atop Nelson's Pillar.
19. British soldiers and a solitary porter guarding Front Gate.
20. The *Marama* leaving Wellington on 5 December 1915.
21. New Zealand troops raising the Union Jack after landing in Samoa.
22. 'The beach at Gallipoli where the men of Anzac had their baptism of fire and took their places as world's heroes'.
23. Volunteer Gerald Keogh.
24. Volunteer Captain Frank Thornton.
25. Alexander Don and his siblings in London.
26. Alexander Don in 1916.
27. Alexander Don's silver cup.
28. The Bank of Ireland facing Trinity College's main entrance.
29. Trinity's West Front building on Peace Day, 19 July 1919.

Credits

1, 2, 3, 4, 6, 7, 9, 10, 16, 28: Trinity College Dublin; 5, 15, 18: National Library of Ireland; 8, 12, 20, 21, 22: Auckland Libraries Heritage Collections; 11: Royal Irish Academy; 13, 19: Imperial War Museum, London; 17: *Irish Sword*; 23, 24: *History Ireland*; 25, 26: Mrs Valerie Gough; 27: Hugh Keane; 29: RTÉ Stills Library.

Acknowledgments

THE GENESIS OF THIS BOOK GOES back some four decades, as do the many debts of honour I have incurred in its making. Pride of place goes to the Trinity Research Centre for Contemporary Irish History, which provided a stimulating and comfortable base for research and writing. My special thanks to the Centre's director, Eunan O'Halpin, and to Tom Brace, for their generous hospitality. I would like to acknowledge the permission of the Board of Trinity College Dublin to reproduce images and documents from its collections. Much of my research was undertaken in Trinity College's superb library, where Paul Doyle, Mary Higgins, Sean Hughes and Simon Lang were unfailingly helpful, as were Aisling Lockhart, Leanne Harrington, Dáire Rooney and the other friendly and efficient personnel of the Manuscripts Department. Staff at several other Irish libraries and archival repositories gave me the benefit of their time and expertise. At the National Library of Ireland, Gerry Kavanagh was a fertile source of ideas and resources, and Linda Hickey helped me solve the mysteries of the Irish Military Archives. Sarah Pouch at the UCD Archives and Susan Hood at the Church of Ireland RCB Library were generous with their advice. At the other end of the world, Peter Stanes (Auckland Grammar School), Rachel Hurd (Presbyterian Archives, Dunedin), Michael Mercer (Hadlow Preparatory School), Bridget Minatel (Sydney Grammar School), Kara Oosterman (Papakura Museum), Keith Giles (Auckland Public Library) and Maureen West (Auckland Public Library) provided valuable assistance.

It was a privilege to speak to the children of two of the Anzacs about their fathers' lives. I am indebted to Margaret Wilson and John Nevin (daughter and son of Fred Nevin) and Valerie Gough (daughter of Alexander Don). My sincere thanks for learned advice on various aspects of the project go to: Miles Dillon, Abel Esterhuyse, Alvin Jackson, the late Keith Jeffrey, Hugh Keane, Donal McCracken, Ida Milne, Chris Pugsley, Geraldene O'Reilly, Vincent O'Sullivan and Richard Stowers. Special mention should be made of Jeff Kildea, whose *Anzacs and Ireland* (Cork, 2007) stimulated my work and who generously shared information with me. Also to my many Irish friends and helpers: Tom Armstrong, Mick Breen, Ciara Breathnach, Turtle Bunbury, Damien Burke, Tom Conlon, Danny Cusack, David Dickson, Catherine Giltrap, James Hammel, Mike and Amanda Kelly, Dáire Keogh, Brian Lambkin, Brian McCabe, Colin McCabe, Peter McDonnell, Fearghal McGarry, Caroline McGee, Mark McGowan, Ronan McGreevy, Robert Marshall, Kay Muhr, Danny O'Donnell, Brendan O Donoghue, Francesca O'Rafferty, Colman Rutherford, Mick and Sarah Sweetman, Brian Thompson and Antony Wheatley. In the United Kingdom I relied upon the generosity of Anna Davin, Max and Tara Elliott, Roger Paulin, Andy and Brigid Sandford-Smith and Janet Wilson.

Among those in New Zealand and Australia who endured my rants about Irish amnesia concerning the Anzac contribution to Easter Week 1916 are Peter Burke, Yvonne Caulfield, Sandy Cleary, George Davis, Ann Elder, Tony Eyre, Craig Freeman, Bryan Harold, Kevin Ireland, Stephanie James, the late Hugh Laracy, Daniel Lark, William McKee, Alan Martin, Karine and Matai Moinaux, Doug Munro, Nicholas O'Flaherty, Warren Parfoot, Jan Slater, the late Stephen Mulqueen, Thomas Schattovits, Ruth Sweetman, and Bob Simpson. Reaching back in time, I cannot forget Anne, who first sent me off to Ireland, and Biddy who helped me to survive there. During my student days my lovely aunt Kitty Kelly supplied lots of tea and comfort, the late Professor Jim Lydon provided wise advice and Colman Rutherford, firm friendship. Later, in Cambridge, Professor D.K. Fieldhouse was a supportive doctoral supervisor, while Peterhouse gave me space, the encouragement to develop my research interests and the opportunity to meet my dear friend Jacques Straetmans.

While I take responsibility for all views expressed herein, including any errors or omissions, the project has benefited greatly from the attentions of the incomparable Austin Gee (Dunedin), who uncomplainingly read several rough drafts. Linda Tyler (Auckland) provided encouragement and moral support throughout the entire project. My gratitude goes to the Trinity College Dublin Association and Trust, to the Embassy of Ireland, New Zealand and to the Auckland Orange Hall Society for grants in aid of publication; also to Four Courts Press, for turning my spotty manuscript into a beautiful book. It is dedicated to my father (and his siblings), seventeen years dead today but not forgotten.

RORY SWEETMAN
1 December 2018

Abbreviations

AIF	Australian Imperial Force
ANZ	Archives New Zealand
ANZAC	Australian and New Zealand Army Corps
BL	British Library
BMH	Bureau of Military History (Ireland)
CEF	Canadian Expeditionary Force
DIB	*Dictionary of Irish biography*
DMP	Dublin Metropolitan Police
DNZB	*Dictionary of New Zealand biography*
GOC	general officer commanding
GPO	General Post Office, Dublin
IRA	Irish Republican Army
IRB	Irish Republican Brotherhood
ITGWU	Irish Transport and General Workers Union
LOI	Loyal Orange Institution
LOL	Loyal Orange Lodge
MP	Member of Parliament
MS	manuscript
MUN	muniments
NAA	National Archives of Australia
NAI	National Archives of Ireland
NLI	National Library of Ireland
NZDF	New Zealand Defence Forces
NZEF	New Zealand Expeditionary Force
NZMC	New Zealand Medical Corps
NZPD	New Zealand Parliamentary Debates
OTC	Officers' Training Corps
PRO	Public Record Office, London
TCD	Trinity College Dublin
WO	War Office
WS	Witness Statement

Foreword

RORY SWEETMAN'S METICULOUSLY researched study of Trinity College and the Rising argues that the institution's importance during the conflict has been gravely understated. The college's strategic location, and its enormous utility as a rallying point for British troops responding to the outbreak have been generally acknowledged – most recently in Tomás Irish's *Trinity in war and revolution, 1912–1923*; nevertheless, an undue reticence infuses many accounts of Trinity's experience, particularly in the first two days of fighting in the city. It has generally been argued that the rebels never mounted a serious assault on the campus, and by implication that the defence of Trinity by a handful of servicemen on leave, by the OTC and by college servants while commendable was not decisive because the rebels never attacked. Sweetman, drawing on the riches of Trinity's archives, of recently released Irish Bureau of Military History and military service documents, of British records, and, importantly, of local newspapers in New Zealand and Australia, has produced a strikingly different analysis. The rebels did mount an assault, albeit in smaller numbers than planned and mistakenly believed to be aimed at the Bank of Ireland building across College Green; it was the disciplined and sustained fire of Trinity's Anzac defenders that drove them off. This, and the almost incomprehensible failure of de Valera's men in control of Westland Row station and of the railway line overlooking the east end of the campus to capture the OTC armoury that stood unguarded under their noses meant that Trinity remained secure.

If Sweetman's analysis is to be accepted, Trinity owes a particular debt to a small core of gritty Anzacs. So too does Ireland, for saving Trinity from the fate that bombardment would ultimately have wrought had the rebels succeeded in gaining control. The gutted GPO on Sackville Street, completed in the early 1800s, was more or less successfully reconstructed; but, just as the great library of Louvain was lost forever in 1914, no human hands could ever have restored the Long Room and its treasures had artillery been used against it.

Sweetman's study, equally, is an important contribution to the history of Anzacs – the military of the dominions of Australia and New Zealand –

during the Great War. Their collective experience and loss during the disastrous Dardanelles campaign in 1915 was so appalling that 25 April has become the national day of commemoration in both countries. Yet a striking aspect of this book is the willingness and sangfroid with which a handful of Anzacs, mainly New Zealanders, entered the fray and conducted themselves during Easter Week. Men who had come through the unremitting hell of Gallipoli emerge not merely as doing their duty, but as able to organize others to conduct an effective defence. Anyone haunted by the horrors they had already experienced was able to push such spectres aside in the forty-eight hours when their presence was crucial to Trinity's security. This reflects a wider truth largely neglected in commemoration of the Great War: soldiers with visceral experience of the horrors, injustices and inhumanity of modern combat remained willing to engage in it. A century later, *plus ça change*.

PROF. EUNAN O'HALPIN
Trinity College Dublin

Introduction

THIS MONOGRAPH IS BASED on a talk I gave at Trinity College Dublin in November 2017, exactly forty years since I first walked through its Front Gate as an innocent junior freshman. I was then 22, around the same age as most of the men whose activities in the Easter Rising I examine in the following pages. Unlike those New Zealanders, I was not driven into Trinity by gunfire, but instead drawn there by curiosity about my native land and by the opportunity to undertake a four-year honours course in history. The timing was fortunate, as among my lecturers were such luminaries of the profession as T.W. Moody, F.S.L. Lyons and R.B. McDowell. I was also able to learn from the coming generation of modern Irish historians, including David Fitzpatrick, John Horne and David Dickson.

My studies were funded through a year's hard graft in the iron ore mines of Western Australia and I had limited financial resources; so it was a shock when paying the first year's fees to be presented with a demand for a 60 per cent surcharge on this sum. Despite my birth certificate, Trinity had deemed me insufficiently Irish to qualify as a local student. My indignant protest at this species of highway robbery, made annually to the college bursar, involved stressing my *Irishness* and pointing out how unfair it was to treat a returning emigrant in this fashion. This book reveals that my claim should have been based squarely on my *New Zealand* citizenship – and on the fact that without the heroic endeavours of my fellow Kiwis during the first two days of the 1916 Rising, there was a very good chance that Trinity College Dublin would have ended Easter Week as a heap of smoking ruins, as did most of the buildings in Sackville (now O'Connell) Street.

In the pages that follow I intend to explore how five New Zealanders, acting as the core of a small squad of colonial troops, provided a vital shield to protect Trinity from capture. Had the college fallen to the rebel attack at midnight on Easter Monday its 324th year may well have been its last. In that case nothing less than a heavy and prolonged bombardment would have sufficed to dislodge and defeat the occupiers. As one acute observer noted, 'it is an almost ideal fortress … and if artillery were not used against its walls it could be held by a few hundred men against almost any numbers'.[1] Any future

1 Walter Starkie, *Scholars and gypsies: an autobiography* (London, 1963), p. 141.

edifice erected on the site would probably have borne as little resemblance to Trinity College as it did to the Augustinian Priory of All Hallows it had supplanted in 1592.

Little has been written on Trinity College's role in Easter Week as – in the words of one of its defenders – 'a loyal nucleus' dividing the insurgents and providing an effective counterweight to the rebel headquarters in the General Post Office.[2] In the immediate aftermath of the rebellion the college magazine, *TCD*, suggested that it was 'a mere freak of circumstance that the defence of Trinity had such a bearing on the safety of the rest of the city'.[3] That may be so, but it is difficult to understand the scant attention paid to it by Irish historians. Most commentators march past Trinity as determinedly as did the Irish Citizen Army en route to St Stephen's Green, with at most a sideways glance towards what one rebel referred to as 'the intellectual centre of West-Britonism in Ireland'.[4] The college is usually mentioned in the context of the rebels' alleged failure to attempt its capture, and its co-option as a barracks in the later stages of the rebellion. One can understand this neglect in what might be termed 'rebel' accounts; no one likes to dwell upon failure, and few of the insurgents chose to do so, even in their recollections three decades later for the Bureau of Military History.

Still more neglected are the men who helped to save Trinity from potential disaster at a time when it was virtually defenceless. The college's colonial defenders have been either entirely overlooked or dismissed as 'a number of scared British soldiers' sheltering behind its solid walls.[5] Confusion reigned, then and now, as to their identity; they are usually referred to as colonials, sometimes 'Anzacs' (after the Australian and New Zealand Army Corps), most often 'Australians'.[6] In fact, five of the six Anzacs were New Zealanders, but the inability of the Irish ear to identify their distinctive accent has led some observers on a wild goose chase for an Australian contingent among the crown forces.[7] Recent historiography has further muddied the waters by focusing on

2 John Joly, *Reminiscences and anticipations* (London, 1920), p. 237. 3 *TCD: A College Miscellany*, 19 June 1916, p. 243. 4 Diarmuid Lynch, *The IRB and the 1916 insurrection* (Cork, 1957), p. 163. G.A. Hayes-McCoy, 'A military history of the 1916 Rising' in Kevin B. Nowlan (ed.), *The making of 1916: studies in the history of the Rising* (Dublin, 1969), pp 255–338. An excellent survey of the historiography can be found in Jeff Kildea's article 'Called to arms: Australian soldiers in the Easter Rising', *Journal of the Australian War Memorial*, 39 (Oct. 2003). 5 Francis P. Jones, *History of the Sinn Fein movement and the Irish Rebellion of 1916* (New York, 1919), p. 310. Michael Foy and Brian Barton, *The Easter Rising* (Stroud, 2000), p. 180. 6 The term was originally applied to all Australian and New Zealand troops who fought on the Gallipoli peninsula. Ian McGibbon (ed.), *The Oxford companion to New Zealand military history* (Oxford, 2000), p. 27. 7 TCD, MS 4456; MS 4874/2. See also Starkie, *Scholars and gypsies*, p. 142. Other sources identify the Anzacs as Canadians. Herbert Fitzgerald's 'Diary of events in Ireland during

the one Australian in the Anzac squad, a man who left no diary, letters or reminiscences of his Dublin experiences.[8]

The appendices to this book offer a rich new source in the shape of letters written home by several New Zealanders caught up in the Rising. Their contents give fresh insight into important aspects of the insurrection and allow us to test some controversial claims made by the Anzacs against both Trinity's own record of its Easter Week experiences and the various rebel accounts contained in Bureau of Military History witness statements and military pension application files. More importantly, they help to answer questions left unasked in previous studies: how close did Trinity come to being a central battleground in the Rising? How and why did it escape this grisly fate? And – not least – what might have happened but for the intervention of the colonial troops? The most apocalyptic vision of Trinity's potential fate was presented by its professor of geology, John Joly, in an account written while the ruins of Sackville Street were still smouldering:

> Was this indeed to be, perhaps, the last night of our ancient University? The question is no mere extravagance of the imagination. For so much of the very existence of so venerable a foundation is bound up with its century-old buildings, with its literary and artistic treasures, that sack and conflagration in a single night might obliterate practically all but its memory from the earth. So might perish Ireland's most priceless treasure – the University of Berkeley, Goldsmith, Burke, Hamilton, and Lecky.[9]

Historians disagree on the extent of the threat posed to the university by the insurgent Volunteers. Tomás Irish, author of *Trinity in war and revolution, 1912–1923*, dismisses Joly's fears as 'misplaced'. 'There was little need to defend Trinity during Easter Week,' he argues, 'The defence was largely an imagined one.'[10] By contrast, Eunan O'Halpin states that the college was 'centrally involved in the events of the 1916 Rising as a site of battle'.[11] This book challenges the historical orthodoxy that Trinity was 'never directly threatened by the rebel forces' during the Rising.[12] It asks what David

the Sinn Fein insurrection', Digital Repository of Ireland, DOI: 10.7486/DRI.p8418p10j-57. Charles Duff, *Six days to shake an empire* (London, 1966), p. 132. Tim Pat Coogan, *Michael Collins* (London, 1990), p. 44. **8** Jeff Kildea, *Anzacs and Ireland* (Sydney, 2007), ch. 2. The recent film *Anzacs and the Easter Rising* is concerned largely with the sole Australian and his alleged role in the killing of a rebel despatch rider. See youtu.be/6qqi4Y_oAys. **9** Joly, *Reminiscences and anticipations*, p. 228. **10** Tomás Irish, *Trinity in war and revolution, 1912–1923* (Dublin, 2015), p. 159. **11** *Trinity and the Rising* (Dublin, 2015), p. 4. **12** Charles Townshend, *Easter 1916: the Irish Rebellion* (London, 2006), p. 185.

Fitzpatrick has called 'the hard questions of history – what actually happened and who thought what, why, and with what consequences'.[13]

Chapter 1 charts the historiography of the college's defence, where a focus on the alleged exploits of its Officers' Training Corps (henceforth OTC) has obscured both Trinity's vulnerability to rebel attack and the role of the colonial troops in its survival. Chapter 2 discusses Trinity's conflicted relationship with Irish nationalism and identifies its manifold attractions as a rebel target. The turbulent first two days of Easter Week are the focus of chapter 3, which describes how the defence of Trinity was accomplished, how haphazard and fortuitous was this process, and how near it came to disaster. Chapter 4 looks more closely at the colonial soldiery, particularly the Anzacs, telling their personal stories, and examining the tales they sent back home about their Easter Week exploits. Chapter 5 is a counterfactual exercise, exploring what *might* have happened had Trinity College become an insurgent stronghold rather than 'the main indigenous centre of resistance to the rebels'.[14] It argues that John Joly's fears were unrealized rather than unrealistic. The final chapter looks at what happened to the Anzacs and probes their motivations, refuting recent scholarship that depicts them as reluctant conscripts, dragged unwillingly into a conflict that was none of their business. It attempts to put this episode of the Easter Rising into an imperial context, with Dublin as a theatre of battle in a global war.

13 David Fitzpatrick, 'Instant history: 1912, 1916, 1918' in Richard S. Grayson and Fearghal McGarry (eds), *Remembering 1916: the Easter Rising, the Somme and the politics of memory in Ireland* (Cambridge, 2016), p. 65. **14** Pádraig Yeates, *A city in wartime: Dublin 1914–18* (Dublin, 2012), p. 105.

CHAPTER 1

Remembering and forgetting

> To be called on to defend our University against the attack of Irishmen, to be forced in self-defence to shoot down our countrymen – these are things which even the knowledge of duty well fulfilled cannot render anything but sad and distasteful.
>
> —*TCD*, 19 June 1916

DESPITE ITS LEADERS' CLAIM to be following a hallowed tradition, the 1916 Rising was a bloody attempt to change the course of Irish history by a small group of radical nationalists. Appalled by the apparent triumph of anglicization over an idealized Gaelic spirit, they preferred to seize Irish freedom rather than accept self-government within the British empire in the form of the long-deferred grant of home rule.[1] The outbreak of a world war provided the means and the rationale – England's difficulty being Ireland's opportunity – for a tiny faction of conspirators within the secret Irish Republican Brotherhood to plan and execute the Rising.

> It was the enduring popularity of constitutionalism, not its failure, that led a motley band of frustrated militants to abandon the Queensberry Rules of conventional nationalism. Only through provocation of a distracted government into insensate coercion might the carefully nurtured modus vivendi between nationalist Ireland and 'Liberal England' be ruptured. Republican visionaries further hoped that the shock of civil conflict would awaken some latent Gaelic pride, and encourage deluded constitutionalists to fling off their English vestments.[2]

For six days around 1,500 rebels fought the forces of the crown in Dublin, mostly their fellow Irishmen, before surrendering on Saturday 29 April. The small turnout was the price of the deception required to fool the head of the

1 The Irish public's enthusiastic response to the war 'brought home to us that the very fever that has possessed us was due to a subconscious awareness that the final end of the Irish nation was at hand ... Our national identity was obliterated not only politically but also in our own minds.' Desmond Fitzgerald, *Desmond's Rising* (Dublin, 2006), p. 58. 2 David Fitzpatrick, *The two*

Irish Volunteers, Eoin MacNeill, who had opposed the sort of reckless and sacrificial undertaking planned by Patrick Pearse and James Connolly.[3] Once alerted to the Rising's imminence, MacNeill countermanded the order mobilizing the insurgent forces, thereby reducing the death toll if not preventing the outbreak itself. The Proclamation of the Irish Republic, declaimed before an uncomprehending crowd by Pearse from outside the General Post Office, was a declaration of war on Britain with the aid of 'gallant allies in Europe'. It called on all Irishmen and women to support the assertion in arms of 'their right to national freedom and sovereignty'.[4] However, Pearse proved to be a more accurate predictor of the British response to the Rising than the Irish one. During Easter Week Dublin was treated like an occupied city to be retaken from the enemy, with artillery used to drive the insurgents out of their strongholds. While the speedy execution of the principal rebel leaders was to be expected, deporting twice as many people as had actually participated in the rebellion was excessive and ultimately self-defeating. The military governor of Ireland, General Sir John Maxwell, defended his policies by citing the destruction caused by the rebels – over three thousand people, mostly civilians, dead or seriously injured, millions of pounds worth of damage to property, and a large part of central Dublin in ruins.[5]

Extolled at the time by those who witnessed it, the contribution of the colonial troops to saving Trinity from this grisly fate was not long remembered.[6] The college chose instead to credit its Officers' Training Corps with preventing the destruction of not only its own buildings but also the surrounding commercial and financial area. On Monday 8 May, a week after the rebel surrender, Trinity's board marked the reopening of the university to students by passing a resolution commending the 'vigor and ability' with which the OTC, Trinity graduates and 'other friends' had secured the safety of the college and its neighbourhood.[7] Over the ensuing months no fewer than three formal ceremonies were held at Trinity to celebrate the OTC's achievements. The first function took place on Monday 1 May, when General Sir John Maxwell 'held a review in the College Park to congratulate the OTC'.[8] He privately told Irish undersecretary Sir Matthew Nathan how impressed he was with its gallant conduct 'at a critical time'.[9]

Irelands, 1912–1939 (Oxford, 1998), p. 58. **3** Brian Hughes (ed.), *Eoin MacNeill: memoir of a revolutionary scholar* (Dublin, 2016), pp 71–6. See also, Michael Tierney, *Eoin MacNeill: scholar and man of action, 1867–1945* (Oxford, 1980), pp 196–209. **4** Liam de Paor, *On the Easter Proclamation and other declarations* (Dublin, 1997). **5** David Fitzpatrick, 'Militarism in Ireland, 1900–1922' in Thomas Bartlett and Keith Jeffery (eds), *A military history of Ireland* (Cambridge, 1996), p. 394. **6** Joly, *Reminiscences and anticipations*, p. 223. Fitzgibbon to Blake, 10 May 1916, TCD, MS 11107/1. **7** TCD, MUN/V/5/21, p. 182. **8** Elsie Mahaffy diary, p. 51, TCD, MS 2074. Elsie was the elder of TCD Provost Mahaffy's two daughters. **9** Brendan O Donoghue,

There was a much larger gathering in the same place on Saturday 13 May, attended by around one thousand men, including the OTCs of both the University of Dublin and the Royal College of Surgeons, the Irish Association of Volunteer Training Corps, and various St John and Red Cross units that had been active during the Rising.[10] Brilliant sunshine alternated with heavy showers as General Maxwell and Major G.A. Harris (OTC adjutant) inspected the assemblage, while a bevy of distinguished guests – including Prime Minister Herbert Asquith – looked on from a platform bedecked with Union Jacks. In his speech Maxwell praised Trinity's OTC cadets for preventing the destruction of the area around College Green: 'It was thanks to their prompt assistance that that part of the city was kept from being ruined.'[11] During the march-past to conclude proceedings Maxwell took the salute of the officers of the various corps, including a body of Indian law students from King's Inns who had performed ambulance work during Easter Week.[12]

Was this second review organized primarily for Asquith's benefit? The prime minister had come over to Dublin a few days earlier to assess the city in the aftermath of the Rising, in what his biographer admits was partly 'an exercise in public relations designed to reassure the Irish parliamentary party'.[13] His evident desire to placate nationalist leader John Redmond was noted by suspicious Irish unionists, who commented sourly on the disproportionate amount of attention he paid to rebel prisoners.[14] (Asquith found those he met in Richmond Barracks to be 'very good-looking fellows with such lovely eyes'.)[15] Although Maxwell assured him that the executions of rebel leaders James Connolly and Sean McDermott, which took place on 12 May, would be the last, Asquith insisted on a drastic comb-out of lower-ranking prisoners before they were deported to England.[16] Annoyed by this interference, Maxwell refused to dine with Asquith at the Viceregal Lodge on the night before the Trinity College review, which occasion some observers saw as a useful way of drawing the prime minister's attention towards loyal soldiers and away from rebels.[17]

Activities wise and otherwise: the career of Sir Henry Augustus Robinson, 1898–1922 (Sallins, 2015), p. 241. **10** *Irish Examiner*, 15 May 1916, p. 5. *Belfast News-Letter*, 15 May 1916, p. 5. The *Sinn Fein rebellion handbook* (Dublin, 1916; republished 1998) misdates the review as 6 May 1916. Trinity College is the sole constituent college of the University of Dublin. **11** *Sinn Fein rebellion handbook*, p. 106. **12** *Irish Times*, 15 May 1916. See Conor Mulvagh, *Irish days, Indian memories* (Sallins, 2016), pp 79–80. **13** Roy Jenkins, *Asquith* (London, 1967), p. 446. **14** Asquith was accused of 'reserving his official attention for [the crown's] declared enemies'. W.A. Phillips, *The revolution in Ireland, 1906–1923* (London, 1923), p. 108. **15** Jenkins, *Asquith*, p. 446. Elsie Mahaffy's diary (p. 73) records that when Asquith 'went to the [Dublin] Castle Red Cross hospital to see the sufferers remaining there since the Rebellion he was most attentive and interested in any wounded Sinn Feiner he could find, but utterly ignored all the wounded soldiers'. TCD, MS 2074. **16** Jenkins, *Asquith*, p. 447. **17** George Arthur, *General Sir John*

Asquith reportedly expressed surprise at the small amount of damage inflicted on Dublin by the rebellion, but most observers were appalled by the massive destruction in and around Sackville Street, which brought Ypres and Louvain to mind.[18] Around 200 buildings, valued at £2.5 million, were in ruins. As historian David Dickson has suggested, the relative immunity of the south side of the city can be explained partly by the more confined sites that the rebels occupied there, which in turn affected the tactics adopted by the crown;[19] artillery was used on the rebel strongholds north of the Liffey, while those on the south side were mostly isolated and contained. Contemporaries preferred to give credit to Trinity's OTC for the fact that damage and looting had been prevented in the most important commercial and banking area in the city. 'But for the action of the Officers' Training Corps in saving the centre of Dublin from destruction, Trinity College and the Bank of Ireland, priceless relics of the past, would have been added to the shambles to which northern Dublin has been reduced.'[20]

A number of banks and other businesses in and around College Green wrote to the press and to Trinity's board to express gratitude to the OTC for protecting their property.[21] Shortly after the second OTC review a committee of businessmen launched an appeal, which raised over £700 towards 'a lasting Memorial to perpetuate the timely and valiant work they had done, which in all likelihood saved the South side of the City from like destruction to that which the Rebellion brought on the North side, where large parts of Sackville St, Abbey St, Henry St, and other places were laid in ruins'.[22] On Saturday 5 August, the largest of the three gatherings took place in the garden of the Provost's House. Sir Maurice Dockrell, chairman of the businessmen's committee, presented two large silver cups to the OTC's commander, Major R.W. Tate, 'in recognition of services rendered during the Easter week rising'.[23] Tate then handed the trophies over to Trinity's provost, to be held in trust in perpetuity. Replica cups were given to Provost J.P. Mahaffy, Major R.W. Tate, Major G.A. Harris and Captain E.H. Alton, while the OTC officers also received specially engraved swords. Each of the large cups carried an engraving of the arms of Trinity College and of the Dublin University Officers' Training Corps, as well as the following inscription:

Maxwell (London, 1932), p. 258. Elsie Mahaffy's diary, p. 68, TCD, MS 2074. **18** Elsie Mahaffy's diary, p. 73, TCD, MS 2074. 'Those who have come back from the front told us that the destruction challenged comparison with the ravaged cities of Belgium.' Starkie, *Scholars and gypsies*, p. 151. Mrs Hamilton Norway, *The Sinn Fein rebellion as I saw it* (London, 1916), p. 68. **19** David Dickson, *Dublin: the making of a capital city* (London, 2014), p. 454. **20** *Sinn Fein rebellion: a souvenir of presentations to the Officers' Training Corps, Trinity College Dublin* (Dublin, 1916), p. 11. **21** TCD, MS 2783/34–6. *Irish Times*, 17/19 May 1916. **22** *Sinn Fein rebellion: a souvenir of presentations*, p. 1. **23** *Sinn Fein rebellion: a souvenir of presentations*, p. 1.

DEFENCE OF TRINITY COLLEGE
Presented by many Loyal and Grateful Citizens of Dublin
To the Officers and Cadets of the
Dublin University Officers' Training Corps
In commemoration of their gallant services during the Rebellion,
Easter, 1916

The man who actually oversaw the defence of Trinity College, Ernest Alton, stated that 'the consciousness that [the defenders] did their best to protect the college and maintain order must be their sole reward', but in fact almost every individual and institution involved during those first critical days was given something tangible to mark their contribution.[24] Trinity's board made special payments to those college servants deemed most deserving, especially the porters who had promptly secured the gates, invited in passing soldiers, and guided the colonial troops to the strategic positions from which the university could best be defended.[25] Donations were made to the Soldiers' Central Club in College Street, from where troops had been directed to Trinity, and to the Irish Volunteers' Training Corps Dependents' Fund. It was also agreed to endow a bed in Sir Patrick Dun's Hospital, to be called 'The OTC Commemoration Bed'. Finally, an inscribed silver replica cup was to be given to every OTC member 'who assisted in the defence on or before Sunday April 30, or who otherwise, during the same period, took an active part in the military operations in the city'.[26]

By such ceremonies, it has recently been suggested, Trinity 'sought to portray itself as an establishment institution, one that had been loyal to Government and Crown in their time of need'.[27] There is dispute among historians over whether Dublin unionists displayed 'exultation' following their victory over the rebels. W.B. Stanford and R.B. McDowell would admit only 'a touch of exhilaration' by loyalists. 'After all, they had shown they could rise to an emergency and stand fire for their principles.'[28] Nevertheless, much relief and self-congratulation were expressed at the Trinity College functions, which were given 'the largest possible social flavour'.[29] The focus was increasingly on Trinity's OTC, which was the only body permitted to carry arms on 13 May and was the undivided centre of attention on 5 August. In describing 'their

24 *TCD*, 19 June 1916, p. 252. **25** TCD, MUN/V/5/21, p. 183. **26** TCD, MS 2783. **27** Irish, *Trinity in war and revolution*, p. 159. **28** W.B. Stanford and R.B. McDowell, *Mahaffy: a biography of an Anglo-Irishman* (London, 1971), p. 233. For a contrary view, see F.S.L. Lyons, *John Dillon* (London, 1968), p. 382. Irish Chief Secretary Augustine Birrell told Asquith on 30 April that 'a good many "loyalists" here are glad things have happened as they have'. Leon Ó Broin, *Dublin Castle and the 1916 Rising* (New York, 1971), p. 114. **29** Arthur, *General Sir* famous defence of Trinity College', Sir Maurice Dockrell used terms that others would soon apply to the dead rebels: 'they will go down to history as showing what a handful of brave and determined men can do'.[30]

The OTC's achievements grew in the telling, and it was even suggested that the rebels had achieved a form of victory by confining the dangerous students to their lair.[31] 'It is said that TCD saved the city,' cadet Robert Tweedy told his mother.[32] Some participants in the awards ceremony were uneasy at what was being left unsaid, and at the undiluted praise heaped on the OTC. 'I am afraid there is a tendency to overestimate very greatly, not what we did, but the way we did it,' wrote Gerald Fitzgibbon, a 49-year-old barrister and OTC cadet-sergeant.[33] *TCD*'s editor also felt that 'the general public have viewed the achievement of the students in, perhaps, too rosy a light'.[34] Despite reports of a shrapnel shell landing in the Provost's Garden, neither the college nor its defenders had suffered any serious injury during Easter Week.[35] Indeed, most of the OTC leaders felt they had successfully bluffed the rebels into believing that the college was an impregnable fortress, teeming with armed men. The vital contribution of the Anzacs towards creating that impression was not publicly acknowledged in the speeches or in subsequent published accounts.

The colonial troops were not completely forgotten, however, as their names were on the list to receive replica cups. One can understand why they were overlooked, as mere tourists in Dublin caught up almost accidentally in the violence of Easter Week. After the rebel surrender on Sunday, they all quickly returned to fight the 'real' war, leaving behind brief and sketchy details concerning their identities and future movements.[36] Their role has continued to be virtually ignored by historians, whose accounts show little awareness of the danger faced by Trinity during the first two days of the Rising, or of the Anzacs' part in preventing disaster.[37] They tend to adopt a reactive

John Maxwell, p. 258. **30** *Sinn Fein rebellion: a souvenir of presentations*, p. 11. **31** Jones, *History of the Sinn Fein movement*, pp 310–11. Valentine Jackson recalled that 'armed members of the OTC of Trinity were moving out in skirmishing order by Merrion Square towards Mount Street'. BMH, WS 409. **32** Robert Tweedy letter, 7 May 1916, TCD, MS 7533/3. **33** Fitzgibbon to Blake, 15 May 1916, TCD, MS 11107/2. **34** *TCD*, 19 June 1916, p. 244. **35** *TCD*, 19 June 1916, p. 257. Elsie Mahaffy's diary, p. 42, TCD, MS 2074. **36** The faulty recording of these details troubled the OTC authorities once word spread of the award of souvenir cups. The Anzacs had to rattle a few cages to ensure their delivery and it is doubtful if the mysterious Private Kinahan (3rd South African Division) ever received his trophy. Georgina Fitzpatrick, *Trinity College and Irish society, 1914–1922* (Dublin, 1992), pp 10–11. **37** According to Peter Fox, *Trinity College Library Dublin: a history* (Cambridge, 2014), p. 259, 'the College … was closed and guarded by members of its OTC'. Kenneth C. Bailey, *A history of Trinity College Dublin, 1892–1945* (Dublin, 1947), p. 47, records that 'Trinity College was occupied by British forces, and partly garrisoned by the Officers' Training Corps of the College.' R.B. McDowell and interpretation – Trinity was attacked, so had to defend itself – dwelling on the OTC's protection of the College Green area, and ignoring the degree to which Trinity soon became 'an oasis of support for the British war effort'.[38] There is some excuse in that the official reports also told a tale of heroic defence.[39] For the rest, no one wished to go into specifics, despite Ernest Alton promising 'on some other occasion it may be possible to give a detailed account of the doings of those days'.[40] Most subsequent commentators echoed the sombre and regretful note of the first post-rebellion issue of *TCD* (cited at the head of this chapter). Its editor, T.C. Kingsmill Moore, preferred to focus on the exploits of Trinity men at the Western Front rather than those who fought for the crown in Easter Week. 'It is rather to the deeds of her sons in Flanders and the Dardanelles that Trinity looks for enduring honour.'[41]

Sadly, both heroic performances would soon fade from Ireland's collective memory. In 1928 Lord Glenavy, Trinity's vice chancellor, warned of a 'growing conspiracy of silence' over the college's huge sacrifice in the war, and this would deepen during subsequent decades.[42] However, Trinity has itself largely to blame for the deafening silence over its role in Easter Week. The three official histories of the college published since 1922 'devote only 8 pages between them, from over a thousand, to Trinity and the rising'.[43] Of course, within six years of the insurrection Trinity had to cope with an Ireland fashioned in the image of the dead rebel leaders. According to Tomás Irish, Trinity was 'a sceptical observer of, rather than an actual participant in, the Irish Revolution', but its students left little doubt over where their sympathies lay by attacking Sinn Féin headquarters on Armistice Day in 1918, and cheering a guard of Auxiliaries on their way to Dublin Castle two years later.[44]

D.A. Webb, *Trinity College Dublin, 1592–1952: an academic history* (Cambridge, 1982), p. 421, says 'the shutting of the gates and the manning of the perimeter by the Officers Training Corps were obvious and necessary precautions before regular troops arrived after two days' fighting'. J.V. Luce, *Trinity College Dublin: the first 400 years* (Dublin, 1992), pp 130–1, states that 'immediate responsibility for the defence of the College rested with the Officers Training Corps'. **38** Yeates, *A city in wartime*, p. 105. **39** Captain Alton's two accounts are in *TCD*, 19 June 1916, and *Sinn Fein rebellion: a souvenir of presentations*, pp 4–8. Major Harris' report to the War Office (10 May 1916) is in WO 32/9576, National Archives, London. A copy is contained in TCD, MS 2783/64. All three documents are reproduced in the appendices to this book, pp 115–21. **40** *TCD*, 19 June 1916, p. 252. **41** *TCD*, 19 June 1916, p. 244. **42** Irish, *Trinity in war and revolution*, p. 261. **43** 'The college itself, however, has remained virtually silent about its role in the period.' Irish, *Trinity in war and revolution*, p. 128. See also, McDowell and Webb, *Trinity College Dublin*, pp 420–1. Bailey, *Trinity College Dublin*, pp 4, 47–8, 158. Luce, *Trinity College Dublin*, pp 130–1. **44** Tomás Irish, 'Students between two states', a paper given to the 'Universities in Revolution and State Formation' conference, University College Dublin, 5–6 June 2015. For the attack on 6 Harcourt Street, see BMH, WS 511 (Michael Lynch); WS 481 (Simon Donnelly); and WS 487 (Joseph O'Connor). The Auxiliaries were a counter-terrorist force mobilized against the IRA by

Trinity eventually agreed – through gritted teeth – to accept the Anglo-Irish Treaty (1921), but found its political and financial position undermined and 'an alien and largely hostile world at its gates'.[45] 'From 1922, the College, crippled by wartime debts and eager to reconcile itself to the new Free State government in the hope of securing financial aid, began a careful policy of quiet cooperation with the new powers.'[46] This may have encouraged gestures like the granting of honorary degrees to the politicians William Cosgrave (1926) and Eoin MacNeill (1928), and the belated introduction of Gaelic games.[47] Trinity's nervousness increased after Fianna Fail took office in 1932. When the president of the executive council, Eamon de Valera, came to open Trinity's new library in 1937, no one was inclined to recall the threat he and his former comrades had posed to the old library twenty-one years earlier.[48]

Running through most of the histories of Trinity is a sense that, as Arthur Luce (later vice provost) put it, the college had 'backed the wrong horse' in 1916.[49] If so, the pendulum had swung far by 1966, as the country marked the fiftieth anniversary of the Rising. Provost Albert McConnell now had a framed copy of the Proclamation of the Irish Republic on the wall of his study ('he knew the contents almost by heart'), while as part of the celebrations a twenty-one-gun salute was fired from the grounds of Trinity – not against the rebels as in 1916, but in their honour.[50] However, the 'deep unease' traditionally felt by Trinity over its actions in 1916 was not entirely to disappear. The author of the most recent study gives this tradition a novel twist by denying the necessity for any such Anzac heroics as described in this book; there was no attack on Trinity, he insists, so no need to defend it.[51] The 'defence' (a word he

the British government in 1920–1. See Fitzpatrick, *Trinity College and Irish society*, p. 17. See also, Paul O'Brien, *Havoc: the Auxiliaries in Ireland's War of Independence* (Cork, 2017). **45** F.S.L. Lyons, 'The minority problem in the 26 counties' in Francis MacManus (ed.), *The years of the great test, 1926–39* (Cork, 1967), p. 98. **46** Irish, *Trinity in war and revolution*, p. 128. According to Terence Brown, 'the 1920s found Trinity financially insecure, intellectually and socially remote for the most part from contemporary Irish concerns, and identified in the popular mind with the former, rejected ruling class'. *Ireland: a social and cultural history, 1922–2002* (London, 2004), p. 104. **47** Irish, *Trinity in war and revolution*, pp 245–50. In fact, Trinity College helped to keep a form of hurling alive when it was virtually extinct in the rest of the country. Trevor West, *The bold collegians: the development of sport in Trinity College Dublin* (Dublin, 1991), pp 53–8. **48** Fox, *Trinity College Library Dublin*, p. 276. **49** A.A. Luce, 'Recollections of Easter Monday 1916', 14 Oct. 1967. TCD, MS 4874/2/1. Luce was vice provost of Trinity College from 1946 to 1952. **50** *Cuimhneachán, 1916–1966: a record of Ireland's commemoration of the 1916 Rising* (Dublin, 1966), p. 69. Roisin Higgins, *Transforming 1916: meaning, memory and the fiftieth anniversary of the Easter Rising* (Cork, 2012), p. 55. Townshend, *Easter 1916*, p. 340. **51** According to Tomás Irish, 'The motley crew present in Trinity on Easter Monday made preparations for an attack, but none ever came … the attacks were metaphorical rather than literal; there was little defending to be done.' *Trinity in war and revolution* (p. 99); also, 'the reality was there was little need to defend Trinity during Easter Week. The defence was largely an keeps firmly in inverted commas) was imaginary, the locking of Front Gate a largely symbolic act, Trinity merely a pantomime villain in the great national drama being staged on the streets of Dublin. A cynical reader might detect here an attempt to drag Trinity out of the British camp, if not quite as far as the General Post Office then at least into the middle of Sackville Street. The college is depicted as confused and conflicted, overwhelmed by the speed and complexity of events – almost itself a victim of the insurrection.[52]

The same note is struck by the college's official publication marking the centenary of the rebellion, which pays more attention to those who attacked Trinity than those who defended it.[53] There *was* a memorial ceremony held outside Trinity's Front Gate in Easter 2016, with a plaque erected nearby to mark the college's actions in the Rising, but this was to commemorate a rebel victim of the Anzacs; there was nothing said or done to mark the actions of the defenders themselves.[54] However, Trinity's current provost, Patrick Prendergast, has recently called for dispassionate historical analysis of the events of Easter Week, in order 'to provide glimpses of alternative viewpoints that may serve to illuminate our pre-conceived ideas'.[55] This book is an Antipodean contribution to the 'big national conversation' on the Rising.

imagined one' (p. 159). **52** 'Trinity's experience of the events of Easter Week – broadly defined – is a complex web of often contradictory motivations and reactions, public gestures and private ruminations, and occasionally erroneous recollections.' Irish, *Trinity in war and revolution*, p. 129. **53** *Trinity and the Rising* (Dublin, 2015). **54** *Sydney Morning Herald*, 27 Mar. 2016. **55** *Trinity and the Rising*, p. 2.

CHAPTER 2

'That English fort in Ireland'

There was a march in the streets of Dublin, right through the city, in front of the foreign College of Trinity and before the Parliament House.[1]

MOST CONTEMPORARIES WERE astonished at Trinity's 'inexplicable' escape from attack during the Rising,[2] with leading rebels ruefully acknowledging that it should have been captured.[3] It was a classic example of Provost Mahaffy's quip that 'in Ireland the inevitable never happens and the unexpected constantly occurs'.[4] Some fairly flimsy reasons have been offered as to why Trinity escaped Easter Week largely unscathed. It was too vast a space to garrison, and therefore difficult to hold once taken. Charles Townshend has suggested that an attack on Trinity, a bastion of Protestantism, would have had sectarian overtones that the rebels preferred to avoid. Finally, the latter may have feared, as McDowell and Webb put it, 'the resistance to be expected from its occupants'.[5] Whatever the strength of these objections, the idea of capturing Trinity should have appealed to the insurgents, either to gain a military advantage or to make a spectacular 'blood sacrifice'. It is worth considering the strategic, symbolic and practical reasons in favour of a rebel attack.

According to John Joly, 'it was obviously the most central and commanding position in the city'.[6] A natural fortress protected by sturdy walls and sitting astride rebel communication lines, Trinity soon became the centre from which the British forces suppressed the rebellion. While it was only one of several potential rebel targets in or near College Green, including Dublin Castle and the Bank of Ireland, Trinity lacked the sentimental associations that gave the former site of Grattan's Parliament immunity from attack. There has been some debate over rebel intentions towards the Bank of Ireland. James

1 Extract from a letter intercepted by the censor, 24 March 1916. *Sinn Fein rebellion handbook*, p. 206. 2 Joly, *Reminiscences and anticipations*, p. 222. 3 W.J. Brennan-Whitmore, *Dublin burning: the Easter Rising from behind the barricades* (Dublin, 2013), p. 25. BMH, WS 6 (Liam Ó Briain); WS 186 (Thomas J. Doyle). 4 Stanford and McDowell, *Mahaffy*, p. 79. 5 Townshend, *Easter 1916*, p. 101. McDowell and Webb, *Trinity College Dublin*, p. 421. 6 Joly, *Reminiscences*

Connolly reportedly saw it as a possible insurgent headquarters, but Patrick Pearse objected, 'as he did not wish to have the old Irish House of Parliament under fire'.[7] Thomas MacDonagh, commandant of the 2nd Battalion, whose area of operations included College Green, is said to have shared Pearse's concerns.[8] Despite the testimony of Trinity's garrison, it is unlikely that the Bank of Ireland was in any serious danger from rebel attack, not least because its lack of windows ruled it out as a defensive outpost.

Nor did an attack on Trinity inspire the fear associated with attempting to storm Dublin Castle, the seat of British administration in Ireland and (to many) the ultimate symbol of alien rule. The hospital attached to the Castle was later cited as a reason why the rebel assault on it was so half-hearted, but it was surely the adjacent military barracks that gave the insurgents greater pause for thought.[9] Still, the Castle *was* attacked, so why should the rebels spare an institution 'widely regarded as a symbol of ascendancy, elitism, inequality and the Union itself'?[10] Declan Kiberd has described the General Post Office as 'an inspired choice' for the 'act of dramatic symbolism' intended by the rebel leaders, but how much more appropriately would Trinity have fitted the bill?[11]

> It embodied everything that political and cultural nationalists claimed to stand against and was frequently cited as an example of British misrule and misunderstanding of Ireland … Following this line of thinking, an attack on Trinity would be an attack on all elements of British rule, be they cultural, military or political.[12]

Of course, this was not how Trinity saw itself. After the fighting was over, *TCD* maintained that 'the honoured fame of our University made the rebels loath to attack it. The love of Trinity and pride in it is the heritage of all Irishmen, and whatever be the form of our government, whatever the party in power, we believe that they will regard our College as one of Ireland's greatest possessions.'[13] A long list of nationalist alumni – including Theobald Wolfe Tone, Henry Grattan and Thomas Davis – was regularly cited to soften Trinity's image as what Douglas Hyde (another Trinity graduate) termed 'that English fort in Ireland'.[14] Critics retorted that these men retained their

and anticipations, p. 222. **7** R.M. Fox, *The history of the Irish Citizen Army* (Dublin, 1943), p. 146. **8** BMH, WS 263 (Thomas Slater). **9** Hayes-McCoy, 'A military history of the 1916 Rising', p. 265. **10** Irish, *Trinity in war and revolution*, p. 135. **11** Declan Kiberd, '1916: the idea and the action' in Kathleen Devine (ed.), *Modern Irish writers and the wars* (Gerrards Cross, 1999), p. 29. **12** Irish, *Trinity in war and revolution*, p. 135. **13** *TCD*, 19 June 1916, p. 244. **14** Gareth W. Dunleavy, *Douglas Hyde* (London, 1974), p. 40. Eoin MacNeill and John Redmond were also patriotism *despite* Trinity, and that their 'strength of character brought them survival out of all that was hostile and inimical to Irish nationalism'.[15]

It has been suggested that both Patrick Pearse and Eamon de Valera retained some residual sense of loyalty to the college from their occasional attendance at lectures within its walls.[16] However, according to his biographer, Pearse's resentment at anti-Gaelic elements within Irish society 'was not lessened by his brief experience of Trinity'.[17] Notoriously, just eighteen months before the Rising, the then vice provost, Mahaffy, had forbidden 'a man called Pearse' from airing his 'traitrous' views on the war in college grounds.[18] For his part, de Valera would hardly have had happy memories of flunking two scholarship exams in mathematics in 1905–6. A future provost of Trinity later linked this failure to de Valera's abandonment of academia for politics.[19] While the experiences of Pearse and de Valera arguably supplied motives to *attack* the college rather than defend it, what was the average Trinity student's political allegiance?

Trinity has been described in this era as 'an unambiguous stronghold of Unionism in a strongly nationalist city'.[20] According to one of its historians, its whole ethos was still staunchly Protestant at the turn of the twentieth century. 'Trinity considered its fortunes to be bound up with those of the United Kingdom, and almost to a man was solidly Southern Unionist in outlook and sympathy.'[21] How was this institutional stance reflected in student behaviour? Most collegians were middle-class Protestants, though the number of Catholics was slowly growing.[22] As the editor of *TCD* wrote in the immediate aftermath of the Rising, 'Here is the one place in Ireland where no one even knows, much less cares, about the religion or politics of his neighbour. Though every type of opinion is here, there is no friction and men are judged by their qualities rather than their views.'[23] Kevin O'Shiel, a Trinity student from 1909 to 1913, agreed that 'politics, particularly Irish politics, were hardly touched on amongst students' in the pre-war years, and that Catholics like himself were treated with tolerance and fairness. He could not help adding, however, that 'in times of strong stress and passions, her fundamental colours escaped and broke out occasionally, and, invariably, on one particular day – 17 March'.

graduates of TCD. **15** *Irish Press*, 9 Nov. 1934, cited in David Fitzpatrick, 'Eamon de Valera at Trinity College', *Hermathena: a Trinity College Dublin Review*, 133 (1982), p. 10. **16** Irish, *Trinity in war and revolution*, pp 136–7. **17** Ruth Dudley Edwards, *Patrick Pearse: the triumph of failure* (Dublin, 1977), p. 41. **18** Luce, *Trinity College Dublin*, p. 129. **19** Irish, *Trinity in war and revolution*, p. 137. **20** Dickson, *Dublin*, p. 439. **21** Peter Boyle, *Trinity College Dublin: the Provosts, 1592–1927* (Dublin, 2015), pp 358, 384. **22** Irish, *Trinity in war and revolution*, pp 26–8, 45. See also, J.F. Hogan, *Irish Catholics and Trinity College* (Dublin, 1906). **23** *TCD*, 19

> The outburst was a piece of organized hooliganism, unworthy of a venerable seat of learning, and it was in double bad taste that the day selected for it was St Patrick's Day. That day was traditionally celebrated by the Lord Mayor's procession through the streets of Dublin. This was a colourful affair ... a completely harmless pageant that no one could take exception to, but, for some extraordinary reason that I could never fathom, its passage past the main gate of Trinity on its way to O'Connell Street was always a signal for a violent attack on it by the Trinity students who had concentrated there in force for that purpose ... This annual occurrence, so provocatively offensive to national sentiment, did much to make Trinity unpopular with the general populace, despite the number of leaders she gave to the nation.[24]

While such episodes could be dismissed as harmless 'rags', a long-standing college tradition, other collective expressions of student allegiances caused a great deal of friction in the Dublin streets. During Queen Victoria's Diamond Jubilee celebrations in mid-1897 a protest meeting addressed by Maud Gonne was attacked by Trinity students.[25] Three years later, after the British relief of Ladysmith, a small riot took place outside the Mansion House between Trinity undergraduates, 'waving Union Jacks and cheering the queen and Generals Roberts and Buller, on the one hand, and a crowd cheering the Boers and their leader Kruger, on the other'.[26] Such tensions were exacerbated by the perennial conflict over university reform, 'which became public and ugly in its final stages'.[27] The long campaign waged for an exclusively Catholic university involved an 'apparent assault on Trinity, a bastion, with its Anglican theological school, of Protestantism in Ireland'.[28] Victory for the 'Hands off Trinity' campaign of 1907 had its price, as the increasingly isolated institution was depicted as an obstacle to national progress, which was implicitly leading towards self-government. Trinity's plight was not helped by 'the crude and ignorant gibes of Provost Mahaffy and others at the renaissance of Irish culture'.[29] The college became a favourite target for cultural nationalists, with the *Leader* accusing it of wanting 'to kill everything Irish in Ireland'.[30]

This image of 'a university unassimilated by a nation' was reinforced by the abortive campaign to exclude Trinity College from the jurisdiction of a

June 1916. **24** BMH, WS 1770 (Kevin O'Shiel). See Eda Sagarra, *Kevin O'Shiel, Tyrone nationalist and Irish state-builder* (Dublin, 2013), pp 52, 56–7. **25** James H. Murphy, *Abject loyalty: nationalism and monarchy in Ireland during the reign of Queen Victoria* (Cork, 2001), p. 272. **26** Murphy, *Abject loyalty*, p. 276. Dickson, *Dublin*, p. 439. See BMH, WS 249 (Frank Henderson). **27** Dickson, *Dublin*, p. 439. **28** Senia Pašeta, *Before the revolution: nationalism, social change and Ireland's Catholic elite, 1879–1922* (Cork, 1999), p. 19. **29** Lyons, 'The minority problem in the 26 counties', p. 97. **30** *Leader*, 24 Nov. 1900, cited in Pašeta, *Before the revolution*, p. 58.

self-governing Ireland.[31] As Eunan O'Halpin has noted, 'Trinity fought tooth and nail to be exempted from Irish self-government between 1912 and 1922.'[32] The crudest attempt to achieve this end came in the shape of an amendment intended to partition off Trinity College from the jurisdiction of a future home rule state. Promoted by Dublin University's two MPs, Edward Carson and James Campbell, and endorsed by Trinity's provost and board, the move was successfully opposed by the college's fellows and professors.[33] During the debate, a vocal body of students circulated a petition declaring that Trinity was 'an Irish university and should stand and fall with the fortunes of the country'.[34] However, the threat posed by home rule, followed shortly by the challenge of world war, sharpened Trinity's unionist, Protestant and imperial allegiances. In a real sense, the college was under siege well before Easter Monday 1916.

Given the strategic and symbolic aspects already discussed, it was no surprise that Trinity had a prominent place in the rebel plans. Joseph Plunkett, the man credited with planning the Rising, is said to have remarked that 'everything was foreseen, everything was calculated, nothing was forgotten'.[35] Although it is impossible to speak infallibly on the subject, as neither the plan nor its architects survived Easter Week, the college was on the original list of sites to be occupied.[36] A practical reason for attacking Trinity was the 300 rifles and five thousand rounds of ammunition held at the OTC headquarters. The Irish Volunteers had secured a detailed map of the armoury several months before the Rising, and the munitions stored therein were to exercise an enduring fascination for the IRA.[37] Was Trinity saved by Eoin MacNeill's countermanding order of Easter Sunday, which drastically reduced the numbers of potential insurgents?[38] The original plans required at least twice as many rebels as were able or willing to mobilize at midday on Monday. Thirty-three years later Volunteer Thomas Slater recalled a conversation with Thomas MacDonagh, his commanding officer.

31 *TCD*, May 1917, cited in Irish, *Trinity in war and revolution*, p. 118. 32 *Trinity and the Rising*, p. 4. 33 Stanford and McDowell, *Mahaffy*, pp 219–20. For a mildly disingenuous version of this episode, see Luce, *Trinity College Dublin*, p. 128. 34 Irish, *Trinity in war and revolution*, p. 53. 35 BMH, WS 6 (Liam Ó Briain). 36 Frank Henderson recalled being 'told after the Rising by Dick McKee, later OC of the Dublin Brigade, that he was to have seized Trinity College with his company'. BMH, WS 249. According to Foy and Barton, 'Trinity College ... was originally a target because it features on a list of strongholds to be occupied by de Valera's 3rd Battalion, only to be excised, suggesting a late abandonment.' Michael Foy and Brian Barton, *The Easter Rising* (Stroud), 1999, p. 27. See Joseph O'Connor's account, MS 13735, NLI. 37 BMH, WS 307 (Thomas MacCarthy). 'We had some 300 rifles and 5,000 rounds of ball [ammunition] and other stores.' Fitzgibbon to Blake, 10 May 1916, TCD, MS 11107/1. See also, BMH, WS 535 (James Francis Hughes); WS 822 (W.J. Stapleton); WS 327 (Patrick Egan). 38 Mixing up her UCD professors, Elsie Mahaffy came to believe that Eoin MacNeill and not

> He told us one of the places which we were to occupy was Trinity College, and an officer named Paddy Walsh of 'D' Company was detailed for this job. As, however, the numbers which could be spared from the main body at Stephen's Green were so small, Tom MacDonagh decided to call off the taking of Trinity College as it would have meant a heavy loss of life with no hope of getting in. All that we could have spared for this job would be about twenty men.[39]

While the countermand caused considerable 'confusion and dispersal' of Irish Volunteer forces, the principal failure appears to have been one of intelligence.[40] 'The rebels neglected to grasp the most elementary advantage available to insurgent forces, local knowledge; they were as much in the dark as their opponents.'[41] In particular, they failed to discover how flimsy were the crown forces holding several key sites. As the next chapter will reveal, twenty men would have easily sufficed to take Trinity College and potentially change the course – if not the eventual outcome – of the Easter Rising.

Thomas MacDonagh was the rebel commandant charged with taking over Trinity College. Elsie Mahaffy diary, p. 122, TCD, MS 2074. **39** BMH, WS 263 (Thomas Slater). See also WS 186 (Thomas Doyle) and WS 249 (Frank Henderson). **40** Brennan-Whitmore, *Dublin burning*, p. 25. **41** Townshend, *Easter 1916*, p. 163.

CHAPTER 3

'Duty well fulfilled'

> It is difficult yet to take a dispassionate survey of the events of that week. The scenes unroll themselves in memory like the mad unrealities of a nightmare.
>
> —Captain Ernest Alton[1]

CORPORAL ALEXANDER DON was enjoying his holiday in Dublin. The sunny weather helped the 21-year-old New Zealander's recovery from a bout of typhoid fever he had contracted at Gallipoli during his country's baptism of fire in the First World War. Just ten months earlier he had left Wellington with the 1st Field Artillery Brigade, part of the 5th Reinforcements of the New Zealand Expeditionary Force.[2] Hoping to land in France, Don and his comrades were disappointed to find themselves disembarking in Suez, and soon afterwards to be fighting the Turkish army on the scrub-covered ridges and steep gullies of the Gallipoli peninsula. Don lasted only three weeks before becoming one of the approximately 36,000 casualties incurred by the Anzac forces (out of an Allied total of around 141,000).[3] Several months of convalescence at the New Zealand base hospital in Hornchurch (20 miles from London) gradually restored his strength. Granted leave at Easter 1916, he decided to visit Ireland. However, as Don described in a long letter to his father, the holiday was soon to come to a very abrupt end.

> On Easter Monday morning I was walking past Dublin Castle, and everything seemed all right, when a couple of shots rang out, and two Tommies, who were in front of me, fell over. I thought I must be dreaming, and went over to where they were lying, and saw that one had got it through the head and the other through the neck. Then I looked up and saw a couple of men in green uniforms and slouch hats, rifles and bandoliers, regarding me from the housetops. It was my hat

1 E.H. Alton, 'Work of the OTC', *TCD*, June 1916, p. 252. 2 NZDF, personnel archives, A.W. Don (2/1745), ANZ. 3 Christopher Pugsley, *The Anzac experience: New Zealand, Australia and empire in the First World War* (Auckland, 2004), pp 117–18.

> that saved my life, because it seemed to puzzle them, being so very like their own, although, of course, not green.[4]

It may have been Don's clothes as well as his slouch hat that confused the Irish Citizen Army snipers, as the uniform then worn by some New Zealand troops was a shade greener than the regular British khaki.[5] The rebels must have thought he was one of their own company, hurrying to take his place in the garrison at St Stephen's Green. If so, Don removed any such suspicion by immediately opening fire on them with his revolver from the next street corner.

> After going up the street a little way I saw more rebels walking on [the roofs of] the houses, and only for the crowd would have been shot. Then a lot of women got round me, crying and wailing for the soldiers, whom they had seen shot before. They pushed me into a place, and I got into civilian's clothes, as I didn't want to stay there all day.[6]

Safe from identification as a 'Tommy', Don joined the throng of Dubliners who were observing the curious goings-on at St Stephen's Green and in Sackville Street. 'At the Post Office I saw the Commander-in-Chief, Connelly [*sic*], standing with folded arms in a doorway,' Don recalled, 'I could have shot him from the crowd, but should have got two or three into me, as rifles and green could be seen from every window.' It was now around 2 p.m. 'I was just turning round to come away when I saw two New Zealanders. They were on holiday. The rebels started shooting at them, so I told them to come along with me.'[7] The men were Sergeant Frederick Nevin and Corporal John Garland, orderlies with the New Zealand Medical Corps, who were staying nearby at Wynn's Hotel in Lower Abbey Street.[8] The three Kiwis hurried across O'Connell Bridge to the Soldiers' Central Club in College Street, where the proprietor told them that 'all the soldiers had gone over to the [*sic*] Trinity College'.[9] They crossed the road and the porter unlocked the gates and allowed them to enter.

4 *Evening Star* (Dunedin), 21 July 1916. 5 Some New Zealand troops on Gallipoli wore the Territorial Force uniform introduced in 1912, which was a darker shade of green than the usual khaki. They also favoured the slouch hat (made of felt, with the left brim turned up); the 'lemon-squeezer' hat that marked out New Zealand troops in Europe was not officially accepted until late 1916. Barry O'Sullivan, 'New Zealand and the peaked felt hat', *Volunteers*, 39:2 (2017), pp 72–9. When Patrick Pearse surrendered he was wearing what a British officer described as 'a hat rather like a Colonial's with one side turned up'. BMH, WS 1019 (Alfred Bucknill). 6 *Evening Star* (Dunedin), 21 July 1916. 7 Ibid. 8 NZDF, personnel archives, J.G. Garland (3/1315); F.L. Nevin (3/1347), ANZ. 9 *Auckland Star*, 28 June 1916.

Don found several other soldiers already gathered in the college, including two more New Zealanders: Lance-Corporal Finlay McLeod and Private Edward Waring. They had also come under fire from rebel snipers, before finding their way to Trinity under the guidance of Lieutenant James Glen, an Irish artilleryman and former member of the OTC. Glen was happy to recruit potential defenders for his alma mater; as well as McLeod and Waring, whom he misidentified as Australians, his group included several South African soldiers and a couple of Canadians.[10] McLeod later recalled how 'on the way [to Trinity] we got eleven more Colonials'.[11] The new arrivals were greeted warmly by their hosts. As soon as news of the rebellion had reached Trinity the college porters realized the danger it posed. George Crawford, on duty at Front Gate, sent an alarm to the OTC headquarters at the eastern end of the campus, and instructed his colleague William Wilmot to lock the Lincoln Place Gate. Chief Steward Joseph Marshall was then 'on his rounds', but after being informed of the outbreak promptly closed the main entrance to the college. 'I took from my Office a large padlock with a strong chain attached and put it on the gate myself.'[12] He sent Crawford to lock the gate to the Provost's House and to confirm that the other entrances to college were equally secure. At both the east and west ends of Trinity, the porters invited in all passing soldiers, less for their own personal safety than to ensure the protection of the practically defenceless university.

Trinity was virtually empty, with most of its potential defenders away for the Easter vacation. Little existed to deter a rebel attack. Besides the six porters then on duty, there was only a four-man guard on the OTC headquarters, instituted a few months earlier in a desultory effort to prevent the pilfering of arms.[13] While it was not stood down a week before the Rising as was a similar guard on the College of Surgeons' armoury, this precaution was laughable as ammunition was not issued to the cadets until an hour after the rebellion had begun.[14] The college porters were more creatively armed, the 70-year-old chief steward having supplied them with several Fenian pikes he had confiscated some fifty years earlier during his days with the Dublin Metropolitan Police.[15] He preferred to rely on 'my old historic revolver and my Tipperary Blackthorn, which I brought into use in the Wild Riots in Dublin in September 1913'.[16]

10 James Glen, 'TCD: Easter Week 1916', 1 Dec. 1967, TCD, MS 4456. **11** *Sydney Morning Herald*, 7 July 1916. **12** Report of Chief Steward Joseph Marshall, 26 June 1916, TCD, MS 2783/19/1. **13** 'Ever since Christmas we kept a night guard in the OTC headquarters.' Fitzgibbon to Blake, 10 May 1916, TCD, MS 11107/1. **14** For the withdrawal of the guard on the College of Surgeons' armoury, see the report of Major G.A. Harris, May 1916, TCD, MS 2783/62. **15** Dublin's *Daily Express* (16 May 1916) later claimed that Marshall had reached the rank of inspector in the Royal Irish Constabulary. Thanks to Turtle Bunbury for drawing my attention to this reference. **16** Report of Chief Steward Joseph Marshall, 26 June 1916, TCD,

Despite their limited numbers, the defenders knew the task before them. 'Trinity must be defended,' declared Arthur Luce, a lieutenant in the Royal Irish Rifles back in Dublin on sick leave from France. A fellow of the college, he had witnessed the rebels attack a party of Lancers in Sackville Street, before hurrying back to warn Trinity. 'It was a spontaneous decision by a few of us on the spot, without any instructions from outside or other communication with civil or military authorities.'[17] Also, Luce might well have added, without the involvement of the OTC's commanding officer, Major Robert Tate, or its adjutant, Major George Harris. Tate was on leave in the North and failed to get back to Dublin that week. Harris was leading the local Dad's Army, known as the 'Gorgeous Wrecks', on a route march in the Dublin mountains, and ended up taking refuge in Beggar's Bush Barracks for the duration of the Rising.[18] In their place were a couple of junior dons, Lieutenant Gilbert Waterhouse and Captain Ernest Alton, professors of German and classics respectively, who were to display similarly relaxed responses to the crisis.

Waterhouse was working in his college rooms in New Square when the rebellion broke out at midday. Hearing 'fairly heavy firing' from the direction of St Stephen's Green, he assumed that the noise came from military operations by the *loyal* Volunteer Defence Corps (the Gorgeous Wrecks) and ignored it as best he could. Stopping work at 1 p.m., he was shocked to discover that it was the *disloyal* Irish Volunteers who were to blame for the disturbance. After alerting the guard at OTC headquarters, Waterhouse went for a quick spot of lunch and to change into his military uniform. On emerging suitably attired from his room, he found Lieutenant Luce knocking without success on Major Tate's door. After a brief discussion, Waterhouse decided to 'take command' of the situation and the two men returned together to OTC headquarters.[19] Arriving at 1.30 p.m., they found that Charles Mein, the 18-year-old cadet-sergeant in charge of the guard, had already issued a rifle and fifty rounds of ammunition to each of his men, posted sentries at strategic points, and begun to fortify the two-storey pavilion that housed the armoury. In case of 'an attack in force' they planned to retire to the upper balcony and hold out for as long as they could.[20] Waterhouse continued these defensive preparations, as later summarized in his official report:

MS 2783/19/1. **17** A.A. Luce, 'Recollections of Easter Monday 1916', 14 Oct. 1967. TCD, MS 4874/2/1. **18** The name was a play on the 'Georgius Rex' badges worn by those members of the Volunteer Defence Corps. Harris report to War Office, 10 May 1916, WO 32/9576. See also TCD, MS 2783/64. *Sinn Fein rebellion handbook*, pp 17–18. Most of the Volunteer Defence Corps were army veterans, including sporting figures like F.H. Browning, 'one of Ireland's great heroes of the cricket field' and twice president of the Irish Rugby Football Union. Starkie, *Scholars and gypsies*, p. 137. See also, Captain E. Gerrard's account, BMH, WS 348. **19** Report by Gilbert Waterhouse, TCD, MS 4875. **20** Report by William Mein, TCD, MS 2783/21. *Sinn*

> I ordered all gates opening on to the premises, including those which were never used, to be barricaded, and used for this purpose all available wagons and a large quantity of barrels and railway sleepers. The open doorway by the Gymnasium was likewise barricaded against a possible attack from the direction of College Park. I then caused all the rifles and equipment to be removed from the Armoury, which is on the ground floor, and carried upstairs into the Officers' Room and the Orderly Room, as it was conceivable that the garrison might be forced to evacuate the ground floor in the last resort. I then proceeded to examine my barricades and was thus engaged when Captain Alton arrived about 3 p.m. and took over the command. The garrison numbered by this time about 25 men.[21]

The paltry garrison was clearly inadequate. The college authorities would later calculate that at least one or two companies of troops – armed with machine guns – were needed for Trinity to be securely protected.[22] Messengers were hurriedly despatched to summon OTC members known to be within reach of Trinity, and as the afternoon wore on a trickle of cadets and alumni came to their college's aid. Many were instinctively drawn to the campus. 'Now it was suddenly clear that I must go to Trinity,' recalled Michael Taaffe, a final-year medical student, in his autobiography written forty-three years later.[23] As soon as he heard of the rising, cadet-sergeant Gerald Fitzgibbon 'knew everyone would be wanted there'.[24] Among those who rallied was John Joly.[25] The 58-year-old don had been cycling along the Dundrum road when he encountered Major Harris and his column of aged reservists. On being told that a rebellion had broken out, Joly turned around and raced back to Trinity. Arriving at 4 p.m. and finding the college 'almost without defenders', he promptly volunteered and would play an active role over the next week. (Joly also kept a close record of events and his response to them, which he wrote up a fortnight later for *Blackwood's Magazine*.)[26] By this time the garrison had grown to around thirty or forty. As well as the Anzacs, it included a handful of soldiers from various serving Irish regiments on leave in Dublin, plus a

Fein rebellion: a souvenir of presentations, p. 5. **21** Report by Gilbert Waterhouse, TCD, MS 4875. Captain Alton had already paid a quick visit to the OTC headquarters, before going home to change into his uniform. **22** TCD, MUN/V/21, p. 183, board resolution of 13 May 1916. See also TCD, MUN/V/21, 3 June 1916. **23** Michael Taaffe, *Those days are gone away* (London, 1959), p. 172. **24** Fitzgibbon to Blake, 10 May 1916, TCD, MS 11107/1. Captain Alton called to summon Fitzgibbon soon afterwards. See also Robert Tweedy's letter to his mother, 7 May 1916, TCD, MS 7533/3. Fitzpatrick, *Trinity College and Irish society*, p. 9. **25** John Joly (1857–1933), *DIB*, iv, pp 1021–2. **26** 'In Trinity College during the Sinn Fein rebellion' by 'One of the garrison', *Blackwood's Magazine*, July 1916, pp 101–25. The account was republished as a chapter

Lancer whose horse had been shot from under him outside the General Post Office. Most, however, were young students with a little part-time military training, dismissed by Joly as 'a few boys in khaki' and as 'raw recruits' by one of the Anzacs.[27]

The fourteen colonial soldiers stood out as a cohesive group among what Fitzgibbon described as 'the queerest military menagerie you ever saw'.[28] While the South Africans and Canadians were recent arrivals in Europe and had yet to see active service, most of the Anzacs – five New Zealanders and one Australian – were combat veterans, whose recent exploits at the Dardanelles were well known in Dublin. Joly privately lamented 'the thousands of these fine soldiers who have left their bones on Gallipoli'.[29] During Easter Week the term 'Anzac' was casually applied to describe the entire group of colonial soldiery in Trinity.[30] The Canadians and South Africans might well have grumbled at thus losing their national identity, but so could the New Zealanders, who were invariably described as 'Australian' in local accounts.[31]

Gallipoli was a very recent and painful memory in Ireland. Exactly one year earlier – on 25 April 1915 – the blood of hundreds of Dublin and Munster Fusiliers had helped to turn the sea red at Sedd-el-Bahr.[32] Although the Anzac sacrifice at the Dardanelles received much wider publicity, more Irish troops than New Zealanders would die during the course of the disastrous campaign. British military despatches dwelt on the impressive performance of the untried New Zealanders and Australians to a degree that even the colonial press deemed unfair to other combatant nations.[33] The *Irish Times* later complained of 'the contemptuous oblivion in which the deeds of Irish troops … on the Gallipoli heights were for a long time condemned to remain owing

in his autobiography and is reproduced in the appendices (pp 121–41). **27** Joly, *Reminiscences and anticipations*, p. 222. Finlay McLeod's letter in the *Grey River Argus*, 22 July 1916. **28** Fitzgibbon identified five Anzacs, two or three Canadians and nine South Africans (one in a kilt). Fitzgibbon to Blake, 10 May 1916, TCD, MS 11107/1. Waterhouse listed the men and their units: TCD, MUN/V/6/5, p. 86. **29** Joly, *Reminiscences and anticipations*, p. 237. **30** 'They took the colonials, whom they called Anzacs (although there were really only six Anzacs), up to the roof', recalled John Garland, 'where we were to snipe'. *Auckland Star*, 28 June 1916. Visiting the Provost's House, Lilly Stokes recalled how Captain Alton came there on Easter Monday afternoon 'to ask for beer for the 30 Anzacs he had collected to help to defend the College'. See her 'Easter Week Diary' in Roger McHugh (ed.), *Dublin 1916: an illustrated anthology* (London, 1976), p. 66. **31** Joly (mis)counted eight Anzacs, who 'by great good luck … had taken harbourage in the College'. *Reminiscences and anticipations*, p. 223. **32** Philip Lecane, *Beneath a Turkish sky* (Dublin, 2015). David Fitzpatrick, 'Imperial loyalties: Irishmen, Anzacs, and the conflict of empires at Gallipoli', *Irish Sword*, 30:121 (2016), pp 305–31. **33** The *Otago Daily Times* (25 Apr. 1916) lamented that praise for the Anzacs had 'the effect … of minimising or obscuring the equally heroic work of troops belonging to the Imperial centres'.

to the neglect or prejudice of officers in high command'.[34] Worse was to come in early August 1915, when the 10th (Irish) Division was practically annihilated after the landings at Suvla Bay, the losses including the celebrated 'Pals Battalion' of the Dublin Fusiliers. Once again the military authorities were accused of failing to recognize the depth of Irish sacrifice. 'There would not have been such bitterness in Ireland if only the British press had given a modicum of praise to Irish regiments,' noted Walter Starkie.[35]

The death toll at Suvla included some fifty Trinity students, staff and alumni.[36] As the war dragged on it slowly drained Trinity's vitality; there were 1,074 students on the books in 1914 but only 535 by the end of the conflict.[37] 'The best men are away and the hearts of the rest of us cannot be wholly in our college life,' *TCD* reflected in late 1914.[38] Some three thousand staff, graduates and undergraduates would eventually join the armed forces, 471 of whom died, a higher proportion than either the British or Irish general death rate.[39] This debilitation was reflected in the parlous state of Trinity's Officers' Training Corps. Formed in 1910, as a means by which students could receive specialized military training in order to secure a commission, it became popular largely as a social club, where cadets could relax and meet friends. There was a band and a sports committee, distinctive cap badges, swagger canes, even specially crested cigarettes. However, the outbreak of war turned the OTC from an occasional object of ridicule to one of deadly purpose as its cadets rushed to the colours.[40] It was later claimed that the corps supplied more than 2,000 trained officers for the fighting line.[41]

The depleted OTC was increasingly made up of older men, including many non-Trinity graduates, and adolescents too young to join the army. Fitzgibbon recalled that 'as time went on all the young men got commissions and the Corps had no young men except recruits'.[42] One cadet described it as 'a somewhat weird body containing, besides many men of fighting age, other old gentlemen whose spirit was magnificent but whose flesh was scarcely equal to it'.[43] Despite its weakened state, the OTC (or those few cadets who could be immediately summoned) was all that stood between Trinity and potential

34 *Irish Times*, 18 Mar. 1916, cited in Pádraig Yeates, *A city in wartime*, p. 84. 35 Starkie, *Scholars and gypsies*, p. 133. 36 Tomás Irish described August 1915 as 'perhaps the darkest [month] in the college's history'. *Trinity in war and revolution*, p. 97. 37 Laura Dooney, 'Trinity College and the war' in David Fitzpatrick (ed.), *Ireland and the First World War* (Dublin, 1986), p. 40. 38 *TCD*, 18 Nov. 1914. 39 Irish, *Trinity in war and revolution*, pp 79–81. Fitzpatrick, 'Militarism in Ireland', p. 392. 40 *TCD* (May 1910), cited in Roger Willoughby, *A military history of the University of Dublin and its Officers Training Corps* (Limerick, 1989), p. 8. 41 Sir Maurice Dockrell made this claim. *Sinn Fein rebellion: a souvenir of presentations*, p. 11. 42 Fitzgibbon to Blake, 10 May 1916, TCD, MS 11107/1. 43 Frank M. Laird, *Personal experience of the Great War* (Dublin, [*c.*1925]), pp 4–5, cited in Willoughby, *A military history of*

disaster on Easter Monday. The police had been immediately ordered off the streets for their own safety, while the army was busily defending its numerous barracks. When the nearest one to Trinity, Beggar's Bush Barracks, was finally contacted around midnight, it was being held by a mere handful of men (including Major Harris and the remnants of his column) with only twelve serviceable rifles between them.[44] 'We knew that help from that quarter was no longer possible,' Joly noted glumly.[45] At Portobello Barracks, despite some 300 soldiers being in occupation, 'it was the general belief that there were not sufficient forces to protect the barracks if an attack was made on it'.[46]

Trinity was well aware of its own vulnerability. Its mile-long perimeter enclosed some 35 acres of grounds, surrounded by thick walls and high fences. However, if Walter Starkie is to be believed, these barriers traditionally proved little obstacle to student ingress and egress.[47] The OTC headquarters and parade ground lay along the eastern boundary of the campus, separated from the main buildings and quadrangles at the College Green end by about a quarter of a mile. Between the two lay the vast expanse of College Park and the football ground. There was no telephone connection between the west and east ends of college. The OTC building was directly overlooked by the high embankment of the Loop Line from the Westland Row railway station, one of the first locations captured by the insurgents. Armed rebel patrols could be seen and heard on the railway line, and Luce recalled that 'there were snipers in the Nassau Street windows, and crossing the [College] Park was not safe'.[48]

The task of organizing a defence now fell to the 42-year-old professor of classics, Ernest 'Tubby' Alton. 'Short in stature, but strong and compact in physique, he was dubbed "the pocket Hercules" by a sports journalist.'[49] Alton's warm and extroverted personality was well suited to the challenge. He promptly posted six guards at Front Gate and strengthened the sentries at all other entrances to the college. The proximity of the rebels convinced Alton that the probable target of any attack would be the contents of the OTC armoury, so from 5 p.m. until 9 p.m. he set the garrison to work sandbagging the windows of the headquarters building. 'This was laborious work,' Joly recorded, 'but the younger men made light of it, filling the bags below and carrying them up the stairs.'[50] Firing platforms were constructed along the walls, and guards, ambulance units, cooking and fatigue details assigned. Joly's

the University of Dublin, p. 11. **44** Rather than receiving aid from Beggar's Bush Barracks, Trinity's OTC arranged to supply Major Harris with a revolver. *Sinn Fein rebellion: a souvenir of presentations*, p. 5. **45** Joly, *Reminiscences and anticipations*, p. 223. **46** *Sinn Fein rebellion handbook*, p. 110. **47** Starkie writes of 'the adventurous expeditions over the wall into the Queen's Theatre' in Great Brunswick (now Pearse) Street. *Scholars and gypsies*, p. 136. **48** A.A. Luce, 'Recollections of Easter Monday 1916', 14 Oct. 1967. TCD, MS 4874/2/1. **49** 'Alton, Ernest Henry (1873–1952)', *DIB*, i, pp 93–5. **50** Joly, *Reminiscences and anticipations*, p. 224.

memoir captures the mood of fear and anxiety felt by Trinity's defenders during that first sleepless night. All street lights were extinguished, and the trams and trains no longer ran. Rebels were known to be in St Stephen's Green, Boland's Bakery, and Jacob's Biscuit Factory; they were also rumoured to have taken Dublin Castle and Guinness' brewery. Trinity felt itself to be surrounded, 'in the midst of rebel-held territory'.[51]

According to Alton, 'it seemed impossible to obtain correct knowledge of the situation'.[52] Talk of a German troop landing circulated in rebel and loyalist camps alike. Desmond Fitzgerald later recalled Pearse's confidence that German submarines were in Dublin Bay.[53] James Stephens heard that 15,000 Germans were now in Ireland and that their warships had defeated the British navy; John Joly that Verdun had fallen and that the Germans had landed on the east coast of England.[54] The *Irish Times* possessed its own gas plant and so was able to appear daily until Thursday. Although it was printed in Westmoreland Street, situated between the warring factions, it carried little information on what was happening in the rest of the city. The edition of Tuesday 25 April limited itself to an official proclamation that 'certain evilly disposed persons and associations' had disturbed the peace, and an assurance that the situation was well in hand. Its main story concerned the opening of the Royal Dublin Society's spring show. Joly did not help matters when he returned to Trinity from a reconnoitre and estimated rebel numbers in St Stephen's Green at around 400 to 500; 'it soon became evident that the rebels were virtually in possession of the city'.[55] The garrison's sense of siege was compounded by rebel sniping from all directions.[56] On several occasions nervous and inexperienced trigger fingers nearly led to incidents of friendly fire.

> Night now slowly closed in. The City without was plainly in a state of chaos. Shots rang out every now and again. Distant shouts and challenges were heard. Sometimes a more rapid succession of shots suggested more serious fighting. Slowly the precincts around became indistinct. Impending dangers, unknown disasters, seemed to fill the gloom. Was this indeed to be, perhaps, the last night of our ancient University?[57]

51 Dooney, 'Trinity College and the war', p. 45. **52** *Sinn Fein rebellion: a souvenir of presentations*, p. 5. **53** Fitzgerald, *Desmond's Rising*, p. 137. **54** James Stephens, *The insurrection in Dublin* (Gerrards Cross, 1978), p. 29. Joly, *Reminiscences and anticipations*, p. 258. 'Dublin was practically in the hands of the rebels,' wrote Elsie Mahaffy in her diary (p. 12). TCD, MS 2074. **55** Joly, *Reminiscences and anticipations*, p. 221. James Stephens heard stories of '3000 well-armed Volunteers in the Green'. *The insurrection in Dublin*, p. 28. **56** 'Sniping shots were fired at us from the roofs of the houses in Westland Row, Nassau Street and Brunswick Street.' Fitzgibbon to Blake, 10 May 1916, TCD, MS 11107/1. **57** Joly, *Reminiscences and anticipations*, pp 227–8.

The same tensions, suppressed fears, and false alarms were being experienced by Eamon de Valera's 3rd Battalion, which was entrenched across the road from the OTC headquarters in or near Westland Row railway station, as in the other rebel strongholds around Dublin. They were also braced for a 'rapid and hard' attack, but the expected British military response never came.[58] Rather than launch an immediate assault, the crown's strategy during the first few days of the Rising was to secure Dublin Castle, the Magazine Fort, and the viceroy's residence in Phoenix Park, then to contain the rebels – isolating what Maxwell called 'the infected areas' – until sufficient reinforcements had arrived to permit an offensive.[59] This policy saw a column of troops from the Curragh actually bypass Trinity on early Tuesday morning en route to the Shelbourne Hotel.[60] The result was a stalemate, as each side waited for the other to attack. 'Will they never come?' was the question on everyone's lips.

However, just as Easter Monday drew to a close so too did the phoney war in College Green as men in both crown and rebel camps – 'impatient for the coming fight' – took decisions that would thrust Trinity College into the very centre of the Rising. First, the rebel leaders in the GPO decided to launch an assault on Trinity's West Front building facing the Bank of Ireland. Late on Monday afternoon Volunteer Captain Frank Thornton and some twenty men had been sent from the GPO in an abortive attempt to reinforce the City Hall garrison.[61] After being ambushed by British troops near the Telephone Exchange in Crown Alley, they retreated to a position near Westmoreland Street. Some hours later James Connolly ordered Thornton to take over several buildings in Fleet Street (east) at the back of the College Restaurant. His task was to provide covering fire for an attack on Trinity, for which purpose Connolly sent reinforcements from the GPO.[62] The Drogheda-born Thornton had come over from Liverpool for the Rising, bringing along a large

58 Townshend, *Easter 1916*, p. 181. **59** Cyril Falls, 'Maxwell, 1916, and Britain at war' in F.X. Martin (ed.), *Leaders and men of the Easter Rising: Dublin 1916* (London, 1967), p. 208. *Sinn Fein rebellion handbook*, pp 97–9. According to one eyewitness, 'The Lodge was left practically undefended'. Owen Dudley Edwards and Fergus Pyle (eds), *1916 The Easter Rising* (London, 1978), p. 202. **60** Joly noted that 'troops of khaki-clad men … occasionally passed the College'. *Reminiscences and anticipations*, p. 238. One wonders if Trinity's defensive 'bluff' also fooled the military authorities into thinking there was no danger of its occupation by the rebels. 'Early Tuesday morning saw one hundred men and a machine gun unit from the Curragh go via Dame, Nassau and Kildare streets to the Shelbourne Hotel.' G.A. Hayes-McCoy, 'A military history of the 1916 Rising', p. 277. **61** Lynch, *The IRB and the 1916 Rising*, p. 161. Liam Reilly, 'Frank Thornton: a Drogheda man's contribution to the 1916 Rising, in Brendan Matthews (ed.), *Reflections on the 1916 Rising* (Drogheda, 2016). Also, https://soundcloud.com/stories-from-1916-podcast/018-frank-thornton. **62** BMH, WS 510 (Frank Thornton); WS 1686 (Ruaidhri Henderson). See also, Military Service Pensions Collection, Dublin, MSP24SP1302 (Frank Thornton); MSP34REF41334 (Gilbert Lynch).

contingent which included three of his siblings.[63] As he recalled in his BMH witness statement:

> Later on in the evening, a further six men were sent to me and at about midnight I received instructions from Seamus [James] Connolly to be prepared to occupy buildings on the other side of the road getting into the rear of the buildings in Fleet Street [west] and so on to the roofs immediately behind the Bank of Ireland. Additional men were to be sent to carry out this job, and from the dispatch I understood that we were to act as a covering party on both sides of the road to enable a force from the GPO to attempt to capture Trinity College. This job was abandoned and on Easter Tuesday morning I was instructed to evacuate the position and return to the Post Office.[64]

What prompted these two decisions by James Connolly? As commandant of the rebel forces in Dublin, he earned deserved praise for his decisive leadership during Easter Week.[65] The messages to Thornton were part of a continuous flow of instructions he sent to all the rebel centres. Connolly had earlier lectured on street fighting and was well aware of Trinity College's strategic importance. Was this attack a belated recognition of the blunder made in not occupying it, as had originally been intended? There had been no sniping from the university's defenders before midnight, so the rebels may have assumed it was there to be taken. The historian G.A. Hayes-McCoy has noted that as the insurgent leaders 'realised they were not going to be overwhelmed immediately … they showed signs – particularly those of them who had not been hard hit – of wanting to pass to the next phase of resistance'.[66] The rebels' move onto the offensive was encouraged by a sense that they were winning. 'As the day ended, Connolly was in an expansive mood, feeling that the rebellion had got off to a good start … Insurgents occupied so many key positions in many parts of Dublin that it could be said that they controlled the city.'[67] In addition, the GPO garrison had swollen

63 Thornton was to serve on IRA headquarters intelligence staff during the war of independence. BMH, WS 615 (Frank Thornton). His sister Nora was active in the Cumann na mBan during the Rising. BMH, WS 655 (Nora Thorton). John M. Heuston, *Headquarters Battalion Easter Week* (Dublin, 1966), p. 65. Padraic O'Farrell, *Who's who in the Irish War of Independence, 1916–1921* (Dublin, 1980), p. 151. Jimmy Wren, *The GPO Garrison Easter Week 1916* (Dublin, 2015), p. 346. **64** BMH, WS 510 (Frank Thornton). **65** According to F.S.L. Lyons, Connolly was 'the real driving-force behind the military efforts of the insurgents'. *Ireland since the Famine* (London, 1982), p. 368. See also Ruth Dudley Edwards, *James Connolly* (Dublin, 1998), p. 139. Donal Nevin, *James Connolly* (Dublin, 2005), ch. 36. **66** Hayes-McCoy, 'A military history of the 1916 Rising', p. 291. **67** Samuel Levenson, *James Connolly* (London, 1973), p. 303. 'Tuesday opened in gloom. Dublin was practically in the hands of the rebels.' Elsie Mahaffy's diary, p. 12, greatly by late Monday night.[68] Did these factors encourage an attempt by Connolly to rectify the mistakes made owing to the confusion and low turnout caused by MacNeill's countermand? Alternatively, perhaps the attack was ordered simply because there was a rebel squad close enough to take on the job.

When Thornton's men began firing on Trinity, at midnight on Easter Monday they were immediately answered by a hail of bullets from the college's West Front building. This had only just been manned by colonial troops, as while Connolly was organizing Thornton's force his opposite number in Trinity had also decided to take the initiative. 'We became convinced of the grave danger which was incurred in leaving the streets to the enemy without challenge,' Alton later explained, 'Dame Street especially seemed to demand protection as large bodies of the enemy were seen marching from Stephen's Green to the north side of the city.'[69] Accordingly, he relocated his garrison to Trinity's front quadrangles at the west end of college, possibly on the urging of his more belligerent (and better experienced) Anzac comrades. By moving the contents of the armoury and concentrating his forces, Alton was able to adopt a more aggressive defence. Before the move of arms and ammunition took place (around 3.30 a.m.), Alton accepted the Anzacs' offer to act as snipers. Just before midnight, guided by porter Philip Donovan, they occupied the most strategic spots on the roof and at the windows of Trinity's West Front. 'The parapets provided excellent cover, and the various buildings are arranged so as to enfilade and subject attackers to a devastating cross fire.'[70] From these elevated positions the colonial troops commanded College Green and Nassau, Grafton, Dame, College and Westmoreland streets, with a line of fire extending across O'Connell Bridge and down Sackville Street.

If, as Tomás Irish argues, the defining characteristic of Trinity's experience from Wednesday onwards was 'passivity', then the preceding two days saw considerable activity by its defenders.[71] Tired of being a target for rebel snipers, the Anzacs seized their opportunity to turn the tables. The gun battle with Thornton's men was fierce and prolonged, as noted by John Joly, who was standing sentry near the OTC headquarters. 'It is now past midnight. A violent fusillade can be heard in the direction of the front gate of the College.'[72] The provost's daughter found it impossible to sleep, as 'all night long there were volleys of rifle shots'.[73] Two of the New Zealanders, Alexander

TCD, MS 2074. St John Ervine felt that 'the Government seemed to have thrown in the sponge'. Keith Jeffery, *The GPO and the Easter Rising* (Dublin, 2006), p. 175. **68** Dickson, *Dublin*, p. 449. BMH, WS 1686 (Ruadhri Henderson). **69** *Sinn Fein rebellion: a souvenir of presentations*, p. 6. **70** Starkie, *Scholars and gypsies*, p. 141. **71** Irish, *Trinity in war and revolution*, p. 150. **72** Joly, *Reminiscences and anticipations*, p. 231. **73** Elsie Mahaffy diary, p. 11, TCD, MS 2074. Fitzgibbon confirmed that 'all night ... we heard firing going on'. Fitzgibbon to Blake, 10 May

Don and John Garland, were stationed on the front parapet, commanding Dame Street and the lower part of Grafton Street. 'We remained on that roof from midnight on Easter Monday till midnight on Thursday,' Garland recalled, 'without a wink of sleep – exactly 72 hours.'[74] Finlay McLeod, Edward Waring and Michael McHugh (the sole Australian) were either on the roof or in the West Front pavilion overlooking the Bank of Ireland and Westmoreland streets. The other colonial troops were posted at different parts of the building. James Stephens was one of several observers who noted 'the unending stream of lead that was pouring from Trinity'.[75] Another nearly caught in the crossfire early on Tuesday morning was Arthur Norway, the secretary of the Irish Post Office:

> Shortly after breakfast … the Police rang me up, by direction of the Under Secretary, asking me to go to the Castle. I asked by what route. 'By Dame Street,' was the answer, 'That is quite safe today.' I was surprised, but to Dame Street I went, and was just turning into it, opposite to Trinity College, when a storm of bullets swept down the street, evidently from rebel rifles, and was answered by sharp successive volleys from Trinity College. The police were wrong.[76]

In their statements to the Bureau of Military History, several Irish Volunteers recalled the effectiveness of the sniping from Trinity College.[77] Domhnall O Buachalla, who would become the last governor general of the Irish Free State, was nearly a victim of the Anzacs' accurate shooting.[78] After being sent from the GPO across Sackville Street to the Dublin Bread Company building on Tuesday, 'I engaged some soldiers on the roof of Trinity College and, while I drew back from the loophole in the barricaded window from which I was firing, a bullet came through and grazed my hair.'[79] The Anzac sniper was probably Frederick Nevin, who later conducted a lengthy duel with Volunteer Captain William Brennan-Whitmore, stationed in the Imperial Hotel, which took on 'an almost personal character'.[80] The rebels had

1916, TCD, MS 11107/1. From his room in the United Arts Club in St Stephen's Green, St John Ervine also noted the increase in gunfire on Monday night. Jeffery, *The GPO and the Easter Rising*, p. 177. At 40 Merrion Square, Molly Woods heard 'a terrific fusillade' just after midnight. Dorothy Dunlop, *1916 and beyond the Pale* (Croydon, 1916), p. 70. **74** *Auckland Star*, 28 June 1916. **75** Stephens, *The insurrection in Dublin*, p. 40. **76** Jeffery, *The GPO and the Easter Rising*, p. 46. **77** BMH, WS 1670 (Seamus Kavanagh); WS 165 (Luke Kennedy); WS 152 (A.P. Agnew); WS 660 (Tom Leahy); WS 361 (Peadar Bracken); WS 660 (Thomas Leahy); WS 694 (Feargus de Burca); WS 724 (Desmond Ryan). **78** 'O Buachalla, Domhnall (1866–1963)', *DIB*, vii, p. 108. See also Brendan Sexton, *Ireland and the crown, 1922–1936* (Dublin, 1989), pp 151–2. **79** BMH, WS 194 (Domhnall O Buachalla). **80** Brennan-Whitmore, *Dublin burning*, p. 120.

strung up a wire across to the GPO to which was attached a small tin to carry messages. After several attempts Nevin succeeded in hitting the canister, as he was delighted to learn when guarding the captive Brennan-Whitmore on the following Sunday in the Custom House.[81]

The best-known incident of 'that night of wild passion and fierce hope' came around 4 a.m. on Tuesday, when three rebel cyclists carrying despatches from St Stephen's Green to the GPO were brought down by fire from Trinity.[82] Two were wounded and escaped, but the third, Volunteer Gerald Keogh, was killed. It was another example of 'the terrible accuracy of the battle-hardened colonial soldiers stationed on top of the college's West Front'.[83] Joly was sufficiently impressed with their 'wonderful shooting' to take a few hasty lessons in marksmanship, while Fitzgibbon noted that 'the Anzacs were given all the eligible situations, which it must be allowed they deserved. They were an outstanding gang. I have never seen their like.'[84] The use of the collective noun was appropriate, as the six men often acted as a mobile unit. Garland recalled that 'if information came to the officer in charge of the Dublin University to the effect that a sniper was on the roofs opposite, the cry was for the "Anzacs"'.[85] Alton and Waterhouse were both academics, more accomplished with the pen than the sword, so it was no surprise that they deferred to the Anzacs. As Luce put it, once the shooting started 'the College authorities faded out and soldiers were in command'.[86]

The results of their lengthy spell of duty drew warm praise from many witnesses. According to Joly, 'there can be no doubt that the accurate fire maintained from the College was an important factor in the salvation of the City ... The many important and stately buildings – banks, insurance offices, business premises – of Dame Street and Grafton Street were protected from the rebel or from the looter.'[87] Shops in Upper Grafton Street, out of range of the College rifles, suffered by contrast. To be sure, there was an element of make-believe involved in all this, as Fitzgibbon later noted. 'The rebels were bluffed by the confident face we put on.'[88] Trinity did a good job of pretending to be an armed camp. On Tuesday morning Min Ryan passed Front Gate on her way to the GPO along with her sister Phyllis, who was concealing their rebel brother Jim's gun under her long coat. She sensed menace from the fortified building. 'I had the feeling that there was something serious going on there. You would see an odd man peeping out from behind sandbags or you

81 Ibid., pp 144–7. **82** This was Arthur Norway's phrase. Jeffery, *The GPO and the Easter Rising*, p. 42. **83** Irish, *Trinity in war and revolution*, p. 140. **84** Fitzgibbon to Blake, 10 May 1916, TCD, MS 11107/1. **85** *Auckland Star*, 28 June 1916. **86** A.A. Luce, 'Recollections of Easter Monday 1916', 14 Oct. 1965, TCD, MS 4874/2/1. **87** Joly, *Reminiscences and anticipations*, p. 237. **88** Fitzgibbon to Blake, 10 May 1916, TCD, MS 11107/1.

would see the muzzle of a gun. There was odd shooting, and people would go off the street and come back again.'[89]

The Anzac squad's most significant service was not recognized at the time and has largely escaped the notice of historians. When Thornton's men launched their attack on Trinity its defenders did not realize what was happening. Both they and most subsequent commentators saw it as a rebel attempt to rob the Bank of Ireland, which they then successfully repulsed. The newspapers later rhapsodized over how Trinity's OTC had saved the bank from capture and possible destruction.[90] The *Daily Mail* carried the most creative account of the rebels making repeated rushes at the doors of the bank, only to be forced back by accurate fire from Trinity's cadets.[91] Cabled reports from London spread the story to New Zealand, though without mentioning the colonial involvement.

> The rebels made careful plans to attack the Bank of Ireland, and marched to the building in great style. They expected it would be an easy matter to overcome the six soldier guards who are always guarding the bank, but the rebels had not reckoned on the preparedness of the Trinity College students, who fired a volley. Several of the rebels fell. The remainder hesitated, and then pressed on with determination; but a second volley caused them to flee.[92]

Attributing rebel action to a desire for plunder indicated a general confusion and ignorance about rebel motives, but how likely was it that the bank was actually attacked? Once the Rising began, its sentries emulated Trinity's porters by locking the iron gates and withdrawing to the portico.[93] The manager and two inspectors were in the bank during Easter Week, as was the resident porter and his wife.[94] None reported an attack. The bank's whole frontage was overlooked by Trinity College, and 'no hostile being could have approached its doors', noted Joly.[95] When asked at the subsequent royal commission of inquiry 'who held the Bank of Ireland against the rebels?', Colonel H.V. Cowan replied simply, 'It was never attacked.'[96] However, rebel

89 BMH, WS 399 (Mary Josephine Mulcahy). **90** *Northern Whig* (Belfast), 1 May 1916, p. 7; *Ballymena Observer*, 5 May 1916, p. 5. **91** *Daily Mail* (Dublin), 1 May 1916. **92** *Evening Post* (Wellington), 1 May 1916, p. 6. Francis P. Jones, *History of the Sinn Fein movement and the Irish Rebellion of 1916* (New York, 1919), p. 310. **93** See 'A citizen's diary' by J.R. Clegg (Rathgar), *Irish Times*, 2 May 1916. **94** BMH, WS 1071 (George Chester Duggan). **95** Joly, *Reminiscences and anticipations*, p. 237. Major Harris reported that the bank was 'completely commanded from the College, and the rebels were prevented from making any attempt on it'. Report of Major G.A. Harris, May 1916, TCD, MS 2783/62. **96** *Sinn Fein rebellion handbook*, p. 179. The bank's historian discovered nothing worth reporting on the matter. Ronan Fanning, gunfire from the rooftops of the Fleet Street buildings immediately behind the Bank of Ireland convinced the Anzacs that it, rather than Trinity College, was the insurgents' target. More perceptively, Joly recorded that 'an attempt was, in fact, made to take possession of [the Bank's] roof, but it was frustrated'.[97] The Bureau of Military History files now reveal the rebels' true objective; yet, while Charles Townshend maintains that Trinity was 'never directly threatened by the rebel forces' during the Rising, the Anzacs' achievement of early Tuesday morning should not be discounted.[98]

The major incident of Tuesday afternoon was the capture by crown forces of the *Daily Express* building opposite City Hall, a drama played out in full view of the college's defenders and of which Joly has left a vivid account:

> We were at the time in ignorance of what was actually happening, for we were possessed with the idea that the Sinn Feiners held the Castle. When, therefore, we saw at the head of Dame Street men in successive waves rush across the street from the City Hall towards the *Express* offices, we thought they represented the enemy in process of expulsion from the Castle. As a matter of fact the waves of men were composed of the troops. From our position in front of the College we could see that a terrific fire was being directed against the *Daily Express* building; plaster and powdered brick were flying in showers from its façade. This fire was to cover the advance of our soldiers. But in spite of this we saw, more than once, one of the running figures pitch forward and fall ... The fight seemed to last a considerable time – about an hour at its greatest intensity – before the firing began to wane. Not till later did we learn that the final phase of the struggle took place, under deadly conditions for the soldiers, in the narrow passages of the newspaper office. But they were not to be withheld, and the Rebels were ultimately bombed out or captured.[99]

Trinity College was finally relieved around 5 p.m. on Tuesday, when a body of troops from the Leinster Regiment arrived. 'You may imagine that we cheered them as they entered the gates,' Robert Tweedy reported.[100] The two machine guns they brought were promptly set up on the roof of the West Front and turned in the direction of Sackville Street. On Wednesday evening

'The impact of independence' in F.S.L. Lyons (ed.), *Bicentenary essays: Bank of Ireland, 1783–1983* (Dublin, 1983), pp 53–4. **97** Joly, *Reminiscences and anticipations*, p. 237. **98** Townshend, *Easter 1916*, p. 185. **99** Joly, *Reminiscences and anticipations*, pp 238–9. **100** TCD, MS 7533/3. A Trinity student who bravely came in to sit an exam, Eileen M. Corrigan, recalled that 'at 5 [o'clock], when we left College, soldiers came trooping in, and formed themselves in a line around the quadrangle'. *Belfast Evening Telegraph*, 5 May 1916.

and throughout Thursday large reinforcements began to stream into the college through the Lincoln Place Gate, many weary and bloody from the battle they had fought in order to cross Mount Street Bridge. By the time General Maxwell arrived to take command on Friday morning there were about 16,000 British troops in Dublin, many of them quartered at Trinity. Ernest Alton could finally relax. 'Anxiety was at an end as regards the safety of the College and the neighbourhood by Thursday, and [OTC] officers who had hitherto slept little and washed less, began again to appear more like their former selves.'[101]

With machine guns and artillery discounting the need for snipers, most of the colonial troops were now placed on guard duty. Two eighteen-pounder field guns arrived from Athlone, so James Glen and five other OTC cadets went out in mufti to dig gun emplacements in Tara Street and act as ammunition porters.[102] Early Wednesday morning the guns targeted Liberty Hall – 'the centre of social anarchy in Ireland, the brain of every riot and disturbance'[103] – then in the afternoon, the rebel strongholds just across O'Connell Bridge. 'At the first report every pane of glass in the street was shattered.'[104] Elsie Mahaffy has left a graphic description of the 'pounding down' of Liberty Hall. 'It lasted some half an hour and was indeed terrible; even the solid Provost's House trembled and in the garden all the birds who had sung and warbled sweetly through all the previous noises became mute, huddling together in terrified clusters.'[105]

Trinity now became what it had always threatened to be – a stronghold from which the crown forces could crush the Rising. Hordes of British troops (what Fitzgibbon revealingly termed 'the Army of occupation') turned the college into a makeshift barracks.[106] As Alton later recalled, 'soldiers invaded the sacred grass plots, horses and mules kicked up the time honoured cobbles, and impetuous Tommies brushed aside impatiently the most august of our academic figures'.[107] College Park, the Engineering School, the Examination Hall and part of the Dining Hall were turned over to the troops. Visiting his alma mater, William Wylie, the lawyer who would soon be tasked with prosecuting the Rising's leaders, was shocked to see artillery in the quadrangles and machine guns on the roofs of buildings.[108] Elsie Mahaffy noted, 'The front

101 *Sinn Fein rebellion: a souvenir of presentations*, p. 8. **102** James Glen, 'TCD: Easter Week, 1916', 1 Dec. 1967, TCD, MS 4456/3. **103** *Sinn Fein rebellion handbook*, p. 19. **104** Ibid. **105** Elsie Mahaffy diary, p. 20, TCD, MS 2074. One Volunteer later recalled how around 2.30 p.m. on Wednesday 'a big gun was in place outside Trinity College and it started sending shells into us beginning with the top storey ... I tried to pick off some of the gunners, with what effect I could not tell, as they kept well behind the shield'. BMH, WS 361 (Peadar Bracken). **106** Fitzgibbon to Blake, 16 May 1916, TCD, MS 11107/1. **107** Ernest Alton, 'Work of the OTC', *TCD*, 19 June 1916. **108** Leon Ó Broin, *William Wylie and the Irish Revolution*, court of Trinity College grew fuller and fuller of soldiers. Here, at all hours, we could see, weary boys, sleeping on the grass, in the sun, or footsore men who had marched into Dublin, washing their feet under the antiquated water taps; others eating "bully" beef and hard biscuit.'[109]

To Joly the college had 'the appearance of a vast open-air stable or horse fair'.[110] Relieved from sentry duty, he took time to talk with the Tommies, mostly Sherwood Foresters and South Staffordshire Territorials. Joly was touched by the plight of these young and fairly recent recruits, many of whom had never fired a rifle before their awful ordeal at Mount Street. 'I heard then the simple narrative of how home and occupation had been left for service of King and Country. Some were anxious as to what might be happening in their absence. But there was no boasting, no display of sacrifice, never a word of regret. They had only done what a brave man should do.'[111] Joly reserved his highest praise for the Anzacs, whose company he regularly sought out during the turbulent week, and whose actions he recorded in terms of breathless admiration:

> The Anzacs listen; they say but little. They are magnificent of physique and lithe of figure. How keen of eye and what unerring shots they were we soon came to know … After being relieved, I joined the Anzacs on the roof. They were undoubtedly men fashioned for the enjoyment of danger. And certainly it would be harder to find nicer comrades.[112]

It is disappointing that historians have paid so little attention to these men. We know less about them than we do of the two smiling Swedish sailors who joined the GPO garrison in order to get some fighting in against the common English enemy before their ship left.[113] They are rarely mentioned in accounts of the Rising. Neil Richardson does not include them in his study of Irishmen who fought in the British army during Easter Week, though he provides fascinating details on the exploits of several of the OTC cadets.[114] They merit

1916–1921 (Dublin, 1989), p. 18. **109** Elsie Mahaffy diary, p. 30, TCD, MS 2074. **110** Joly, *Reminiscences and anticipations*, p. 248. **111** 'Just realise what he has done for the terrified citizens of Dublin,' Joly noted of the average Tommy; 'After my few days with him I like him very much indeed.' Joly, *Reminiscences and anticipations*, pp 254–5. Sadly, the South Staffordshires were soon to achieve notoriety for what they did *to* the terrified citizens of North King Street. **112** Joly, *Reminiscences and anticipations*, pp 230–1. This recalls the description of the Anzacs in Egypt by Maxwell's biographer. 'Tall of stature, broad-chested, loose of limb and easy of gait, to many an open-mouthed spectator they appeared as supermen.' Arthur, *General Sir John Maxwell*, p. 151. **113** Fitzgerald, *Desmond's Rising*, p. 134. Townshend, *Easter 1916*, p. 235. A Swede and a Finn, according to Volunteer Liam Tannam, BMH, WS 242. **114** Richardson discusses the Dublin-born Canadian, George Webb, but not Blackburn Charlton, the 33-year-old Irishman fighting with the 3rd South African regiment. *According to their lights: stories of Irishmen in the* a mere footnote in Roger Willoughby's history of Trinity's Officers' Training Corps,[115] while in his *Anzacs and Ireland*, Jeff Kildea concentrates on the one Australian in the squad, a man who left no known letters or diary recording his Dublin experiences.[116] Of the Anzacs, Tomás Irish says only that the OTC members 'were both impressed and taken aback by their battle-hardened professionalism'.[117] The next chapter will attempt to put some flesh on their bones.

British army, Easter 1916 (Cork, 2015), pp 361–2. **115** Willoughby, *A military history of the University of Dublin*, p. 22. **116** Kildea, *Anzacs and Ireland*, pp 62–8. **117** Irish, *Trinity in war and revolution*, p. 133.

CHAPTER 4

From the uttermost ends of the Earth

> We are a portion of the dominant family of the world. We are of the English-speaking race. Our kindred are scattered in dispersed parts of the globe, and wherever they are, no matter how far distant apart, there is a feeling of affection – that crimson tie, that bond of unity existing which time does not affect – and in the end will become indispensable.
>
> —Richard Seddon, New Zealand premier (28 Oct. 1899)[1]

TO THE IRISH REPUBLICAN BROTHERHOOD the First World War was an opportunity to take advantage of 'England's difficulty'. However, the global conflict swiftly led to the creation of a massive military machine, with over 1 million troops arriving from the white settler dominions to aid Britain in her hour of need. By the end of 1918 around 458,000 Canadians, 332,000 Australians, 136,000 South Africans and 112,000 New Zealanders had taken up arms for king and empire.[2] Together with more than 1 million troops from India, they made up a substantial part of the serving British forces, estimated at over 8.5 million. It was a human and material tribute freely offered, with all (except South Africa) paying their own way. As James Belich puts it, the dominions 'fought for Britain as though they co-owned it'.[3] During the four years of war many of these troops would use Ireland as either a base for training, a place for convalescence or a holiday destination.

Of course, the dominions (like Ireland) had no choice but to enter the conflict once their head of state, King George V, on the advice of the Westminster government, declared war. Despite some resistance from Afrikaner and French Canadian elements, who had no reason to love the British empire, these colonial communities largely agreed on what was at stake and why they ought to go to war.[4] They generally defined themselves as

1 *NZPD*, vol. 110, pp 75–6. 2 Steven Loveridge, *Calls to arms: New Zealand society and commitment to the Great War* (Wellington, 2014), p. 38. See also, Stephen Garton, 'The dominions, Ireland, and India' in Robert Gerwarth and Erez Manela (eds), *Empires at war, 1911–1923* (Oxford, 2014), pp 152–77. 3 James Belich, *Replenishing the Earth: the settler revolution and the rise of the Anglo-World, 1783–1939* (Oxford, 2009), p. 467. 4 Phillip Buckner and R. Douglas Francis (eds), *Rediscovering the British world* (Calgary, 2005), chs 8 and 11 on Canada;

British and saw the empire as their joint creation. Participation in the war would hopefully give them a voice in the future of an emerging commonwealth of nations. Despite horrendous casualties, Britain's white dominions raised, fielded and maintained large forces throughout the long and weary conflict. It has been noted that British-born men dominated the ranks of the dominion forces. Around 70 per cent of the members of the first Canadian contingent were British-born, while the 70,000 white South African troops who served overseas were 'overwhelmingly' drawn from the English-speaking community.[5]

This phenomenon was also reflected among Trinity's colonial defenders. Four of the five South African and Canadian soldiers whose birthplace is known were British- or Irish-born. Both of the Canadians had volunteered in late 1915, but had little obviously in common besides sporting a tattoo on their left shoulder. The 28-year-old George Alfred Webb was a clerk from Calgary, who had been born in Dublin, where his mother still lived. His comrade in the 56th Battalion, Howard Francis Cassidy, only 19, was a railway fireman born in Ontario. Cassidy had arrived in England in November 1915, only to badly injure his knee on manoeuvres two months later. After his discharge from hospital he was given leave at the end of April 1916. It is likely that Webb suggested to Cassidy that they take the opportunity together to explore his native city.[6]

The six South Africans were also a tight unit. Most were British-born, while three shared their first name with their monarch. As reinforcements for the 1st South African Infantry Brigade, George Gibson, Blackburn Charlton, George Moffitt and Eric King all left Cape Town on 25 March 1916, arriving in England on 14 April. George Russell had made the same journey at the end of February. All except King were enrolled with the 3rd Regiment, recruited largely from the Transvaal and Southern Rhodesia. King was a member of the 4th Regiment, raised from the Transvaal Scottish and the Cape Town Highlanders. He fought in a kilt of the Murray of Atholl tartan, and was remembered in Trinity largely for this reason. Moffitt was lucky to have been allowed to sail with the reinforcements, as he had spent most of March in the Military Hospital, Potchefstroom, suffering from gonorrhoea, a malady that

ch. 13 on South Africa. **5** John Darwin, *The empire project: the rise and fall of the British world-system, 1830–1970* (Cambridge, 2009), pp 336, 345. The British-born in Australia were also more likely to join up than their colonial-born counterparts. Malcolm Campbell, 'Emigrant response to war and revolution, 1914–21: Irish opinion in the United States and Australia', *Irish Historical Studies*, 32:25 (May 2000), p. 80. **6** Webb's tattoo was of a snake, but Cassidy's remains a mystery. Personnel records of the Canadian Expeditionary Force: George Webb (447766), RG 150, Accession 1992–3/166, Box 10177–44; Howard Cassidy (454045), Accession 1992–3/166, recurred shortly after his Easter Week experiences. Based in Shorncliffe, near Folkestone, the South Africans were granted furlough from 19 to 25 April, and appear to have made a collective decision to visit Dublin.[7]

The predominance of British-born men among the colonial soldiery also reflected tensions within Canada and South Africa, which were well illustrated by the divisive issue of conscription. Legislation for compulsory military service overseas was enacted in Canada but split the country; a similar proposal was twice rejected in Australia, while the Afrikaner voter majority ensured that it was never attempted in South Africa.[8] By contrast, New Zealand was exceptional in both the large number of native-born volunteers – four out of five Kiwis in the Trinity College garrison were New Zealand-born – and its general acceptance of compulsory military service. The historian Steven Loveridge has suggested that 'being raised in New Zealand may have been a comparable motivating factor to being British-born' in terms of recruitment.[9] There was little opposition to the 1916 Military Service Act, as conscription was regarded as necessary to ensure equality of sacrifice; overall there were about three volunteers for every conscript in the New Zealand Expeditionary Force.[10]

On the outbreak of war, New Zealand's press, priests and politicians largely sang from the same loyal song sheet. The influential *New Zealand Herald* saw the conflict as 'a war for the liberties of the world'.[11] John Grimes, Catholic bishop of Christchurch, declared it to be 'one of the most just wars we have ever entered upon'.[12] After hearing that the Canadians intended to send an expeditionary force to Europe, New Zealand's Prime Minister William Massey immediately promised in parliament that his government would match the offer, after which the entire House rose and sang 'God save the King'.[13] The Ulster-born Massey was in no doubt where New Zealand's loyalty lay: 'When the Empire calls it is for the citizens of the Dominion to respond [and] obey.'[14] The leader of the other major political party was Sir

Box 1568–9, Canadian Library and Archives. **7** The sixth South African, Kinahan, remains a mystery as it has proved impossible to locate his records. Military files of George Russell (7624), Blackburn Charlton (9343), Eric King (9380), George Gibson (9405), and George Moffitt (9435), Department of Defence Archives, Pretoria, South Africa. On King's kilt, see Fitzgibbon to Blake 10 May 1916, TCD, MS 11107/1. **8** Darwin, *The empire project*, p. 344. **9** The British-born (21.6% of the population in 1911) constituted 25.6% of enlistees by November 1914 and 19.6% of volunteers awaiting call up in October 1915; the New Zealand-born (71.1% in 1911) comprised 74.1% of enlistees by November 1914 and 73.4% of volunteers in October 1915. Loveridge, *Calls to arms*, p. 51. **10** Loveridge, *Calls to arms,* p. 26. See Paul Baker, *King and country call: New Zealand, conscription and the Great War* (Auckland, 1988). **11** *New Zealand Herald* (Auckland), 6 Aug. 1914. **12** *New Zealand Tablet*, 27 Aug. 1914. **13** *NZPD*, 169, 31 July 1914, p. 369. **14** Loveridge, *Calls to arms*, p. 45. See Rory Sweetman, 'Beery Bill the Orangeman: another look at William Ferguson Massey' in James Watson and Lachy Paterson

Joseph Ward, an Australian-born Catholic of Irish parentage, who during a long political career 'turned the identification of Catholicism with Imperialism into almost an art form'.[15] These loyal sentiments were widely shared; more than half of the country's eligible males eventually presented for service, with those mobilized representing over 10 per cent of the total New Zealand population, possibly the highest proportion of enlistment among the dominions.[16]

Stranded at the very edge of empire, 'the smallest and most isolated of the white Dominions was the most effusively loyal to Britain and the most determined to prove its worth to her'.[17] The war was seen as 'a conflict fought by a pan-British people for the survival, or triumph, of a British Empire to which New Zealanders had contributed and in which they excelled'.[18] Victory would protect the empire and the values it was believed to embody. The historian Ian McGibbon has argued convincingly that 'New Zealand's participation in the First World War was the logical outcome of a defence policy which depended on the power of Great Britain.'[19] British command of the seas was deemed vital for regional security in a time of Great Power competition in the Pacific. Accordingly, in 1903 New Zealand began paying Britain an annual naval subsidy of £40,000, which was raised to £100,000 in 1908. 'There is but one sea around our shores', declared Ward, 'and with one sea and one Empire, there should in reality be but one Navy'.[20] In March 1909, he offered to gift Britain 'one first-class battleship of the latest type'. The result was an Indefatigable-class battle-cruiser, the HMS *New Zealand*, launched on 1 July 1911 and costing almost £2 million.[21]

There was a strong material incentive for such conspicuous displays of loyalty. The New Zealand economy depended on the demands of the British market, and British goods made up 60 per cent of the dominion's imports in 1913.[22] Cultural ties were even closer than economic ones. Most citizens embraced a concept of 'Greater Britishness', allowing them to be both proud New Zealanders and loyal members of an empire that covered one-quarter of

(eds), *A Great New Zealand prime minister? Reappraising William Ferguson Massey* (Dunedin, 2011), pp 77–86. **15** Rory Sweetman, 'New Zealand Catholicism, war, politics and the Irish issue, 1912–1922' (PhD, University of Cambridge, 1990), p. 39. See also Michael Bassett, *Sir Joseph Ward* (Auckland, 1993). **16** Loveridge, *Calls to arms*, pp 12, 50. **17** Baker, *King and country call*, p. 11. Newfoundland was, in fact, smaller in size. **18** Loveridge, *Calls to arms*, p. 66. **19** Ian McGibbon, *The path to Gallipoli: defending New Zealand, 1840–1915* (Wellington, 1991), p. 259. **20** R.A. Loughnan, *Life of Sir Joseph Ward* (Dunedin, 1928), pp 145–6, cited in Matthew Wright, *Shattered glory: the New Zealand experience at Gallipoli and the Western Front* (London, 2010), p. 36. **21** McGibbon, *The path to Gallipoli*, pp 171, 179. **22** New Zealand exemplified James Belich's 'recolonization' thesis, where Anglophone settler populations gravitated towards the economic and cultural pull of the metropolises. *Replenishing the Earth*, pp 179–80, 208–9.

the globe and encompassed one-quarter of the world's population. According to their Dublin-born governor, Lord Plunket, New Zealanders were 'fellow citizens of the Empire … British in thought and blood'.[23] This relationship was symbolized by the national flag officially adopted in 1902, which ranged the Southern Cross alongside the Union Jack. The dominion had just made its first 'blood sacrifice' for empire, despatching some 6,000 men to fight in the Anglo-Boer War (1899–1902), 230 of whom died. Premier Richard Seddon described the ten contingents sent to South Africa as fighting for 'one flag, one queen, one tongue, and for one country – Britain'.[24] The claim that such actions earned New Zealand its right to membership of the imperial club was to be repeated after the disastrous Dardanelles campaign. On the first anniversary of the Anzac landings, 25 April 1916, A.W. Averill, Anglican archbishop of New Zealand, insisted that 'our boys' had not 'died in vain' on Gallipoli: 'They represented New Zealand's sense of honour and gratitude … [and show] the worthiness of the nation to take its place in the great family of free nations in the Empire.'[25]

It was in such a climate of opinion that Alexander Don, John Garland, Frederick Nevin, Finlay McLeod and Edward Waring made their decisions to volunteer for service in the war. While their individual personal motivations are unknown, they may well have included a desire to escape from poverty and unemployment, or merely from a humdrum colonial life, taking the chance to experience the wider world. It was a rare opportunity to visit Britain, referred to as 'home' by even the New Zealand-born. Most Kiwis had been brought up hearing about the glories of London, at that time the largest city in the world.[26] These men were also part of a generation groomed from childhood for their role in the First World War. Nurtured on schoolboy fantasies of imperial glory in a culture that exalted military adventure, they had been taught that their duty was to fight for community, nation and empire. (One could compare the indoctrination at St Enda's school by Patrick Pearse and Thomas MacDonagh.)[27] As in Ireland, informal peer pressure was perhaps the most compelling factor in their decision to enlist.[28]

Such conditioning helps to explain the rapid recruitment and despatch of two New Zealand expeditionary forces – the first to German Samoa, the

23 Loveridge, *Calls to arms*, p. 42. William Lee Lord Plunket was New Zealand's governor from 1904 to 1910. Educated at Trinity College, he was the son of the Protestant archbishop of Dublin (1884–97). Gavin McLean, *The governors: New Zealand's governors and governors-general* (Dunedin, 2006), pp 157–64. **24** *NZPD*, vol. 110, pp 75–8, 95–6. **25** *New Zealand Herald*, 26 Apr. 1916. **26** Felicity Barnes, *New Zealand's London: a colony and its metropolis* (Auckland, 2012), pp 53–69. **27** Elaine Sisson, *Pearse's patriots: St Enda's and the cult of boyhood* (Cork, 2004). See also, John C. Mitcham, *Race and imperial defence in the British world, 1870–1914* (Cambridge, 2016), ch. 6. **28** David Fitzpatrick, 'Home front and everyday life' in John Horne second to Europe – within ten weeks of the declaration of war. It also reflects how completely New Zealand had been drawn into a systematic project of 'imperial defence' since the chaotic years of the Anglo-Boer War.[29] In 1909 New Zealand broke with British precedent by introducing compulsory military training for every male between 14 and 25 years of age. A school cadet system was established that fed into an adult territorial force; by mid-1911 there were some 29,991 cadets and 21,838 territorials on the books.[30] The aim was to standardize the dominion's forces on the British regular army model, thereby ensuring the provision of an efficient expeditionary force. In February 1910, Field Marshal Lord Kitchener, 'the Empire's leading military personality', examined New Zealand's defences, and soon afterwards Major-General Alexander Godley was named as commandant of the New Zealand forces. A nephew of one of the founding fathers of Canterbury, Godley was born in England but considered himself 'by birth and upbringing an Irishman'.[31] With the assistance of a clutch of imported Imperial staff officers and instructors, he transformed the ramshackle dominion units into a body that impressed the Inspector-General of the Overseas Forces, General Sir Ian Hamilton, when he visited New Zealand in 1914. The man who was to command the Anzacs on Gallipoli in less than a year then remarked of his future charges, 'the human material is second to none in the world'.[32]

During their schooldays, Don, Garland, Nevin, McLeod and Waring would have passed through junior cadets (from age 8 to 12), where the focus was mostly on physical training with the occasional opportunity to fire miniature small-bore rifles. On graduating to senior cadets they would have participated in more combat-oriented activities, organized now by the military authorities.[33] An emphasis was placed upon marksmanship, the cadets using the same .303 Lee-Enfield rifles destined to be employed at Gallipoli. Garland's cadet training at Auckland Grammar School and three years' service with the Territorials helped to win him selection for the Samoan Expeditionary Force. This body was hastily organized after Britain asked New Zealand to perform the 'great and urgent Imperial service' of seizing the German territory.[34] Within ten days of the request being made, a 1400-strong

(ed.), *Our war: Ireland and the Great War* (Dublin, 2008), pp 134–5. **29** Douglas E. Delaney, *The imperial army project: Britain and the land forces of the dominions and India, 1902–1945* (Oxford, 2017). **30** Wright, *Shattered glory*, p. 39. **31** Terry Kinloch, *Godley: the man behind the myth* (Dunedin, 2018), p. 12. Alexander Godley, *Life of an Irish soldier* (London, 1939). **32** McGibbon, *Path to Gallipoli*, p. 205. **33** Finlay McLeod completed his primary education in Wellington, before moving to Australia with his parents. He spent his last year of schooling (1911–12) at Sydney Grammar School, where he is pupil number 7632 in the school register. **34** Stephen J. Smith, *The Samoa (NZ) Expeditionary Force, 1914–1915* (Wellington, 1924), p. 14.

party landed at Apia on 29 August 1914, meeting no resistance from either German officials or the local population. The operation was not without risk, however, as Germany's East Asia squadron was in the vicinity; two weeks later the SMS *Scharnhorst* and *Gneisenau* appeared off shore, trained their guns on the new occupiers but then withdrew without opening fire.[35] Papeete in French Tahiti was soon to feel their wrath, being left half-destroyed after a prolonged bombardment on 22 September.

The 20-year-old Garland enlisted as part of the 3rd (Auckland) Regiment, whose journey to the port of embarkation at Wellington saw residents turning out en masse at the various railway stations, accompanied by bands and bunting. On landing in Samoa, the Auckland contingent was ordered to march inland to capture the vital wireless signal station. First, as staff bugler, Garland had to sound 'the officers' call, which signalized the taking of possession of the former German territory'.[36] (Thirty years later he would present the bugle he had used, suitably inscribed, to the Auckland War Memorial Museum.)[37] The news that Samoa had fallen was greeted joyfully in New Zealand, as it was believed – wrongly, it turned out – to be the first overseas German territory captured by British forces.[38] Samoa's occupation was to prove more problematic than its capture, however, as tropical downpours and the 'maddeningly persistent mosquitos' began to take their toll.[39] Eye and ear diseases spread among the troops, along with cases of dysentery and typhoid. Garland survived the conditions for just over seven months, before returning home sick in mid-April 1915. He then transferred to the Trentham Rifle Brigade before being discharged as medically unfit on 16 September. Garland's 'swollen knee' healed quickly, however, as six weeks later he signed up for training as an orderly with the New Zealand Medical Corps.

Who was John Godwin Garland? His parents, Thomas Henry Garland (a grocer) and Harriet Threader, had emigrated from London to Christchurch in 1884, settling soon afterwards in Auckland, where Thomas established a baking powder factory. They had seven children, including three boys, of whom John was the youngest. The family were strong Methodists, four of Garland's uncles becoming ministers. When he enlisted with the Samoan Expeditionary Force he was working as a clerk with the New Zealand Dairy Association and living with his parents in Mount Eden, an Auckland suburb. While he was somewhat fortunate to pass the medical for selection (the hearing in both of his ears being deemed 'bad'), service in Samoa appears to

35 J. Bryant-Haigh, 'The military occupation of German Samoa, 1914–19', *Volunteers*, 40:2, pp 9–15. 36 *Auckland Star*, 26 Aug. 1944. 37 Ibid. 38 The Togoland Colony, West Africa, had fallen to French and British forces three days before. David Killingray, 'The war in Africa' in John Horne (ed.), *A companion to World War I* (London, 2012), pp 112–26. 39 Smith, *The Samoa*

have cured Garland's deafness and added twenty pounds to his weight.[40] One wonders what prompted his decision to become a medical orderly. The prospect of serving on a hospital ship clearly appealed to one who enjoyed shipboard life. He had probably observed medical orderlies in action, as there was a large NZMC contingent in Samoa, including a small base hospital and a field ambulance unit.[41] After being attested at Palmerston North on 28 October 1915, Garland underwent brief training at Awapuni camp before being assigned to the ambulance unit of the *Marama*, the second of two hospital ships contributed by the New Zealand government to the British war effort.

The day after Garland signed his attestation form in Palmerston North, another 20-year-old recruit for the *Marama*'s ambulance unit arrived at Awapuni camp. Frederick Leslie Nevin was a machinist at the government railway workshops in Christchurch, the son of Irish-born Catholic immigrants who brought up their six children in the working-class suburb of Linwood. He appears to have suffered from health problems in his youth, which may have led to his involvement with the local Red Cross society. He acquired several qualifications in first aid and served four years with the New Zealand Mounted Field Ambulance.[42] This experience was recognized by a speedy promotion to corporal at Awapuni, then to acting-sergeant after the *Marama* had begun operations in the Mediterranean. According to his commanding officer, Nevin 'proved himself a most conscientious and careful ward sergeant, capable in handling orderlies, and punctilious in the performance of all his duties'. In the same report Lieutenant-Colonel Percy Cook noted laconically that Garland, by contrast, was 'allowed to remain an acting-corporal, which rank he held at Awapuni'.[43]

Larger and faster than its sister ship *Maheno*, the *Marama* was a twin-screw steamer of 6,437 tons which had been on the Auckland-San Francisco service before its rapid refit as a hospital ship. It was painted white with a yellow funnel, and along its sides were a green band and large Red Cross markings, while the cabin fittings were replaced by some 600 beds. It left Wellington on 5 December 1915, and after stops in Adelaide, Albany, Colombo and Aden, reached Suez two months later. Passing through the canal to the cheers of thousands of troops lining its banks, the *Marama* arrived in Egypt on 18 January 1916 to find 471 sick and wounded soldiers awaiting transportation from Alexandria to Southampton. Thus began a commission in which the ship would steam around 52,251 nautical miles and carry some 13,000 patients.[44]

(NZ) Expeditionary Force, p. 81. **40** NZDF, personnel archives, J.G. Garland (1/636) and (3/1315), ANZ. **41** Smith, *The Samoa (NZ) Expeditionary Force*, p. 20. **42** NZDF, personnel archives, F.L. Nevin (3/1347), ANZ. **43** Lieutenant-Colonel Percy Cook's report to GOC, 22 Oct. 1916, AD1 887 39/182, Archives New Zealand. **44** J.S. Elliott, 'The New Zealand

Many of those who walked or were carried on board the *Marama* in Alexandria had just been evacuated from the Dardanelles, where the Allied campaign had ended in humiliating withdrawal. The New Zealand forces had around 8,000 casualties, including 2,800 dead, while the Turkish defenders suffered around a quarter of a million casualties.[45] Four survivors of the campaign would later share the first anniversary of the Anzac landing, with Fred Nevin and John Garland, on the battlements of Trinity College Dublin. Edward Waring, Finlay McLeod, Michael McHugh and Alexander Don had already left the Mediterranean before the *Marama* arrived on the scene, but collectively they had experienced the full trauma of the recent campaign: Waring amid the confusion and terror of the initial landing on 25 April; McLeod enduring the worst of a brutal summer in the trenches; McHugh in the prolonged battle for the Sari Bair range; and Don during the forlorn fight for Chunuk Bair in early August.

Edward Waring was a 23-year-old Aucklander, a blacksmith of English parentage and a private in the 6th Hauraki Company of the Auckland Battalion.[46] When leaving New Zealand with the 2nd Reinforcements on 14 December 1914, he and his comrades expected to land in Europe, but Turkey's decision to enter the war on Germany's side led to a change of destination. This was deemed to pose so great a threat to the Suez Canal – 'the jugular vein of the British empire'[47] – that the Australian and New Zealand contingents were ordered to disembark and train in Egypt, recently proclaimed as a British protectorate. Waring arrived just in time to participate in the defence of the canal, his infantry brigade assisting Indian forces in repelling an Ottoman attack in early February 1915.

The British commander in chief in Egypt, General Sir John Maxwell, was dismissive of the Turkish threat ('it required no great effort on our part to throw those who reached the Canal back in confusion'), but heaped praise on 'the splendid qualities of the New Zealand contingent'.[48] This brief action led to New Zealand's first combat casualty of the war, the Wicklow-born William Ham, who had emigrated from Ireland with his family in 1903, coincidentally on the same ship in which he returned to Europe with the NZEF.[49] After his

hospital ships' in H.T.B. Drew (ed.), *The war effort of New Zealand* (Auckland, 1924), p. 135. Letters from John Garland are cited by Gavin McLean, *The white ships: New Zealand's First World War hospital ships* (Wellington, 2013). See also, Anna Rogers, *With them through Hell: New Zealand medical services in the First World War* (Auckland, 2018), ch. 9. **45** Richard Stowers, *Bloody Gallipoli* (Wellington, 2005). See also his *Heroes of Gallipoli* (Christchurch, 2015). **46** NZDF, personnel archives, Edward Waring (12/1523), ANZ. **47** Arthur, *General Sir John Maxwell*, p. 153. **48** General Sir John Maxwell, 'Introduction' in C.G. Powles, *The New Zealanders in Sinai and Palestine* (Auckland, 1922), p. x. **49** Wright, *Shattered glory*, p. 62.

baptism of fire, Edward Waring settled down as one of 'Massey's Tourists', based in a tent camp at Zeitoun, some four miles from Cairo. By this time rumours were circulating that the newly formed Australian and New Zealand Army Corps would be heading to the Dardanelles as part of a Mediterranean Expeditionary Force led by Lieutenant-General Sir Ian Hamilton.

The rumours were true. On 12 April 1915, Waring embarked from Alexandria to join the numerous transports assembled in Mudros harbour. As a fellow Anzac, Ormond Burton, later recalled, 'in this floating city were Australians and New Zealanders from the southern Pacific, the regulars of the 29th Division, battalions of English Territorials, long-haired bearded Sikhs, smiling Gurkhas, blue-coated Frenchmen and big, black Sinhalese'.[50] Waring survived the initial landing at Anzac Cove only to be shot in the left thigh nine days later. Reported as 'wounded and missing', he was evacuated within a few days. He next surfaces in the military records as a patient in the 1st Southern Hospital, Birmingham, from where he was transferred to the New Zealand War Contingent Hospital at Walton-on-Thames on 25 August 1915. Six months later he had recovered sufficiently to be sent to the New Zealand base hospital at Hornchurch.

Of the three 'Trinity Kiwis' on Gallipoli, Finlay McLeod served the longest there. He was a 20-year-old motor mechanic, born in Otago. A lance-corporal with the 2nd Company, New Zealand Field Engineers, McLeod left Wellington on 17 April 1915 with the 4th Reinforcements. Arriving in Egypt on 25 May, he was sent to Gallipoli five days later. McLeod was wounded on 25 July and evacuated first to hospital in Malta, suffering from neuritis, then to England in the *Carisbrook Castle*. McLeod was fortunate in avoiding both the brutal early battles of the campaign and the awful bloodletting of the August offensive. He was admitted to Netley Hospital (near Southampton) on 23 October 1915 suffering from enteric fever, now more commonly known as typhoid, before being transferred to Hornchurch for convalescence.[51]

Alexander Don and Michael McHugh both fought in the bloody summer offensive of August 1915 that saw two divisions of the Anzac Corps virtually wiped out within a week, while the 10th (Irish) Division was being decimated nearby at Suvla Bay. Don had been a clerk with Whitcombe and Tombs (booksellers and publishers) in his native Dunedin, when he volunteered for

50 Ormond Burton, *The silent division: New Zealanders at the front, 1914–1919* (Sydney, 1935), p. 34. 51 McLeod has been identified as one of the gallant band of sappers who laid telephone lines from the Apex to the summit of Chunuk Bair, an episode that saw Corporal Cyril Bassett win New Zealand's only Victoria Cross of the campaign. Stowers, *Heroes of Gallipoli*, p. 210. His military file says otherwise, however, and Christopher Pugsley and Charles Ferrall identify a different Sapper McLeod. *Remembering Gallipoli* (Wellington, 2015), p. 183. NZDF, personnel

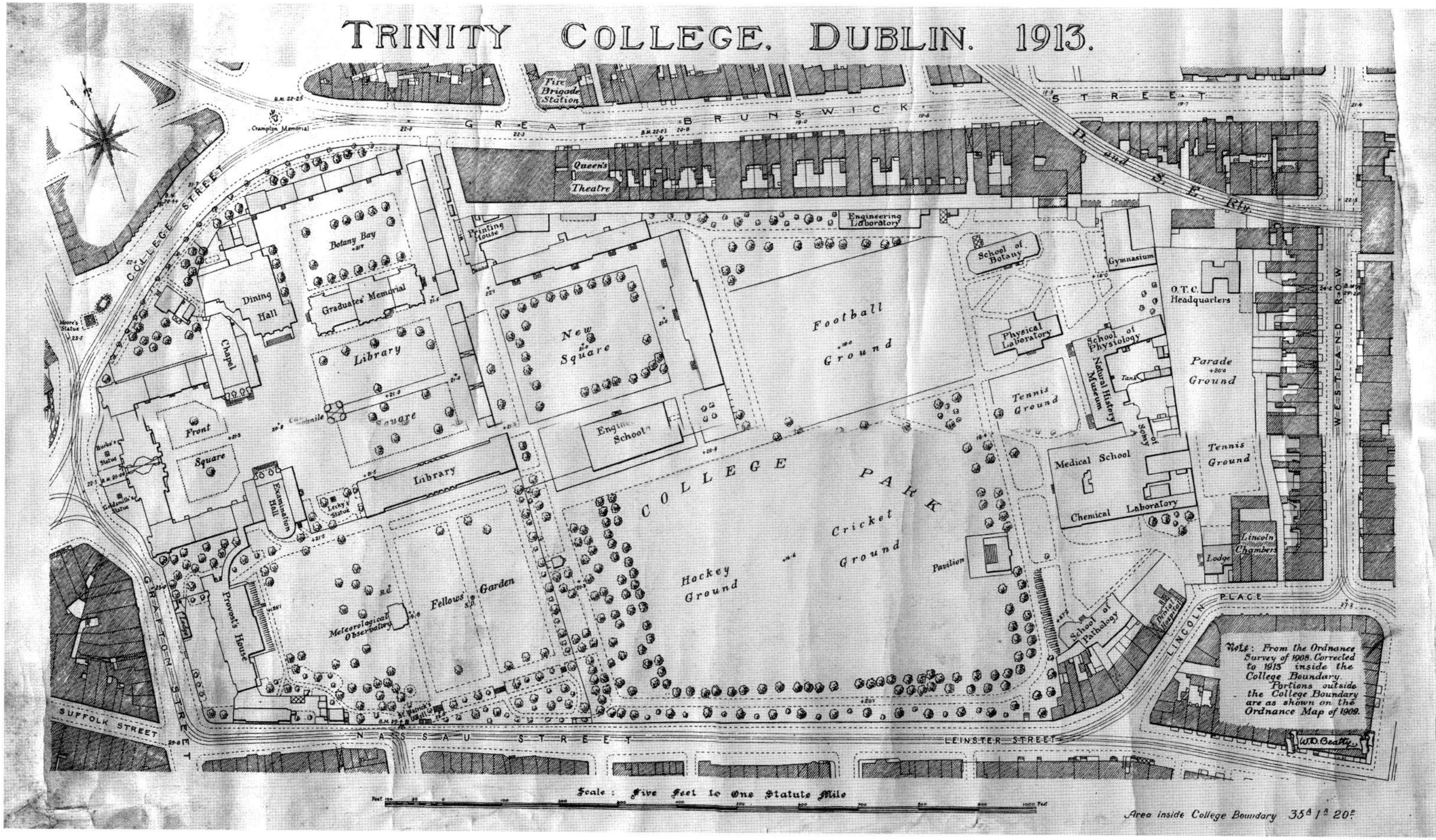

1. Map of Trinity College (1913).

2. The official party at the OTC review in College Park on 13 May 1916. From left: Provost Mahaffy, Prime Minister Asquith (obscured), Lady Wimborne and General Maxwell.

3. General Maxwell inspecting the OTC with Provost Mahaffy looking on.

4. Major R.W. Tate speaking at the cup presentation ceremony on Saturday 5 August 1916.

5. Prime Minister Asquith leaving Richmond Barracks.

6. Professor John Joly *c.*1905.

7. Captain Ernest Alton, the man who oversaw the defence of Trinity College.

8. Corporal John Godwin Garland.

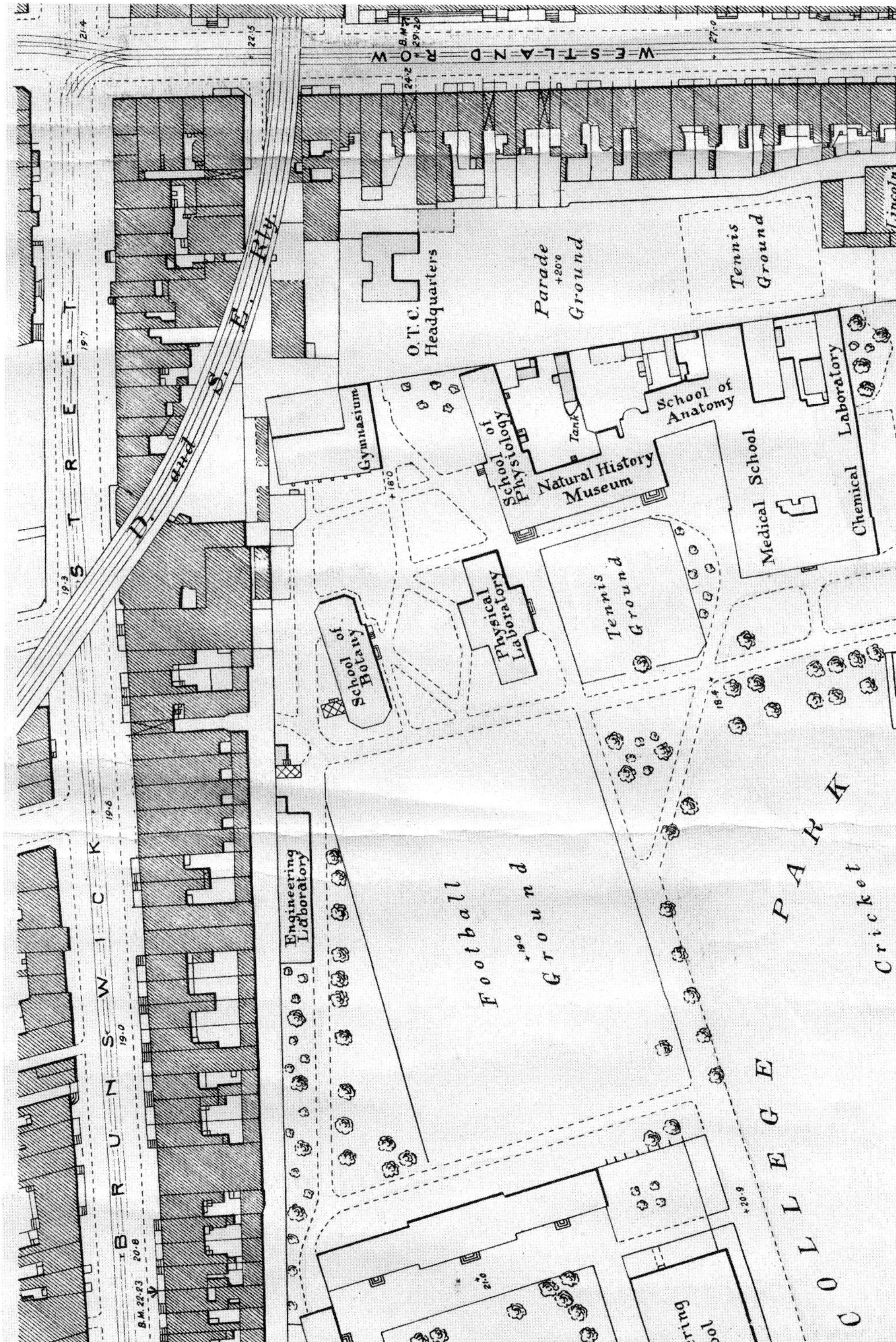

9. Map showing the OTC headquarters and parade ground.

10. British troops in Parliament (Front) Square during Easter Week.

11. 'The morning wash – Troops in Trinity College'.

12. 'The British Lion and his cubs aroused'. *Auckland Weekly News*, 20 August 1914.

13. Anzacs crossing College Green after the Rising ended. From left: Finlay McLeod, Edward Waring, unknown, and Michael McHugh.

14. 'These Anzacs assisted in quelling the Dublin disturbances. One is holding a rifle taken from a Sinn Feiner.' *Sheffield Independent*, 10 May 1916. From left: Edward Waring, Finlay McLeod and Michael McHugh.

15. The ruins of Wynn's Hotel, Lower Abbey Street, where John Garland and Fred Nevin were staying. The IRB's military council met here occasionally when planning the Rising.

16. The north-eastern corner of Trinity College's grounds, showing the OTC headquarters in the bottom right corner.

17. A map showing the dispositions of the crown and rebel forces in Dublin in 1916.

DRUMCONDRA
All Hallows College
Convent
College
St. Joseph's
St. Mary's College
Monastery
O'Brien's Institute
Clontarf Golf Course
Station
MARINO
St. Vincent's
Archbishop's House
Holy Cross College
Tolka River
Clontarf Castle
VICTORIA RD.
FAIRVIEW PARK
FAIRVIEW STRAND
Croke Park
CLONLIFFE ROAD
PORTLAND PL.
SUMMERHILL
SEAN MACDERMOTT STREET
School
Clontarf Baths
EAST WALL ROAD
SHERIFF STREET
MAYOR ST. LOWER
MAYOR STREET UPPER
TOLKA QUAY
ALEXANDRA QUAY
ALEXANDRA BASIN
CUSTOM HOUSE QUAY
NORTH WALL QUAY
RIVER LIFFEY
CITY QUAY
SIR JOHN ROGERSON'S QUAY
HANOVER QUAY
Ferry
Lighthouse
O'CONNELL
G.P.O.
BACHELORS WALK
ASTON QUAY
TRINITY COLLEGE
NASSAU
PEARSE STREET
RINGSEND ROAD
RINGSEND
RINGSEND PARK
Stadium
PIGEON HOUSE ROAD
IRISHTOWN
ELECTRICITY WORKS
Greyhound Race Course
BATH AVENUE
LONDON BRIDGE
BEGGARS BUSH BARRACKS
Hockey Gd.
Lansdowne Rugby Gd.
MERRION SQUARE
ST. STEPHEN'S GREEN
UNIVERSITY COLLEGE
Hospital
Hosp.
FITZWILLIAM
WILTON TERRACE
Station
PEMBROKE
RIVER DODDER
SANDYMOUNT
SANDYMOUNT AVENUE
STRAND
GRAND PARADE
CANAL RD
Monastery
Hospital
HERBERT PARK
R.D.S. Headquarters
BALLSBRIDGE
DONNYBROOK
Convent
Town Hall
RATHMINES
Schools

18. The ruins of the GPO from atop Nelson's Pillar (showing the step in which so many Irish historians disbelieve).

19. British soldiers and a solitary porter guarding Front Gate.

20. The *Marama* leaving Wellington on 5 December 1915, with Fred Nevin and John Garland on board.

21. New Zealand troops raising the Union Jack after landing in Samoa, 29 August 1914. *Auckland Weekly News.*

22. 'The beach at Gallipoli where the men of Anzac had their baptism of fire and took their places as world's heroes.' *Auckland Weekly News.*

23. Volunteer Gerald Keogh.

24. Volunteer Captain Frank Thornton.

25. Alexander Don and his siblings in London (August 1916). Don is seated next to his sister, Amelia, who was a nurse.

26. Alexander Don in 1916, wearing the hat that helped to save his life.

27. Alexander Don's silver cup.

28. The Bank of Ireland facing Trinity College's main entrance, *c.*1914.

29. Trinity's West Front building, replete with Union Jack and crowd celebrating Peace Day (19 July 1919).

service. A corporal with the 1st New Zealand Field Artillery Brigade, he left Wellington with the 5th Reinforcements in the *Maunganui* on 13 June 1915.[52] Arriving in Egypt on 24 July, he and his comrades reached Gallipoli in time to participate in the dying stages of the battle for Chunuk Bair. On the day he landed Turkish troops led by Mustafa Kemal (later Ataturk) drove the Allies off the heights, from which the New Zealanders had earlier caught a brief, tantalizing glimpse of the Narrows, control of which was the ultimate goal of the Dardanelles campaign. Don was 'taken on the strength' of 4th Battery on 13 August, but lasted only a week before falling ill with dysentery. He was evacuated first to Mudros (on the Greek island of Lemnos) and then England, where he was admitted to the military hospital in Fulham on 1 September 1915, suffering from enteric fever. He arrived at the Hornchurch convalescent hospital on 11 January 1916.

Michael McHugh, the one Australian among the Anzacs at Trinity, survived on Gallipoli the longest. He was a 21-year-old labourer from Queensland, who had enlisted in the Australian Imperial Force on 9 January 1915. He reached Gallipoli in mid-June and remained there for nearly thirteen weeks (his brother Willie lasted just nine weeks). A bout of influenza and enteric fever then saw him spend a month in the Imtarfa Military Hospital, Malta, before being admitted to the 1st Southern General Hospital, Edgbaston, England. He wrote to his mother in March 1916 telling her that his convalescent camp was in isolation as some of his mates were suffering from the measles. It took him nearly four months to recover his health, during which time he chose to go for a rest cure to Ireland.[53]

It was no surprise that the four Anzacs succumbed to one or other of the numerous hazards to health presented by life on Gallipoli – Waring (bullet wound), McLeod (neuritis), Don (dysentery) and McHugh (enteric fever). Conditions were horrendous on the peninsula, with the combatants squeezed into a tiny area of less than six square kilometres. At some points the opposing trenches were only a few metres apart. The distance from beach to front line was barely one thousand metres at its furthest point; nowhere was safe from enemy fire, shell or shrapnel, and snipers took a regular toll on the incautious or foolhardy. Hundreds of corpses – rotting or horribly bloated – littered no-man's-land. Chronically short of water, the men subsisted on a woeful diet of tinned bully beef and army biscuit – 'it was like chewing rock', one Anzac recalled.[54] The increasingly exhausted men had little resistance to diseases that

archives, Finlay McLeod (4/666), ANZ. **52** *Maunganuian*, 1:1 (28 June 1915), p. 7, D 526.2 MAU, Auckland War Memorial Museum. **53** Kildea, *Anzacs and Ireland*, pp 62–8. Military file of Michael McHugh (1985), B2455, NAA. **54** Russell Weir, cited in Jane Tolerton, *An awfully big adventure: New Zealand World War One veterans tell their stories* (Auckland, 2013).

flourished in such insanitary conditions. Ormond Burton graphically described daily life for the Allied troops:

> Scorching heat, swarms of venomous flies, hosts of never-resting lice, thirst, the pervading stench of the unburied dead, and then a new experience – the frightful monotony of war … The bad food, the tropical heat, the smell, wore down the physical condition. Then came the spectre of disease. In June scores of men were going down with diarrhoea, dysentery and enteric; in July they were being evacuated in [their] hundreds.[55]

By April 1916, Gallipoli was just a horrible memory for all four Anzacs. The three New Zealanders were convalescing at Hornchurch, out of hospital but not sufficiently recovered to return to action. The camp was a cluster of huts around an ivy-covered manor house called Grey Towers, nestled in an estate of almost one hundred acres. Medical cases requiring no further treatment at the big general hospitals were transferred there for convalescence. Once fit for discharge from Hornchurch the men would be transferred to the command depot at Codford to be retrained for active service at the front:

> Three comfortably fitted large halls – the Y.M.C.A., the New Zealand War Contingent Association, and the Church Army Hut – vied in their attractions for the men in games, concerts, picture-shows, reading and writing rooms, billiards, and in the sale of food, and articles soldiers required. As in all the camps, there was a 'wet' canteen which tended to keep in camp those who liked a glass of beer … For advanced convalescents football, cricket, and hockey were played daily; there was pulling in light boats on a small river adjacent; a large concrete swimming-bath near the same river offered further sport; tennis and croquet were played on the lawns; a post and telegraph office was available in the camp.[56]

For these men Easter 1916 was a last opportunity to enjoy the pleasures of peacetime before being plunged once more into the horrors of war. McLeod, Waring and McHugh appear to have teamed up, not unusual for veterans of Gallipoli, where whenever possible a man paired off with a mate and established a 'bivvy'.[57] The holiday was a chance to spend some of the wages their service had earned. (Anzacs were paid 5 or 6 shillings a day, several times

55 Burton, *The silent division*, p. 85. **56** Drew, *The war effort of New Zealand*, p. 265. **57** A bivouac, meaning a temporary encampment.

the rate of a British Tommy.) Garland and Nevin had also earned a well-deserved break. After unloading its first lot of patients in England, the *Marama* was fitted with new appliances at Southampton. It then spent March 1916 being used as a base hospital in Salonika, enduring a Zeppelin raid on the morning of its arrival. Returning to Southampton with around 520 patients on 20 April, 'the ship required painting, coaling and refitting, and while this work was being carried out the personnel was given leave in sections, and had the opportunity of seeing their friends in England'.[58] Rather than travel to London to attend the Anzac Day commemorative service at Westminster Abbey, where some 2,000 New Zealand and Australian troops paraded before the king and queen, Nevin and Garland decided instead to use a railway concession by which servicemen got return tickets for the single fare and take the train from Southampton to Holyhead and the boat across to Dublin. It was to be a fateful decision.

What did the five New Zealanders have in common? They were all approximately 21 years in age, 5 foot 9 inches in height, and eleven stone in weight. All were young and unmarried, city-dwellers, not career soldiers but ordinary civilians drawn from a range of occupations (a blacksmith, a motor mechanic, two clerks and a machinist).[59] They came from right across the country – Garland and Waring from Auckland, McLeod from Wellington, Nevin from Christchurch and Don from Dunedin. They professed different varieties of the Christian faith – two Presbyterians (Don and McLeod), two Methodists (Garland and Waring) and one Catholic (Nevin). War service in a national unit had helped to cement their sense of collective identity; an Australian soldier visiting Trinity College during Easter Week easily identified their group as 'Enzedders'.[60] Their dominion had won the race to send the first colonial expeditionary force, and this early military experience was reflected in their ranks; four of the five New Zealanders were non-commissioned officers, while all the other colonial troops in Trinity were privates. Their 'battle-hardened professionalism' helps to explain how they took the lead in the defence of Trinity and why they were deferred to by the OTC officers as well as cadets.[61]

In many ways service on Gallipoli was excellent preparation for Dublin in rebellion, given the constant sniping, wretched food and utter exhaustion experienced by the soldiers in both locations. Fortunately for the historian, the New Zealanders were unusually willing to write and talk about their

58 Earl of Liverpool, *The voyages of his majesty's hospital ships 'Marama' and 'Maheno'* (Auckland, 1917), ii, p. 32. **59** One can compare the Irish Volunteers, 58% of whom were skilled workers, clerks and shop assistants, while 36% were semi- or unskilled workers. Dickson, *Dublin*, p. 449. **60** Kildea, *Anzacs and Ireland*, p. 60. **61** Irish, *Trinity in war and revolution*, p. 133.

experience of Easter Week. Their letters from soon after the event have the immediacy of eye-witness testimony and give a glimpse of the brutal realities of urban warfare. They also contain elements of fantasy and exaggeration, inflating – and in Garland's case, inventing – episodes for the benefit of a colonial audience that had no means to assess their veracity.[62] By comparing their accounts with Irish sources (both crown and rebel), however, we can test some of their more surprising assertions.

Arriving in Dublin on Thursday 20 April, Finlay McLeod 'noticed a very bitter feeling against England. Soldiers were even jeered at, and the following Saturday … a man was arrested for threatening to shoot anyone in khaki'.[63] This threat became a reality from midday on Easter Monday, as all five Kiwis came under fire from the rebels, confounding later claims that 'the Irish Volunteers did not believe in firing on unarmed men'.[64] The response of the civilian population was surprisingly sympathetic. Several women hustled Alexander Don into a shop in Dame Street to get him out of the line of fire, and other colonial troops in danger of being hit by snipers were similarly protected.[65] Standing together on the corner of Sackville and Abbey streets, Fred Nevin and John Garland were shot at from the GPO. While Nevin noticed only that a nearby civilian was wounded, Garland told his father a much more alarming tale:

> We were standing in the main street about 2 p.m., just about 100 yards from our hotel. Shots were being fired, and a soldier from the Dublin Fusiliers was killed while walking with his young lady. There were thousands of people in the streets, and all of a sudden a large motor car whizzed past us. In it was the noted Countess, dressed in a green uniform. As she went past she fired two shots at us. One went above our heads; the other caught an elderly man in the arm. It seemed to be a signal to the other Sinn Feiners, for bullets started to whizz all round us. As we were unarmed, and had our Red Cross badges on, we went for our lives to the Soldiers' Club.

Why Countess Markievicz should be firing at soldiers displaying Red Cross insignia is a puzzle. The New Zealanders were also wearing slouch hats, part of the Irish Citizen Army uniform she herself had designed. The countess

62 Some of Garland's claims clearly fall into the category of 'unsustainable'. See Catriona Crowe (ed.), *Guide to the Military Service (1916–1923) Pensions Collection* (Dublin, 2012), pp 154–5. **63** *Grey River Argus*, 22 July 1916. The *Irish Times* (31 Mar. 1916) carried a complaint from a wounded Irish Fusilier of being spat at in Grafton Street. **64** Brian O'Higgins, *The soldier's story of Easter Week* (Dublin, 1925), p. 27. **65** 'Onlookers implored the Australians [George Davis and Bob Grant] to hide, telling them they would be shot.' Kildea, *Anzacs and Ireland*, p. 59.

was indeed a passenger in Kathleen Lynn's open-topped car on Easter Monday, but this was over two hours earlier and on the other side of the Liffey. Whatever the truth of her possible involvement in the death of Constable Michael Lahiff at St Stephen's Green, she is clearly blameless in this case.[66] Garland's long letter (published in several New Zealand newspapers) is a curious mixture of precision and invention, verifiable detail and sheer fantasy. In it he describes the exhausting vigil kept by the Anzacs on Trinity's West Front. 'I left Dublin at 8 p.m. on Tuesday [2 May], after doing nine days' duty, living on biscuits and water the whole time, and only having about twenty hours' sleep.'[67] The food situation worsened as the week dragged on. 'Conditions suggesting famine reigned in the College by Friday,' according to Joly, while 'the hardness of the ship's biscuits was something of scientific interest'.[68] Garland noted instances of looting – 'small boys of 10 to 14 who were brought in and searched had cameras, watches, diamond tiepins, etc.' – but concedes that 'the rebels themselves did not do much looting'. Joly recorded the activities of another youthful offender in his memoir:

> In the midst of the broad pavement in front of the College a small ragged boy was rejoicing in a toy motor car which was certainly value for three or four guineas. It was rather small for him, but he managed to sit in it and to pedal himself round Grattan's statue. Bullets were nothing to him. For the nonce he was one of the fortunate ones, and a lordly toy was his to play with. In after-years this trivial sport will stand for the Great Rebellion in his memory.[69]

After regular troops arrived in large numbers on Wednesday, Trinity's garrison was employed largely in escort, sentry and guard duties. 'We were then relieved and patrolled the city', McLeod told his father, 'getting prisoners and doing house searching, and it was not an easy job'.[70] Don was also involved in clearing the area near Trinity of suspected rebels. On Saturday, Nevin and Garland were ordered to guard around fifty prisoners being held in the enclosed courtyard of the Custom House. Nevin was clearly curious about why the rebellion had taken place; he spent most of the weekend quizzing the rebel leaders and rank and file, some of whom remembered him several decades

66 Lauren Arrington, *Revolutionary lives: Constance and Casimir Markievicz* (Princeton, 2016), pp 128–32. It was noted of Markievicz, 'there were few places where she had not allegedly been sighted during Easter Week, either lying dead on the steps of the City Hall, dressed in men's clothing, or arrested at bayonet point in George's Street'. Foy and Barton, *The Easter Rising*, p. 70. **67** *Auckland Star*, 28 June 1916. **68** Joly, *Reminiscences and anticipations*, p. 252. **69** Ibid., p. 224. Patrick Pearse blamed the looting on 'hangers-on of the British army'. *Sinn Fein rebellion handbook*, p. 45. **70** *Grey River Argus*, 22 July 1916.

later.[71] (They recalled his expressions of sympathy with their cause, but this was not evident in the interview Nevin gave to a *Liverpool Daily Post* reporter on Monday 1 May, when he was on his way back to rejoin his ship at Southampton.)[72] William Brennan-Whitmore was surprised to discover that Nevin was the British sniper with whom he had duelled from the roof of the Dublin Bread Company building. Frank Thornton remembered how their captors (again misidentified as 'an Australian unit') 'divided their own rations with us and acted in quite a decent fashion'.[73] The historian can only regret that Thornton did not enlighten Nevin as to the real objective of the attack he led at midnight on Easter Monday.

Garland preferred to chat with some of the 300 civilian refugees in the Custom House, 'who had been burnt out of their homes'. Among them was a troupe from the D'Oyly Carte Opera Company, whose scheduled performance at the Gaiety Theatre had been overtaken by events. Their baritone, Fred Hobbs, was a New Zealander (from Christchurch) and wrote home soon afterwards telling of his meeting with the New Zealand 'sharpshooters' who 'did deadly work' defending Trinity College.[74] One wonders if Hobbs, while telling Garland how his lodgings on Eden Quay had burned down on Thursday, mentioned that the fire had spread from Lower Abbey Street, having earlier destroyed Wynn's Hotel, where Nevin and Garland had been staying.[75] The Dublin travails of the D'Oyly Carte troupe, later amusingly retold by Sir Henry Lytton, had already come to Joly's notice:[76]

> It was, I think, on the Thursday that a strange demand was made on the hospitality of the College. An operatic company, of well-known excellence, unaware of the extraordinary conditions prevailing in the City of Dublin, had reached the City on Wednesday. They found all the hotels closed and no possibility of getting accommodation. Eighteen members of the company took refuge with the Police. The Police sent across to my gate to know if hospitality – mere housing within the College – could be extended to them. Under the conditions, to grant this request was clearly impossible. Accordingly the stranded actresses and actors had to abide in the premises of the Dublin Metropolitan Police.

71 BMH, WS 510 (Frank Thornton); WS 360 (Seamus Daly); WS 1766 (William O'Brien). Brennan-Whitmore, *Dublin burning*, pp 101–6, 144–9. **72** *Liverpool Daily Post*, 2 May 1916. **73** BMH, WS 510 (Frank Thornton). **74** Frederick Hobbs' letter, *Christchurch Sun*, 12 July 1916. Hobbs (1874–1942) was the son of a former mayor of Christchurch. **75** The fire that consumed both Dalby's lodging house (12 Eden Quay) and Wynn's Hotel had started in the *Irish Times* print shop. Levenson, *James Connolly*, p. 311. **76** Sir Henry Lytton, 'Innocent bysinger' in Roger McHugh (ed.), *Dublin 1916* (London, 1976), pp 145–57. Drawn from his autobiography,

> Then a change came over that house of retribution. Strains of clever song and sounds of pleasant laughter reached my gate, mingled with the crack of distant rifles and the crash of bombs. Cheerful faces peered from door and window. Inexorable duty brought me across to the DMP barracks that afternoon. The scene within was worthy of Gilbert and Sullivan at their best. The gigantic uniformed Inspectors – grey of hair and upright of bearing – beamed with parental indulgence upon the graceful forms which tripped down the stone stairs or laughed and sang in groups in the hall. Among all the experiences of a week of novelties this was not the least novel. It may safely be predicted that such a scene of mingled gaiety and tragedy will never again visit the halls of that building.[77]

Two episodes described in the Anzacs' letters raise troubling questions. During the week there had been intermittent sniper fire coming from the tower of St Andrew's (Church of Ireland) in St Andrew's Street, and on Friday 28 April the Anzacs decided to do something about it. Both Don and Garland told pretty much the same story about what happened next:

> We were troubled by a sniper on our left in the direction of St Andrew's Church, but as we were not quite sure we did not like to fire on that building. On Friday, after we had been relieved from the roof, a man living opposite the church came over and said he had seen the rifles pointing out of the belfry, so we six Anzacs were sent across to his house, and from his kitchen window we put about 100 rounds into the small triangular window they were firing from. Half an hour after they had ceased firing we decided to climb the tower. On the way over we were fired on by our own men, who mistook our slouch hats for those of the Sinn Fein. When we got to the belfry we found two men. One was already dead, and the other so badly wounded that he died an hour afterwards.[78]

There is no record of Volunteer activity in St Andrew's, and no press report of the incident, nor are the dead snipers included in the rebel necrology.[79] It may have been a case like that of Ernie O'Malley, who with an unnamed chum

Wandering minstrel (London, 1933), this account is fuller and more coloured than his earlier reminiscences of the Rising in *The secrets of a Savoyard* (London, 1922). **77** Joly, *Reminiscences and anticipations*, pp 256–7. **78** John Garland in the *Auckland Star*, 28 June 1916, corroborated independently by Alexander Don in the *Evening Star* (Dunedin), 21 July 1916. **79** Nor is anything about the incident recorded in the St Andrew's church vestry minutes, 1916–17, lodged decided to borrow a rifle and do some irregular sniping in the insurgent cause.[80] Don's slouch hat helped him to escape injury on Monday, but its similarity to the Irish Citizen Army uniform was now a liability. Another incident in the 'mopping up' stage of the Rising concerns the recapture of Westland Row railway station. In his letter home McLeod mentioned how the Anzacs assisted regular British troops in this operation. Garland, predictably, had a much more thrilling tale to tell:

> On Saturday afternoon the colonials were given the honour of capturing Westland Row Station. We entered the Grosvenor Hotel, which faces the station, and by means of a ladder climbed over the railway arch and then over to the station. We got four there, and I had a narrow squeak. Two of us were going through the ticket office, and as soon as we entered the Sinn Feiners tried to bayonet the chap behind me. They just missed him, and caught me in the hand – just a mere scratch. Then we both got him together with our bayonets. The same night we were on duty on the [college] roof doing two hours on and four off, and I had just taken my boots off and was going to sleep, when a ricochet bullet caught me just below the left ankle. It only went in a little over half its length. The doctor pulled it out with a pair of forceps.[81]

Again, there is no other record of a fight over the retaking of the railway station, which the rebels had effectively abandoned after the first night in favour of digging trenches further along the line towards Beggar's Bush Barracks, awaiting 'the onslaught that was never delivered'.[82] None of the witness statements or military service pension applications by members of the Dublin Brigade's 3rd Battalion mentions the conflict described by Garland.[83] While Volunteer George Lyons boasted that the Westland Row area was 'the first to be occupied and the last to be evacuated', there was no actual fighting at the station. Those captured on the railway platform (including four British officers) were initially confined in the waiting rooms, then ushered out the main gates onto Great Brunswick Street. ('It was with some difficulty that I got them to take the matter seriously,' Lyons recalled.) On Friday de Valera actually ordered Volunteer Sean Quinn to set fire to the station, before

in the Representative Church Body archives, Dublin. **80** Ernie O'Malley, *On another man's wound* (Dublin, 1979), pp 38–41. **81** *Auckland Star*, 28 June 1916. **82** George Lyons, 'Occupation of Ringsend area in 1916', *An tÓglách*, 10, 17, 21 Apr. 1926. **83** The 3rd Battalion Volunteers who saw service in Westland Row railway station include John Edward Bracken, John Bracken senior, Thomas Joseph Kelly, George A. Lyons, Patrick McBride, Michael Meagher, Patrick Meagher, Laurence Moore, John J. (Sean) Murphy, Andrew O'Neill, Richard Pearle and John (Sean) Quinn. Military Service Pensions Collection, Dublin. Joseph E.A. Connell, *Who's* countermanding the order once Quinn had got a good blaze going. The Boland's Bakery garrison surrendered without a fuss or a fight early on Sunday afternoon.[84] Significantly, neither of Garland's injuries was deemed serious enough to be mentioned in the report made to the New Zealand authorities by his commanding officer on the *Marama*.[85]

Similar doubts arise over the alleged number of victims of Anzac fire during Easter Week. Garland told his father that 'altogether we Anzacs were responsible for 27 rebels (twenty-four men and three women)'.[86] McLeod came up with an even higher toll after the fighting on Tuesday 25 April: 'During that day we killed six in one building, 26 in another and snipers here and there.'[87] As Jeff Kildea has noted, these figures are scarcely credible; if true they would represent around half the total insurgent fatalities in Easter Week.[88] Garland boasted of his 'kills' at the time, evidently believing that every bullet he fired had found its mark.[89] It is possible that McLeod is referring to the dead from the crown forces' attack on the *Daily Express* building, where the bodies of 26 rebels were reportedly found on the premises.[90] The body count might have been higher had the Anzacs been clear about their orders.[91] Initially they were told not to fire until attacked, but once Frank Thornton's covering party began sniping at midnight on Monday all restraints were removed.[92]

Another puzzle concerns Garland's account of a female sniper's body being brought into college:

> On Saturday morning we killed a woman who was sniping from an hotel window in Dame street. When the RAMC brought her in we saw she was only a girl about 20, stylishly dressed and not at all bad looking. She was armed with an automatic revolver and a Winchester repeater.[93]

who in the Dublin Rising, 1916 (Dublin, 2015). **84** However, the *Sinn Fein rebellion handbook* (p. 27) claims that the rebels remained in possession of the railway station until Wednesday 3 May. **85** Lieutenant-Colonel Cook's report to GOC, 16 May 1916, AD1 887 39/182, ANZ. **86** *Auckland Star*, 28 June 1916. Garland estimated crown losses at around 700 casualties, with 500 on the rebel side. **87** *Grey River Argus*, 22 July 1916. **88** Jeff Kildea, '"We personally had no quarrel with the rioters": Anzacs in Dublin during the Easter Rising 1916', paper given at the conference 'The 1916 Rising: Australasian Perspectives', University of Melbourne, 7–8 Apr. 2016, p. 4. **89** Garland boasted to Fred Hobbs of his prowess and is probably the soldier of whom Fitzgibbon wrote, 'one Anzac got nine, but he was a marksman'. Fitzgibbon to Blake, 10 May 1916, TCD MS 11107/1. **90** *Sinn Fein rebellion handbook*, p. 12. Such claims were not infrequent. Elsie Mahaffy was told by a soldier that 'he counted 45 Sinn Feiners dead' around Boland's Bakery on Saturday 29 Apr. Diary, p. 36, TCD, MS 2074. **91** F.L. Nevin interview, *Liverpool Daily Post*, 2 May 1916. **92** The strict order given to all sentries and patrols was not to fire until attacked. Joly, *Reminiscences and anticipations*, p. 229. **93** *Auckland Star*, 28 June 1916.

Both the date and the detail are unconvincing, as by Saturday the Anzacs had completed their sniping duties and Garland himself was retaking Westland Row station before being posted to the Custom House. The weapons allegedly found with the dead sniper have a decidedly exculpatory ring, although Alton also stated that 'a couple of women were seen to fire revolvers – out of sheer gaiety of heart – into the College Park'.[94] Joly mentioned a female sniper operating from the top floor of an insurance office in Dame Street. James Connolly had distributed revolvers among the female members of the Irish Citizen Army, which unlike the Irish Volunteers permitted women to bear arms, then considered a very radical act.[95] Other than Gerald Keogh, there is no record of a dead rebel being taken into Trinity.[96] There is, however, Joly's harrowing tale of the mortally injured woman brought by ambulance through the Brunswick Street gate on Thursday 27 April:

> A woman was lifted out. The stretcher dripped with her blood. A glance showed that death was not far from her. It was a face without hope. A shocking wound was hers. Shot through the lower part of her abdomen, the infernal bullet used by the Sinn Feiners had done work which must surely be fatal. They tried to plug the wound. A little later she was brought on to hospital, where she died. This woman had done no wrong. She was probably seeking food for her six little children when death met her. There will be no one to sing her sorrows in modulated verse. The guilty 'Countess' may possibly one day evoke the strains of the bard. But this woman's anguish of farewell to her little children will be absorbed unnoticed – save by these poor words – in that great total of human sorrow which the mind cannot evaluate or even conceive.[97]

Joly's evident emotion stemmed from witnessing the death of innocents and the destruction of his beloved Dublin. On Saturday night he climbed the lookout tower of the Fire Brigade Station on Tara Street.

> The view northward was sublime and terrible. Acres of flame and red-hot buildings stretched across the middle distance. The lurid light, reflected on rolling clouds of smoke, rose and fell as roof and walls toppled over. Fresh fires appeared to be springing into existence at a point to the north-east, and it really looked as if we were witnessing the

94 *Sinn Fein rebellion: a souvenir of presentations*, p. 6. **95** Arrington, *Revolutionary lives*, p. 128. **96** Connell, *Who's who in the Dublin Rising*, p. 45. **97** Joly, *Reminiscences and anticipations*, pp 250–1. See also, Elsie Mahaffy diary, pp 33–4, TCD, MS 2074.

> wholesale destruction by the devouring flames of the entire northern side of the City.[98]

The Anzacs shared Joly's sense of horror, if not his personal grief. Writing to his father, Garland described 'a town in ruins' with 'bodies of soldiers, horses, civilians, and Sinn Feiners lying about Sackville Street until Saturday'.[99] Don reported on the final act of the Easter Week drama. The first New Zealander to come under rebel fire on Monday, he had arrived in Sackville Street just too late to hear Patrick Pearse proclaim the Irish Republic, and was far too sensible to fire his own revolver at James Connolly soon afterwards. Six days later Don was back outside the General Post Office to witness the surrender of the defeated rebels: 'It was a grand sight, the whole of Sackville Street being in flames, and the fire flashing on the bayonets of the guards ranged round the prisoners.'[100]

98 Joly, *Reminiscences and anticipations,* pp 261–2. **99** *Auckland Star*, 28 June 1916. **100** *Evening Star* (Dunedin), 21 July 1916. Don misremembered the day of the surrender as Thursday.

CHAPTER 5

Whatiffery

I had a nightmare vision of a last stand at the Library windows, ammunition spent, while a horde of rebels with fixed bayonets swept in line across the Fellows' Garden.

—Michael Taaffe[1]

HOW CLOSE WAS THIS NIGHTMARE to coming true? What would have happened had Michael Mallin shouted 'left wheel! CHARGE!' once his Citizen Army column reached Trinity's Front Gate?[2] Or had members of Eamon de Valera's 3rd Battalion rushed past the sole porter at the Lincoln Place Gate, or dropped down silently from the Loop Line bridge behind the OTC headquarters, unseen and unheard by its corporal's guard? Or simply entered Trinity's grounds by climbing over the northern wall, as multitudes of students were wont to do when patronizing the Queen's Theatre in Great Brunswick Street?[3] Or taken advantage of the railings on the southern side of college, described by an acute observer as 'by no means unscalable'?[4] Who would have stopped them? A handful of porters armed with pikes? Four young cadets wielding empty rifles? Once the shooting began on Easter Monday, the military and police fled Dublin's streets for their respective barracks, the latter emerging occasionally to collar an unsuspecting looter.[5] Trinity was largely empty, its students all on vacation, so the first armed group to arrive in force would almost certainly have won the day, especially after taking control of the OTC armoury.

Even after the alarm was raised, the gates were secured, and armed sentries posted, Trinity was still not safe from invasion. John Joly recalled that 'no unknown person was [then] allowed to enter', but merely waving an academic gown at the porter was sufficient to secure admission to college on Tuesday, while those students who entreated Ernie O'Malley to help to defend the

1 Taaffe, *Those days are gone away*, p. 173. 2 The Irish Citizen Army was founded in the Trinity College rooms of Robin Gwynne, a TCD fellow, in 1913. Reid, *The lost Ireland of Stephen Gwynn*, p. 117. 3 Starkie, *Scholars and gypsies*, p. 136. 4 Joly, *Reminiscences and anticipations*, p. 226. 5 BMH, WS 1280 (Eamon Broy).

university from 'those damn Sinn Feiners' on Monday afternoon did not know their man – before the week was out O'Malley would be sniping at the crown forces.[6] Either he or one of Walter Starkie's 'Sinn Fein friends' in college could have expedited a rebel incursion, providing the 'kindly traitor' whose existence so concerned the provost's elder daughter.[7] For that matter, the rebels needed only to capture Trinity's well-known professor of geology on one of his incautious spying expeditions to their strongholds to have secured a key to one of the several side gates to college.[8] Had the rebels gained entrance to Trinity, its defenders had few illusions about the likely outcome. According to Gerald Fitzgibbon, 'they could have had [the college] for the asking up to two o'clock on Monday, and at very small cost up to two o'clock on Tuesday'.[9] James Glen agreed that 'it is very doubtful whether with the small number of defenders a really determined attack in the dark could have been successfully resisted'.[10]

Once secure in occupation, the rebels would have done just as Alton and his comrades did: relocate the contents of the armoury, fortify the front quadrangles, and prepare for a siege. As in the other rebel strongholds, this would have involved a considerable amount of damage: smashing windows, boring holes in internal walls, using books to construct barricades, throwing furniture downstairs to block access.[11] However, this destruction would pale in comparison to the likely effect of the British response. Chief Secretary Augustine Birrell privately warned Asquith that artillery was needed in order to reduce crown casualties when retaking the city.[12] On his arrival in Dublin, General Maxwell made this threat public, declaring in his first proclamation as military governor that 'if necessary, I shall not hesitate to destroy all buildings within any area occupied by rebels'.[13] Maxwell had spent most of his career on the African continent, where his experience in dealing with colonial subjects reputedly gave him 'insight into, and sympathy with, racial characteristics'.[14] His friend Earl Kitchener chose him to deal with the Irish

6 Joly, *Reminiscences and anticipations*, p. 221. O'Malley, *On another man's wound*, pp 32–41. Tomás Irish interprets the O'Malley incident as illustrating 'the contingent nature of Easter Week' and suggests that the future guerrilla leader could just as easily have been fighting for the British. *Trinity in war and revolution*, p. 133. **7** Starkie, *Scholars and gypsies*, p. 134. 'To [the rebels] it was a strange and unknown territory, into which they did not care to adventure themselves rashly without at least one kindly traitor inside to help them from within.' Elsie Mahaffy diary, p. 8, TCD MS 2074. **8** 'I left Trinity cautiously by one of the side gates of which I possessed a key.' Joly, *Reminiscences and anticipations*, p. 219. **9** Fitzgibbon to Blake, 10 May 1916, TCD MS 11107/1. **10** TCD, MS 4456. **11** Possibly imprisoning its loyal defenders and celebrating Mass in the College chapel, as had occurred in 1689. McDowell and Webb, *Trinity College Dublin*, pp 27–9. Lisa Marie Griffith, *Stones of Dublin: a history of Dublin in ten buildings* (Cork, 2014), p. 82. **12** Leon Ó Broin, *The chief secretary: Augustine Birrell in Ireland* (London, 1969), p. 174. **13** Townshend, *Easter 1916*, p. 208. **14** Arthur, *General Sir John Maxwell*, p. 247.

natives, a selection 'clearly intended as a signal that the most resolute steps would be taken'.[15]

Trinity's defenders applauded the use of artillery against rebel strongholds instead of the 'expensive tactics' of a frontal assault by troops.[16] They agreed that only intensive shelling would drive the rebels from their fortresses. Joly rejoiced as Liberty Hall 'received its quietus', but would surely have changed his tune had the heavy guns been turned instead on his beloved university.[17] He correctly foresaw that 'once captured, nothing but the wholesale destruction of buildings, containing the most precious heirlooms of the ancient university, would suffice to dislodge the enemy'.[18] As Michael Taaffe's nightmare scenario suggests, Trinity's library was a symbol to generations of graduates. The destruction of 'the College's greatest asset' would have been a tragedy on the scale of the loss of the University of Louvain's library in August 1914.[19] No-one would have intended this outcome, but war is no respecter of culture. Trinity meant little to soldiers like Lowe and Maxwell, and as the historian Charles Townshend notes, 'an alien kind of militarism was in the ascendant' during the Rising.[20] Joly conceded that rebel occupation would have consigned Trinity to 'the same fate which befell every public building into which the Sinn Feiners entered'.[21] Fire would probably accomplish what shelling did not. By the end of Easter Week at least some of the university's fine buildings would have resembled the shell-like remnants of the recently refurbished General Post Office.

What of the wider strategic implications? Rebel occupation of Trinity would not only have deprived the crown of a vital troop-concentration centre, but also prevented the division of rebel forces planned by Brigadier-General Lowe. British troops would no longer be able simply to bypass and ignore rebel strongholds like Boland's Bakery and Jacob's Biscuit Factory. Attacks on these places would have driven the surviving rebels towards the centre of the city, accentuating a natural centripetal tendency as the British cordon tightened. For the increasingly beleaguered rebel outposts Trinity would then have become a place of refuge; even the headquarters garrison at the GPO and Ned Daly's 1st Battalion at the Four Courts might have made it across the Liffey, especially with rebel snipers commanding O'Connell Bridge from the heights of Trinity. Given General Maxwell's refusal to accept anything less

15 Townshend, *Easter 1916*, p. 207. **16** Joly, *Reminiscences and anticipations*, p. 239. **17** Ibid., p. 245. **18** Ibid., pp 222–3. **19** Fox, *Trinity College Library*, p. 1. Louvain was to lose its library once again during the next world conflict. **20** Townshend, *Easter 1916*, p. 271. **21** Joly, *Reminiscences and anticipations*, p. 245. William Wylie agreed: 'If the OTC had not held it for the first three days of the rebellion, and it had been occupied by the IRA, it would probably have been shelled and set on fire as Sackville Street and the GPO were.' William Wylie, Autobiographical notes, pp 20–1, PRO 30/89/2, National Archives, London. My thanks to than unconditional surrender, and the rebel leaders' desire for as spectacular a 'blood sacrifice' as possible, the stage was set for a fight to the death, possibly across the Fellows' Garden as Taaffe had envisaged. There would be no civilians dying in tragic circumstances to dishearten Patrick Pearse, only a straight-out showdown between the armed forces of the crown and what Thomas MacDonagh called the 'zealous martyrs' of the new Irish republic.[22]

Trinity would have become first a funeral pyre for the rebels, and then – rapidly – a shrine to their memory. There would be fewer insurgent leaders for General Maxwell to execute, but the shock of their grisly deaths would contribute to shifting public opinion in their favour. With the rebels' ashes mixed in the rubble of the university's once splendid buildings, who would then be in a hurry to rebuild the college of the Holy and Undivided Trinty? It took thirteen years to reconstruct the GPO, and over a decade to restore the Custom House; within six years of the Rising most of Ireland was under new management, a Free State created in the image of the dead rebel leaders. During the Rising a rumour spread in the suburbs of Dublin that, should the rebels succeed in their audacious enterprise, Patrick Pearse was to be Trinity's new provost. Elsie Mahaffy scoffed at the idea, but Pearse ended Easter Week as 'Commandant-in-Chief of the Army of the Republic and President of the Provisional Government',[23] and within a few years the railway station and main street on Trinity's northern boundary would both bear his name (over the energetic protests of Trinity's board).[24] Is it entirely fanciful to suggest that any new educational establishment erected on the former site of Trinity might then have been called 'Pearse College Dublin'?

While this book focuses on the defence by the Anzacs and their comrades of an otherwise unprotected college, Trinity's survival owes almost as much to the fateful decisions of three Irish Volunteer leaders: Eoin MacNeill, Thomas MacDonagh and Eamon de Valera. MacNeill was the villain of the piece for many involved in the Rising. Elsie Mahaffy heard that he was to lead the insurgents in attacking Trinity, but the chief of staff of the Irish Volunteers was as much in the dark over the rebel leaders' intentions as the British authorities.[25] His countermand of Volunteer mobilization on Easter Sunday meant, among other things, that insufficient men were available for Thomas MacDonagh to carry out the original plan of occupying Trinity College.

Robert Marshall (Dublin) for this reference. **22** Shane Kenna, *Thomas MacDonagh* (Dublin, 2014), p. 175. James Ryan claimed that Pearse decided to surrender on seeing three elderly men 'lying dead on the opposite footpath of Moore Street with white flags'. James Ryan, 'In the GPO: the medical unit' in F.X. Martin (ed.), *The Easter Rising 1916 and University College Dublin* (Dublin, 1966), p. 89. **23** *Irish War News*, 1:1, Tuesday 25 Apr. 1916, cited in *Sinn Fein rebellion handbook*, p. 46. Elsie Mahaffy diary, p. 42, TCD, MS 2074. **24** Fitzpatrick, *Trinity College and Irish society*, p. 3. **25** Elsie Mahaffy diary, p. 122, TCD, MS 2074. See also, Tierney, *Eoin MacNeill.*

While initiative was rare among the rebel leaders, MacDonagh's remarkable passivity as commandant of the 2nd Battalion also contributed to Trinity's salvation. Reportedly 'obsessed with the study of military textbooks', he remained ignorant of the college's vulnerability, refused to risk what would have been an unopposed entry at midday on Easter Monday, and failed to support the belated attack later that night organized by James Connolly.[26]

These criticisms could be equally made of MacDonagh's disciple, Eamon de Valera, whose 3rd Battalion occupied the area immediately adjacent to Trinity College. Subsequently pilloried by some historians for his inadequate performance during the Rising, de Valera appears to have had a nervous breakdown, issuing contradictory and confusing orders and alarming his subordinates.[27] His major blunder was not providing more support to the Mount Street Bridge unit, where seventeen men held off a regiment of British soldiers for almost five hours. 'De Valera, like MacDonagh, was reluctant to reinforce outposts such as Mount Street Bridge because he was convinced that the British would ultimately launch a major assault on his main position and he would need to conserve his manpower.'[28] His decision illustrates how the rebel plan tied the various commanders 'rigidly to the defence of the positions they first occupied'.[29] This defensive mentality was compounded by a severe shortage of men, with less than one-fifth of the battalion responding to the mobilization order, and a lack of expertise in deploying those who did turn up.[30]

While de Valera's passivity was not untypical, its consequences were arguably the most severe for the rebel cause. None of his critics mentions Trinity as one of his failures, as its occupation was entrusted to MacDonagh, but for a commander who reportedly 'knew every inch of the area under his command', leaving the OTC armoury unmolested was blameworthy.[31] The patrols that so alarmed Trinity's garrison concealed an effective rebel abandonment of the Westland Row station, as the insurgents dug in further along the railway line to await an expected British onslaught. A more proactive commander might have risked a raid on Trinity on Monday afternoon, or liaised with Frank Thornton in the belated attack on the college later that night. As Hayes-McCoy observes, such failures 'indicate that the insurgents were indeed amateur soldiers'.[32]

26 Kenna, *Thomas MacDonagh*, p. 165. **27** Townshend, *Easter 1916*, p. 255. Owen Dudley Edwards, *Eamon de Valera* (Cardiff, 1987), pp 46–59. David McCullagh, *De Valera: Rise 1882–1932* (Dublin, 2017), pp 81–96. **28** Yeates, *A city in wartime*, p. 101. **29** Brennan-Whitmore, *Dublin burning*, p. 27. **30** Connell, *Who's who in the Dublin Rising, 1916*, p. 169. **31** Lyons, 'Occupation of the Ringsend area in 1916', *An tÓglách*, 17 Apr. 1926, p. 4. De Valera and Connolly walked through the 3rd Battalion's area of operations shortly before the Rising. *Sunday Press* (Dublin), 10 Apr. 1966. By Thursday 27 April, the battalion was reportedly running low on ammunition. **32** Hayes-McCoy, 'A military history of the 1916 Rising', p. 266.

Over a long political career – lasting some sixty years after the Rising – de Valera became one of Trinity College's staunchest supporters, opening not only its various libraries, but also the state's coffers. When the college requested funding from Liam Cosgrave's government in 1923 it received a 'humiliating rebuff'.[33] While de Valera's advent to power in 1932 'caused a tremor' in Trinity, there was no reason for concern.[34] He had long been conscious of the university's painful isolation from the new Irish state. Provost McConnell later recalled how de Valera 'often expressed to me his great admiration for the contribution that Trinity College had made to Irish scholarship and learning and his desire to help bring that isolation to an end'.[35] This was accomplished in 1947 when his administration approved an annual grant of £35,000 to the college; the generous act came – by happy coincidence – during the provostship of Ernest Alton, who would have been de Valera's potential opponent had he chosen to attack Trinity during Easter Week.

33 McDowell and Webb, *Trinity College Dublin*, p. 474. **34** Ibid., p. 444. **35** Luce, *Trinity College Dublin*, p. 179.

CHAPTER 6

Epilogue

> [I]n all the disturbances of the past centuries Trinity has never passed a more anxious time than on that fateful first night of the rebellion, when the houses held by the enemy loomed ominously over the low building [OTC headquarters], where a handful of students watched and waited for an attack; while the tramp of rebel feet and the sound of rebel challenges came clearly through the darkness; while the outposts of the enemy rattled the gates of the College.
>
> —*TCD*, 19 June 1916

TRINITY'S OTC WAS NOT LONG to bask in the glory of its alleged achievements during the Rising. Over the next few years it would look on helplessly as Irish politics radicalized; the rise of a reinvented Sinn Féin and the demise of constitutional nationalism, the British government's refusal to recognize Sinn Féin's victory in the 1918 election, and its subsequent outlawing of Dáil Éireann, which led to a bloody conflict that ended in the signing of the Anglo-Irish Treaty (1921). Despite repeated urgings, Trinity's board did not attempt to make the college a fortress once again during these years.[1] Instead, the OTC's armoury was quietly removed by the military authorities and the institution morphed back into a social club. It was finally disbanded in mid-1922, along with several of the 'southern' Irish regiments of the British army, whose soldiers had helped to defeat the rebels in 1916.[2] Trinity's doughty defenders fared slightly better, although Chief Steward Joseph Marshall was asked to resign in 1922, to make way for someone of a 'higher social position'.[3] Three years earlier John Joly became the first fellow of Trinity to be elected rather than gain the accolade through examination, but his impressive performance in Easter Week did not advance his candidature

1 TCD, MUN/V/5/22, Minutes of the board, 10 June 1920. Fitzpatrick, *Trinity College and Irish society*, p. 16. The two cups presented to the OTC in August 1916 were melted down and made into nine large dinner plates in 1953. Douglas Bennett, *The silver collection Trinity College Dublin* (Dublin, 1988), p. 62. **2** The regiments disbanded in 1922 were the Royal Irish, Connaught Rangers, Leinsters, South Irish Horse, Royal Dublin Fusiliers and Royal Munster Fusiliers. **3** Fitzpatrick, *Trinity College and Irish society*, p. 8. It should be mentioned that Marshall was then aged 75.

for the vacant provostship after Mahaffy's death in 1919. By contrast, Arthur Luce was to serve as Trinity's vice provost (1946–52), and Ernest Alton as provost (1942–52), both men also being awarded the Military Cross soon after the Rising ended.

Gerald Fitzgibbon's career might stand as a barometer of Trinity College's response to the new political dispensation in Ireland. His furious opposition to 'that accursed Home Rule Bill' and scorn for Sinn Féin and its leader ('the Portuguese half-breed') was accompanied by a strong sympathy for Protestant Ulster. ('The Irish scum will not dare to lay a finger upon N[orth] E[ast] Ulster.')[4] Despite considering emigration to Canada to ensure that he continued living under the British flag, Fitzgibbon agreed in 1921 to act as unionist MP for Trinity in the short-lived parliament of 'Southern Ireland'.[5] However, he saw the Anglo-Irish Treaty as the ultimate betrayal of his country, writing to his Canadian relative: 'I regard myself as absolved from all loyalty and allegiance to the King and Empire that have cast me out … I shall without the least hesitation vote for Ireland and let the Empire go to hell.'[6] True to his word, Fitzgibbon became an independent member of Dáil Éireann (1922–4) and sat on the supreme court of the Irish Free State (1924–38), the last member of three successive generations to serve on the Irish bench.[7]

Meanwhile, the colonial troops who had rallied to Trinity's aid were making their own 'blood sacrifice' on the Western Front. The six South Africans landed in France in time to participate in the murderous battle for Delville Wood, a series of small-scale attacks from mid-July to mid-September 1916 that cost around 82,000 casualties. Fighting as part of the 9th (Scottish) Division, they all survived the campaign, but George Gibson, Eric King and George Russell were killed in action before the war's end. Blackburn Charlton, the Limerick-born man, was badly wounded and later discharged as 'permanently unfit for war service'. George Moffitt was luckier, if flat feet, trench fever and a recurrence of venereal disease can be considered fortunate; he eventually returned to South Africa in April 1919. Both of the Canadians made it through the Great War: the Dubliner George Webb emerged relatively unscathed, but Howard Cassidy was shot through the lung and spine on 15 September 1916 while fighting with the 18th Battalion. He was invalided back to Canada, his medical file noting 'a large element of shell-shock also'. Discharged as unfit, Cassidy tried to re-enlist but his back injury proved too severe; he was given a pension of $7.50 per month, and died in Toronto in 1979, aged 83.[8]

4 Fitzgibbon to Blake, Apr. 1921, TCD, MS 11107/21; Easter Monday 1920, TCD, MS 11107/23. 5 Fitzgibbon to Blake, 14 May 1921, TCD, MS 11107/29. 6 Fitzgibbon to Blake, 10 Dec. 1921, TCD, MS 11107/31. 7 He appears briefly in the *DIB*, iii, p. 930. 8 Personal

Fred Nevin and John Garland found themselves plunged into the horrors of the battle of the Somme. Nevin left Dublin on Monday 1 May, but Garland waited another day in order to replace some of his possessions destroyed when Wynn's Hotel burned down. The two medical orderlies appear to have made no official claim for compensation, unlike Fred Hobbs (the D'Oyly Carte baritone), who received £49 from the Property Losses (Ireland) Committee in January 1917.[9] Typically, Garland's departure was not without incident: 'The next night (Tuesday) I left the College at 6 p.m. in a motor-bicycle side-car. On our way three shots were fired at us, but no damage was done.'[10] Three months later, Nevin and Garland were rather surprised to find themselves back in Dublin, as the *Marama* was ordered to transport 482 Irish casualties from Le Havre. Arriving on 22 July 1916, the ship was met on the wharf and inspected by General Maxwell, and its staff driven around the ruins of the city by members of the Automobile Association.[11]

The visit was a welcome break from the *Marama*'s gruelling schedule during the early months of the Somme campaign, which saw the overloaded hospital ship constantly shuttling from Boulogne and Le Havre to Southampton. On one occasion it carried no fewer than 1,636 patients, more than double its normal capacity.[12] Garland described the awful conditions on board in letters to his father: 'All our men were straight from the trenches, and they were mostly in a bad way.'[13] Filthy, lice-infested and frequently suffering from shell shock, the patients often bore septic and smelly wounds by the time they came aboard. The overworked orderlies soon showed signs of strain. 'There are no soft jobs going about this boat now,' Garland reported on 14 July. 'Sometimes we don't get any sleep for 48 hours. Of course, if this keeps up long we will all be knocked out: it's too much. I am so tired now that I can't sleep and in twelve hours from now we will be back in [Le] Havre, loading up again.'[14] He lasted another fortnight before succumbing to illness, and was admitted to the New Zealand General Hospital at Brockenhurst, which he had helped to relocate from Egypt some months earlier.[15]

The other three New Zealanders were no more fortunate with their health. Alexander Don had another bout of typhoid fever after returning to Hornchurch from Dublin. Apparently recovered, he crossed to France in

records of George Webb (447766) and Howard Cassidy (454045), Canadian Expeditionary Force. Military files of George Russell (7624), Blackburn Charlton (9343), Eric King (9380), George Gibson (9405) and George Moffitt (9435), Department of Defence Archives, Pretoria, South Africa. **9** Property Losses (Ireland) Committee record, PLIC/1/1469, National Archives, Dublin. **10** *Auckland Star*, 28 June 1916. **11** Lieutenant-Colonel Percy Cook's report to GOC, 25 July 1916, AD1 887 39/182, ANZ. **12** Elliott, 'The New Zealand hospital ships', p. 134. **13** McLean, *The white ships*, p. 113. **14** McLean, *The white ships*, p. 113. **15** During the *Marama*'s first commission (1915–16) over 60% of the orderlies fell ill at some point, as did

February 1917, but soon returned sick to England. By early October he was well enough to 'march into camp' at Étaples, and spent the next year with the 2nd New Zealand Field Artillery Brigade. Wounded in October 1918, Don had sufficiently impressed his superiors to be selected for officer cadet training, but the end of the war intervened, and he had to settle for promotion as temporary sergeant for the voyage home to New Zealand.[16] Edward Waring was not to see active service again, his leg wound from Gallipoli restricting him to the role of company cook at Codford camp. In November 1917 he returned to Auckland after being deemed 'no longer physically fit for war service on account of wounds received in action'.[17] Waring died of pneumonia during the influenza pandemic in November 1918, aged 26. Finlay McLeod went to France in late September 1916 with the New Zealand Field Engineers and had two brief spells in hospital before being badly gassed during the battle of Messines on 26 July 1917. Evacuated to England, he was admitted to hospital at Walton suffering from severe attacks of vomiting and headaches. He had lost so much weight that a medical board recommended an immediate return to New Zealand. After McLeod landed in Wellington in January 1918, he was given a permanent disability pension (at half 'full livelihood' rate) and soon moved to Australia, where his family now lived.[18]

The strain of hospital-ship work eventually proved too much for both Nevin and Garland, neither of whom signed on for a second commission after the *Marama* returned to New Zealand in November 1916. Garland was discharged, suffering from an unspecified injury 'sustained on active service'. Nevin, who had shown symptoms of rheumatic fever prior to enlistment, was given extended leave without pay before being discharged a year later. Nevin's father had died while Fred was in Europe, so increased family responsibilities may have been a factor in his decision to remain at home.[19] Both men should have had a 'Sinn Fein rebellion cup' in their luggage on arrival in Wellington, but Trinity's OTC adjutant had only just begun to despatch these trophies because of concerns about possible losses in transit. One wonders if the two orderlies were introduced to General Maxwell during the *Marama*'s Dublin visit in July 1916; if so, it would appear that neither Nevin nor Garland chose to disclose their Easter Week adventures, possibly through embarrassment at so flagrantly breaking Red Cross rules by taking up arms. Had Maxwell realized that they were part of the Anzac sniping squad, he would surely have told them about the ceremony due in a fortnight's time at which Trinity's defenders were to be recognized.

40% of the nurses and all but one doctor. McLean, *The white ships*, p. 114. **16** NZDF, personnel archives, A.W. Don (2/1745), ANZ. **17** NZDF, personnel archives, Edward Waring (12/1523), ANZ. **18** NZDF, personnel archives, Finlay McLeod (4/666), ANZ.

John Garland first read about the award of replica cups to Trinity's garrison in the *Irish Times* of 7 August, whereupon he wrote to the OTC adjutant telling him how he 'did duty' there, 'mostly on the roof of the college'.[20] After hearing the news, Alexander Don informed his fellow convalescent Edward Waring, who promptly applied for his replica cup. After it arrived, Waring wrote back in thanks: 'I shall always value it as a souvenir of one of the troublous times in British history, which I hope will never occur again.'[21] The responses of the other three Kiwis differed significantly. While Garland and Don regularly boasted of their service to Ireland and the empire, Nevin remained silent on his activities during Easter Week. On returning home, Nevin found that his (largely Irish-descended) Catholic community was coming to embrace a view of the 1916 Rising that reflected Irish nationalist opinion at home.[22] This may explain why he made no mention of his Dublin adventure to his children, and left no written record besides a brief newspaper interview on 1 May.[23] By contrast, Garland lectured on 'My Experiences in the 1916 Rebellion in Ireland' to his local Orange Lodge in Auckland,[24] and Don often regaled the pupils of the preparatory school he founded with tales of his Irish exploits (unwittingly encouraging the widespread belief that he had served there as a 'Black and Tan').[25]

Were these New Zealanders – as recent scholarship has suggested – mere pawns in a game of which they knew nothing, dragged into a fight that was none of their business? ('We were in a very unenviable position,' wrote another New Zealand-born Anzac, who took refuge in Portobello Barracks, 'for we personally had no quarrel with the rioters.')[26] They are described as being 'called to arms', 'ordered back into combat', reluctant participants in somebody else's quarrel, paid for their service with miniature trophies like so many pieces of silver.[27] In this view, the replica cups were a reward for betrayal, a source of shame and a reason for silence. 'Now hidden under my bed that silver chalice

19 *Press* (Christchurch), 22 Jan. 1916. **20** J.G. Garland (Southampton) to OC DU OTC, 30 Aug. 1916, TCD, MS 2783/100. **21** Edward Waring, NZ (Command) Depot, Codford, Wilts, to the Adjutant DU OTC, 1 Oct. [1916], TCD, MS 2783/80. **22** Rory Sweetman, 'Who fears to speak of Easter Week? Antipodean Irish Catholic responses to the 1916 Rising' in Ruan O'Donnell (ed.), *The impact of the 1916 Rising: among the nations* (Dublin, 2008), pp 71–90. **23** Interviews with Margaret Wilson and John Patrick Nevin, daughter and son of Fred Nevin, Sept. 2017. *Liverpool Daily Post*, 2 May 1916. **24** Minutebook of City of Auckland (No. 1) Lodge, 3 May 1922, Loyal Orange Order Archives, Auckland. **25** In 1929, Don set up the Hadlow Preparatory School for Boys in Masterton, around 100 km from Wellington. *Hadlow, 1929–1979* (Masterton, 1979), p. 23. Susan Price, *A mind of his own: the childhood of Hugh Price* (Wellington, 2012), p. 124. **26** Private George Davis, New Zealand-born but serving in the Australian Imperial Force. Kildea, *Anzacs and Ireland*, p. 74. **27** *Trinity and the Rising*, p. 18. Jeff Kildea, 'Called to arms: Australian soldiers in the Easter Rising', *Journal of the Australian War Memorial*, 39 (Oct. 2003).

lies,' as Kevin McCarthy's (recent) song 'Digger in Dublin' goes.[28] This interpretation is contradicted by both the actions and writings of the Anzacs. Far from being reluctant recipients of the small cups, most of the New Zealanders had repeatedly to remind Trinity College of their claim to one; Michael McHugh, the supposedly remorseful subject of the song, cheekily asked the OTC adjutant to inform his commanding officer that his presence was required at the awards ceremony in Dublin.[29]

Those facing a worse dilemma during Easter Week were the thousands of Irishmen in British uniform, often the brothers and cousins of the rebels.[30] The insurrection placed the Irish serviceman in a 'no-man's-land',[31] as most of the British units stationed or drafted into Dublin were reserve battalions of Irish regiments.[32] The majority of troops who suppressed the Rising were not only Irish, but also drawn from Dublin and its surrounds, which helps to explain the hostile reaction to the rebels displayed by numerous 'separation women' with sons or husbands at the front. (Although, as David Dickson observes, 'the early contempt for the rebels was much broader than that', as evidenced by the assistance offered by civilians to the endangered Anzacs when the Rising began.)[33]

Some observers doubted whether Irish troops would fire on their fellow Irishmen.[34] Lieutenant Arthur Luce was unequivocal on the matter – 'at the time there was only one course of action open to law-abiding citizens in College, especially to those wearing British uniform'.[35] One Irishman in British uniform, Charles Duff, begged to differ with the English-born Luce, telling his superiors that he had enlisted in the British army to fight Germans not Irishmen. As a result, he was quietly shipped back to England together with a large group of Irish and colonial soldiers.[36] Duff's account provides some partial corroboration of Patrick Pearse's claim that 'Irish regiments in the British Army have refused to act against their fellow-countrymen.'[37] There

28 The song was composed by Kevin McCarthy and Geoff McArthur. **29** Kildea, *Anzacs and Ireland*, p. 67. **30** Gerald Keogh, the Volunteer despatch rider, had three brothers involved in the Rising, while his elder brother had been killed in action in France in October 1914. Raymond M. Keogh, 'Well dressed and from a respectable street', *History Ireland*, 17:2 (Mar./Apr. 2009), pp 32–3. **31** Tom Burke, 'Fancy the Royal Irish captured Moore Street': attitudes to the Easter Rising of Irish soldiers serving in the British army in Dublin', *Irish Sword*, 28:112 (2012), p. 187. **32** Jane Leonard, 'The reactions of Irish officers in the British army to the Easter Rising of 1916' in H. Cecil and P.H. Liddle (eds), *Facing Armageddon: the First World War experienced* (London, 1996), p. 258. **33** Dickson, *Dublin*, p. 455. **34** Leon Ó Broin, *Dublin Castle and the 1916 Rising*, p. 109. See also, Burke, 'Fancy the Royal Irish captured Moore Street', p. 190. **35** A.A. Luce, 'Recollections of Easter Monday 1916', 14 Oct. 1965, TCD, MS 4874/2/1. **36** Charles Duff, *No angel's wing* (London, 1947), pp 44–6. **37** 'Manifesto of the provisional government to the citizens of Dublin', cited in *Sinn Fein rebellion handbook*, p. 41.

was widespread sympathy and admiration for the rebels among their opponents. While serving as a medical orderly in Trinity College, Conn O'Grady reported that 'all troops there [are] Irish and not at all bitter against the volunteers, though no question of not obeying orders … All [are] unanimous in praising the fighting of the volunteers.'[38] Irish soldiers at the front were less favourably impressed by the insurrection, their letters expressing feelings of 'disgust, betrayal, revenge and downright hostility towards the men who carried it out'.[39] The week of the Rising saw the 16th (Irish) Division suffer a German gas attack at Hulluch, costing more lives than were lost in Dublin, with thousands of other soldiers left incapacitated.[40]

The sense of betrayal felt by Irish troops was sharpened by widespread reports of unarmed soldiers being shot down on Dublin's streets. The worst case was the slaughter of five members of the Gorgeous Wrecks on Haddington Road; by Monday evening the bodies of twelve soldiers were reported to be lying in various Dublin hospitals.[41] Such reports infuriated many troops, and may have helped to tip one officer into temporary insanity. Captain J.C. Bowen-Colthurst later attempted to justify his murder of several civilians by citing these killings: 'I knew also that men on leave home from the trenches, although unarmed, had been shot down like dogs in the streets of their own city, simply because they were in khaki, and I also heard that wounded soldiers home for convalescence had been shot down also.'[42] Gerald Fitzgibbon was equally appalled by the needless deaths of men who could not defend themselves: 'I have felt very bloodthirsty about those rebels since I saw the men they shot down in St Stephen's Green and Haddington Road, and saw all Sackville Street in flames.'[43]

When interpreting the actions of the colonial soldiery during Easter Week, the instinct of self-preservation needs to be considered. Members of Trinity's garrison soon swapped stories of their close shaves with injury or death. The shock of seeing their fellow soldiers killed and of being shot at themselves clearly stimulated a desire to shoot back. After being holed up in the OTC headquarters for several hours under rebel sniping, the Anzacs volunteered to return fire from the college's West Front building. Even the two medical

38 Diarmid Coffey papers, MS 21193, 2, NLI. Captain E. Gerrard later recalled that 'Every officer I ever met who was ever in Dublin was so impressed by the extraordinary gallant bearing of the insurgents.' BMH, WS 348. 39 Burke, 'Fancy the Royal Irish captured Moore Street', p. 197. Stephen Sandford, *Neither unionist nor nationalist: the 10th (Irish) Division in the Great War* (Sallins, 2015), p. 185. 40 Burke, 'Fancy the Royal Irish captured Moore Street', p. 198. 41 Yeates, *A city in wartime*, p. 95. See also, Phillips, *The revolution in Ireland*, p. 99. 42 *Sinn Fein rebellion handbook*, p. 219. Bowen-Colthurst is alleged to have said that 'in any other country except Ireland it would be recognised as right to kill rebels'. James W. Taylor, *Guilty but insane* (Cork, 2016), p. 119. 43 Fitzgibbon to Blake, 10 May 1916, TCD, MS 11107/1.

orderlies chose to pick up rifles rather than bandages. Garland and Nevin could have worked in the casualty clearing station set up in Front Square, but preferred to join their comrades on the roof, covering up their Red Cross insignia with an OTC armband. This act of solidarity reflected their sense of collective identity, first as soldiers and then as New Zealanders; it expressed a camaraderie forged in training, during the voyage out, and on active service, a sense of mutual obligation, in a word, of mateship. 'New Zealand's war effort was in many senses a national project. New Zealand troops fought as New Zealanders (with plans that they be subsumed into an Australasian force rejected).'[44]

The Anzacs' initial ignorance of rebel motives was illustrated by Fred Nevin's alleged belief that the Rising stemmed from an industrial dispute by munitions workers.[45] Other defenders of Trinity interpreted the occupation of the GPO as driven by a criminal desire for loot. In fact, few Irish people knew quite what was happening on Easter Monday. The insurrection was immediately (and erroneously) described as a 'Sinn Fein' rebellion. Protected from rebel attack by sniping from the roof of Trinity College – 'like the Devil [it] took care of its own'[46] – the *Irish Times* was quick to condemn 'an attempt, instigated and designed by the foreign enemies of our King and Country to incite rebellion in Ireland'.[47] The failed effort to land arms from Germany led to fears (and hopes) that the rebellion would soon be followed by an invasion. In the House of Commons, Prime Minister Asquith referred to 'this most recent German campaign', while John Redmond condemned the Rising as 'a dastardly German plot'.[48] Nevin was allegedly convinced that he had duelled with a band of German snipers.[49] Typically, John Joly discounted the rumours of German involvement after inspecting the rebel stronghold at St Stephen's Green: 'No German officer was responsible for such strategy. For no officer in his senses would shut his men in an enclosure commanded by tall buildings on every side, from any one of which almost every corner of the Green could be reached.'[50] He did not pause to consider that – under professional leadership – those rebels digging useless trenches in the Green could easily have been occupying his beloved university.

44 Loveridge, *Calls to arms*, p. 65. **45** BMH, WS 360 (Seamus Daly). The 1913 labour disturbances in Dublin received wide publicity in New Zealand. Richard P. Davis, *Irish issues in New Zealand politics, 1868–1922* (Dunedin, 1974), pp 188–90. **46** 'The *Irish Times* on the Easter Rising' in Owen Dudley Edwards and Fergus Pyle (eds), *1916: the Easter Rising* (London, 1968), p. 243. **47** Lord Wimborne's proclamation, *Irish Times*, 25 Apr. 1916. **48** *Sinn Fein rebellion handbook*, p. 38. Redmond told the press that 'Germany plotted it, Germany organized it, Germany paid for it.' Denis Gwynn, *The life of John Redmond* (London, 1932), p. 481. **49** Brennan-Whitmore, *Dublin burning*, p. 145. **50** Joly, *Reminiscences and anticipations*, p. 221.

Despite the Proclamation's reference to 'gallant allies in Europe', the rebel leaders were keen to assert the autonomy of their actions and to root their enterprise in Irish history rather than the world conflict, especially given the odium in which all things German were currently held.[51] The Volunteer and Citizen Army ranks were filled with the 'respectable' working class, who prided themselves on their soldierly qualities. Goaded by inactivity and a desire to prove their manliness – a chance to escape being seen as 'figures of fun in worn uniforms'[52] – they responded eagerly to Patrick Pearse's rhetoric on 'the valour, self-sacrifice and discipline of Irishmen and women [who] are about to win for our country a glorious place among the nations'.[53] As Owen Dudley Edwards puts it:

> In fighting against Britain, the Easter insurgents responded to the same mood which led so many to fight for Britain. The ideals were the same: militarism, honour, patriotism, self-sacrifice, manhood, adventure, and above all a desire to testify to spiritual yearnings defying the grey calculations of a secure and cautious life. Combat and death had become world-wide faiths. Ireland had taken her place among the nations of the earth. She had simply chosen to do so when the nations of the earth were at the height of suicidal irrationality.[54]

Pearse's injunctions had their effect, as even Sir Matthew Nathan, undersecretary for Ireland, testified to the rebels' skill and courage.[55] John Dillon, Redmond's deputy, voiced his admiration in the House of Commons, arguing that the rebels were not murderers but 'insurgents who have fought a clean fight, a brave fight, however misguided'.[56] This brought a sharp rebuke in the *Times* from Trinity's provost, whose views probably reflected those of the numerous British officers he had hosted during Easter Week. Writing to congratulate Mahaffy on challenging 'that fiend Dillon', General Maxwell concluded, 'the tendency here is to try to attribute every death that occurred in Dublin during the revolt to the brutality of the soldiery'.[57] Both sides accused the other of firing on women and of not respecting the Red Cross flag.[58] 'Women and children were hit by the stray bullets of snipers occupying roofs in many respectable parts of the city,' asserted Mahaffy.[59] However, if

51 John Horne and Alan Kramer, *German atrocities, 1914: a history of denial* (New Haven, 2001), pp 292–4. Stuart Wallace, *War and the image of Germany: British academics, 1914–1918* (Edinburgh, 1988). **52** Elsie Mahaffy diary, p. 119, TCD, MS 2074. **53** *Sinn Fein rebellion handbook*, p. 45. **54** Dudley Edwards, *Eamon de Valera*, p. 48. **55** *Sinn Fein rebellion handbook*, p. 161. **56** Lyons, *John Dillon*, p. 382. **57** Maxwell to Mahaffy, 16 May 1916, in Elsie Mahaffy diary, p. 67, TCD, MS 2074. **58** *Sinn Fein rebellion handbook*, p. 45. **59** *Times* (London), 16

Garland, Don and McLeod are to be believed, the crown forces were as culpable as the rebels for the high death toll, the Anzacs having sniped at everything that moved for most of Easter Week from the building adjacent to the provost's own house.

The use of artillery and the location of rebel strongholds in crowded working-class neighbourhoods contributed to civilian casualties. Another factor was the sheer recklessness of Dubliners. 'They persisted in walking about the street while bullets were flying and a good many were hit while engaged in looting,' Dillon informed Redmond.[60] Joly was equally appalled: 'Here were bullets flying about, death lurking at every corner, and yet troops of foolish people [were] running about the street.'[61] The *Irish Times* advised its readers that 'the present military operations are not public entertainments, but a grim and dangerous business'.[62] Then there was the problem of distinguishing rebels from ordinary citizens, as few wore an easily identifiable uniform. It was 'a nerve-wracking business to fight a largely unseen enemy'.[63] Maxwell claimed that rebels deliberately mixed with peaceful civilians in order to ambush the troops.[64] Elsie Mahaffy's diary contains all sorts of outlandish accusations against the insurgents and their sympathizers, including deliberately poisoning the tea they offered to unsuspecting British troops (three of whom allegedly died as a result).[65] One charge that seems proved was the rebel use of 'expanding bullets of the sort used for killing big game'.[66] The German Mauser rifles imported by the Irish Volunteers at Howth in 1914 took large-calibre ammunition; according to one rebel, 'you could clearly distinguish the heavy boom of the "Howth" rifle from the sharper crack of the Lee-Enfield'.[67] Patrick Pearse admitted that the use of such bullets was 'against the rules of civilised war'.[68]

The Anzacs were painfully familiar with the destructiveness of 'dumdum' bullets, as the Turks had used them freely on Gallipoli. That campaign was on the minds of many in Trinity's beleaguered garrison, not only because it was the exact anniversary of the first landings at Sedd-el-Bahr and Anzac Cove. Many veterans considered that Dublin was more dangerous than the Dardanelles. 'Several of the chaps from Gallipoli reckon that one had a far better chance of getting off with his life there,' Garland recorded.[69] At the front you at least knew the direction from which a bullet might be expected to

May 1916, p. 9. **60** Lyons, *John Dillon*, p. 376. **61** Joly, *Reminiscences and anticipations*, p. 244. **62** *Irish Times*, 27 Apr. 1916. **63** Lyons, *Ireland since the Famine*, pp 372–3. **64** Townshend, *Easter 1916*, p. 27. **65** Elsie Mahaffy diary, p. 25, TCD, MS 2074. **66** *Sinn Fein rebellion handbook*, pp 10–11. **67** Dick Humphreys in Jeffery, *The GPO and the Easter Rising*, p. 144. **68** Townshend, *Easter 1916*, p. 91. The Hague Convention (1899) prohibited the use of expanding bullets in international warfare. **69** *Auckland Star*, 28 June 1916.

come, Joly was told. 'Here the enemy is all round you. He lurks in dark passages and among chimney-stacks, and when at last you think you have hunted him down, you find yourself in possession of a peaceful citizen who gives some plausible reason for his presence.'[70] In fact, most of the Allied forces on Gallipoli were represented in the ramshackle Trinity garrison: Anzacs, Canadians, the Royal Naval Reserve, Irish Guards, Dublin Fusiliers, Royal Irish Rifles – there was even an Indian ambulance unit bringing casualties into the college and a French cook supplying meals.[71] Indeed, the Anzacs might have found themselves under their old commanding officer, General Sir Ian Hamilton, had not 'damaging Irish memories of Suvla Bay' ruled him out of contention as Ireland's military governor.[72]

'As surely as Verdun or the Somme, Dublin in 1916 was a First World War battlefield,' wrote the late Keith Jeffery.[73] The Proclamation defiantly ranged the Irish republic against Britain, France and Russia, and alongside Germany, Austria and Turkey – its 'gallant allies in Europe'. The *Freeman's Journal* made the link with Gallipoli explicit by noting that 'the 4th and 10th Dublins [Fusiliers] kept the glorious anniversary of their regiment's heroic landing at Sedd-el-Bahr by defending their own city against the blind, self-devoted victims of the Hun'.[74] Finlay McLeod considered that Anzac Day was being 'well kept up' as he and his fellow Kiwis defended Trinity from rebel attack.[75] In fact, the Anzacs could also have been fighting advanced Irish nationalists on the banks of the Suez Canal had Sir Roger Casement's Irish Brigade accepted an invitation to join the Turkish campaign to 'liberate' Egypt.[76]

According to the *Irish Times*, defeating the rebels in Dublin helped to save the British empire, so it was only fitting that troops from the British dominions played their part. The imperial dimension, like the First World War itself, should not be seen as a 'mere exotic backdrop for Irish politics' in this period.[77] Rather than unwelcome intruders in a domestic quarrel, the colonial soldiers were precisely where they were most needed. They had travelled across the world to fight for king and empire, and their 'blood sacrifice' – at Gallipoli, Delville Wood and Vimy Ridge – matched the Irish ones in Dublin and on the Somme. They acted from a belief in the justice of the Allied cause, and to

70 Joly, *Reminiscences and anticipations*, pp 248–9. 71 TCD, MS 7533/3. Of course, the Newfoundlanders on Gallipoli would have denied they were Canadians (before 1949). 72 Townshend, *Easter 1916*, p. 207. 73 Keith Jeffery, *1916: a global history* (London, 2016), p. 104. 74 *Freeman's Journal* (Dublin), 5 May 1916. 75 *Grey River Argus*, 22 July 1916. 76 The option was put to the brigade on 3 Dec. 1915, but only 38 of 56 agreed. Townshend, *Easter 1916*, p. 116. Casement believed that 'short of directly fighting to free Ireland from British rule, a blow struck at the British invaders of Egypt, to aid Egyptian national freedom, is a blow struck for a kindred cause to that of Ireland'. Brian Inglis, *Roger Casement* (New York, 1973), p. 296. 77 Paul A. Townend, *The road to home rule: anti-imperialism and the Irish national*

save themselves from possible German domination. They were keen to demonstrate their loyalty and commitment to the empire, and to ensure that their voice would be heard in discussions over its future direction. Some of them also hoped that a short victorious war would help to heal their internal divisions.

All the above was equally true of Ireland's constitutional nationalist leaders, who regarded the dominions' war service as a model to be followed. For John Redmond it was 'a just war … for the defence of the sacred rights and liberties of small nations, and the respect and enlargement of the great principle of nationality'.[78] Its outbreak had not only averted looming civil conflict with the Ulster unionists, but might also bring Orange and Green together at home while their representatives were fighting side by side in the trenches. 'A war to unite us all' could dissolve centuries of suspicion and enmity in Ireland, as well as demonstrating the compatibility of home rule with loyalty to empire.[79] Unlike advanced nationalists, who focused on the subject non-white races suffering under the British flag, constitutional nationalists looked to the white settler dominions and insisted that similar treatment for Ireland would ensure a comparable loyalty. Erskine Childers, in his pre-republican days, argued that an 'imperial' answer to the Irish problem could 'provide a framework in which both autonomy and allegiance might be accommodated'.[80] 'Throughout the Empire', according to Alvin Jackson, 'it seemed that self-government propagated imperial swans out of Anglophobic, nationalist ducklings'.[81] Paul Townend has recently demonstrated the centrality of anti-imperialism to the revival of Irish nationalism in the late nineteenth century, but as the prospects of home rule revived from 1910, Redmond and his colleagues adopted a softer approach towards the British empire, one that recalled Daniel O'Connell and Isaac Butt. In doing so, they occasionally acknowledged Ireland's role in conquering, populating, evangelizing and administering what Irish separatists termed 'the pirate empire'.[82]

The placing of home rule on the statute book in 1914 redoubled Redmond's loyal outpourings. Ireland was now pledged to prove 'that this concession of liberty would have the same effect in our country as it has had in every other portion of the Empire'.[83] In the House of Commons, Redmond declared it as his objective 'to combine local and Imperial patriotism', thus

movement (Madison, 2016), p. 9. **78** Cited in Deirdre McMahon, 'Ireland, the empire, and the commonwealth' in Kevin Kenny (ed.), *Ireland and the British empire* (Oxford, 2004), p. 200. **79** Adrian Gregory and Senia Pašeta (eds), *Ireland and the Great War* (Manchester, 2002). **80** Keith Jeffery, *'An Irish empire'? Aspects of Ireland and the British empire* (Manchester, 1996), p. 6. **81** Alvin Jackson, 'Irish unionists and the empire, 1880–1920: classes and masses' in Jeffery, *'An Irish empire'?*, p. 124. **82** *Irish Volunteer*, 21 Nov. 1914. **83** Keith Jeffery, 'The Irish military furthering both the liberties of Ireland and 'the unity, strength and best interests of this Empire'.[84] Of course, both Redmond and Sir Edward Carson expected to reap a post-war reward in the form of Irish self-government implemented to their satisfaction. Nationalist Ireland answered Redmond's call by flocking to the recruiting offices – by April 1916 there were more than 150,000 Irishmen on active service, around one hundred times the number of insurgents who turned out on Easter Monday. Redmond's brother William, MP for East Clare, joined the colours in 1915 and perished at Messines two years later. Three months before his death he told the House of Commons of his dream to see Ireland – like Canada, Australia and New Zealand – 'standing side by side in the common cause'.[85] On the scrubby slopes of Gallipoli in April 1915 and on Dublin's streets a year later, Irish nationalists took this very opportunity; the vast majority of Irishmen 'out' in Easter Week were dressed in khaki, fighting for what they perceived to be Ireland's best interests.

Easter 1916 brought the awful reality of war to Ireland's door and forced its people to decide which side they were on. 'To each comes the same thought', declared John Joly, 'to seek his duty and to do it'.[86] The impulse that took John McBride into Jacob's Biscuit Factory, The O'Rahilly to the General Post Office, and Ernie O'Malley onto a railway bridge with a borrowed rifle also brought the Anzacs to the windows and parapets of Trinity College. The rebel proclamation stated that 'the Irish Republic is entitled to, and hereby claims, the allegiance of every Irishman and Irish woman'. However, most Irish soldiers had already decided their allegiance and, despite some sympathy for the insurgents, remained true to it.[87] It was not an easy decision, as the conflict was 'that worst of all forms of strife – civil war'.[88]

The centrality of the Rising to the subsequent narrative of Irish history has tended to mute the voices of these men and their colonial comrades. In particular, the New Zealanders' part in the drama of Easter Week has been erased from the historical record; if there was no defence of Trinity College

tradition and the British empire' in Jeffery, *'An Irish empire'?*, p. 109. **84** Cited in Darwin, *The empire project*, p. 355. 'Just as it had proved to be for the Australians and New Zealanders, Redmond saw in the actions of Irishmen at Gallipoli material through which his increasingly imperially tinted version of Irish nationalism could be articulated.' Conor Mulvagh, *The Irish Parliamentary Party at Westminster, 1900–18* (Manchester, 2016), p. 196. **85** Terence Denman, *A lonely grave: the life and death of William Redmond* (Dublin, 1995), pp 106–11. **86** Joly, *Reminiscences and anticipations*, p. 219. **87** One recalls the words of the Irish non-commissioned officers at the German prisoner-of-war camp at Limburg who rejected the offer of special treatment if they deserted the ranks, because 'in addition to being Irish Catholics, we have the honour to be British soldiers'. Only 56 of the 2,300 Irish prisoners agreed to join Casement's 'Irish Brigade'. Ronan McGreevy, *Wherever the firing line extends: Ireland and the Western Front* (Dublin, 2016), p. 73. **88** Joly, *Reminiscences and anticipations*, p. 219.

during the Rising, or no one to defend it from, then why bother with the defenders? Is this perhaps a case where the historian Ernest Renan's concept of 'shared forgetting' – including the occasional embrace of historical error – might be employed in order to reconcile conflicting historical traditions and allow us all to live in peace?[89] Such recourse can come only at the price of an honest appraisal of what actually happened in Dublin during Easter 1916.

89 Ernest Renan, 'What is a nation?' in Geoff Eley and Ronald Grigor Suny (eds), *Becoming national: a reader* (Oxford, 1996), pp 41–55. 'Though often morally desirable, the use of history to promote intercommunal or international reconciliation may involve the suppression of ugly or inconvenient facts.' David Fitzpatrick, 'Historians and the commemoration of Irish conflicts, 1912–23' in John Horne and Edward Madigan (eds), *Towards commemoration: Ireland in war and revolution, 1912–1923* (Dublin, 2013), p. 132.

Appendices

APPENDIX 1: NEW ZEALAND LETTERS

1. John Godwin Garland (*Auckland Star*, 28 June 1916, p. 8)
2. Finlay McLeod (*Grey River Argus*, 22 July, p. 8)
3. Alexander Don (*Dunedin Evening Star*, 21 July 1916, p. 5)
4. Frederick Nevin (*Liverpool Daily Post*, 2 May 1916, p. 5)
5. Frederick Henry Hobbs (*Christchurch Sun*, 12 July 1916, p. 9)
6. 'A Canterbury lady' (*Christchurch Press*, 25 July 1916, p. 8)

APPENDIX 2: IRISH LETTERS

1. Mr McDermott (*Evening Post*, Wellington, 1 May 1916, p. 7)
2. Mr Rentoul Brown (*Christchurch Star*, 22 June 1916, p. 3)

APPENDIX 3: OTC LETTERS AND REPORTS

1. Robert Tweedy to his mother, 7 May 1916, TCD MS 7533/3
2. Gerald Fitzgibbon to William Hume Blake, 10 May 1916, TCD MS 11107/1
3. Gerald Fitzgibbon to William Hume Blake, 15 May 1916, TCD MS 11107/2
4. Ernest Alton, 'Work of the OTC', *TCD*, 19 June 1916
5. Ernest Alton's report in *Sinn Fein rebellion: a souvenir of presentations to the Officers' Training Corps, Trinity College Dublin* (Dublin, 1916)
6. Major G.A. Harris' report to War Office, 10 May 1916, in WO 32/9576, National Archives, London
7. John Joly, *Reminiscences and anticipations* (London, 1920), ch. 8, 'In Trinity College during the Sinn Fein rebellion' by 'One of the Garrison'

APPENDIX 1

New Zealand letters

1. John Godwin Garland (*Auckland Star*, 28 June 1916, p. 8)

In the Dublin Riot: Grammar School Old Boy: Has an Exciting Time: Went to Visit, Had to Fight: Fired at by Rebel Countess: Sniping Sinn Feiners.

A vivid description of the exciting time when the Sinn Fein riot was in progress in Dublin is given by Bugler JG Garland in a letter written to his father, Mr Thomas H. Garland, of this city. Bugler Garland, it may be mentioned, was formerly a member of the Grammar School Senior Cadets, and left with the Expeditionary Force for Samoa. Having been invalided back to Auckland, he was subsequently appointed to a hospital ship. Having a few days' leave, he ran across to Dublin, and happened to be in the thick of the fight, but escaped with a spent bullet wound in his ankle and a clean cut in his hand from a bayonet thrust.

'We arrived in England the day before Good Friday, and were given railway concession by which we could get return tickets for single fare. Sergeant Nevin, of Christchurch, and myself took tickets for Dublin. On Easter Monday we left the hotel at 8 a.m., and went by tram to Killiney Park. Half an hour after we were clear of Dublin the rebellion started. Our first intimation of it was when we were half-way back, and the electric power was cut off. We walked back to our hotel. We were standing in the main street (Sackville) about 2 p.m., just about 100 yards from our hotel. Shots were being fired, and a soldier from the Dublin Fusiliers was killed while walking with his young lady. There were thousands of people in the streets, and all of a sudden a large motor car whizzed past us. In it was the noted Countess, dressed in a green uniform. As she went past she fired two shots at us. One went above our heads; the other caught an elderly man in the arm. It seemed to be a signal to the other Sinn Feiners, for bullets started to whizz all round us. As we were unarmed, and had our Red Cross badges on, we went for our lives to the Soldiers' Club. The proprietor of the place told us that all the soldiers had gone over to the Trinity College, which is the headquarters of the Dublin University Officers' Training Corps. We reported there at 3 p.m. There were only about thirty of us, and we filled sandbags from 5 p.m. until 9 p.m. By that time our strength had grown to nearly sixty, including five New Zealanders, one Australian, five from South Africa, and two Canadians. At 11 p.m. they woke us up and took the colonials, whom they called Anzacs (although there were really only six Anzacs), up to the roof, where we were to snipe. We remained on that roof from midnight on Easter Monday till midnight on Thursday without a wink of sleep – exactly 72 hours. From the roof we could command a view of the main streets

– Sackville, Grafton, and Dame. Four of us were on the front parapet, commanding Dame Street, also part of Grafton Street.

'We got our first bag on Tuesday morning, at 4 a.m., when three Sinn Feiners came along on bikes, evidently going from Shepherd's [Stephen's] Green to the GPO. The men on my left, as soon as they saw them coming, told us to mark the last man, and they would get the first two. We all fired at once, killing two and wounding the other. When they were brought in the chap we killed had four bullet marks in the head, which meant that we all got him, and that he must have been killed instantly. A peculiar thing had happened. After he was killed he still sat on his bike and continued on for about 30 yards on the free-wheel. In fact, we thought we had missed him, when all of a sudden the bike swerved and he came off. This chap was a platoon leader, and on him they found a list of the names and addresses of the members of his platoon, and two despatches, together with some money that he had evidently taken from the GPO.

'On Wednesday we got two more in Sackville Street. They were armed with double-barrelled fowling-pieces, and had taken the small shot from the cartridges, replacing it with four slugs of lead about three-quarters of an inch by a quarter of an inch. We were troubled by a sniper on our left in the direction of St Andrew's Church, but as we were not quite sure we did not like to fire on that building. On Friday, after we had been relieved from the roof, a man living opposite the church came over and said he had seen the rifles pointing out of the belfry, so we six Anzacs were sent across to his house, and from his kitchen window we put about 100 rounds into the small triangular window they were firing from. Half an hour after they had ceased firing we decided to climb the tower. On the way over we were fired on by our own men, who mistook our slouch hats for those of the Sinn Fein. When we got to the belfry we found two men. One was already dead, and the other so badly wounded that he died an hour afterwards.

'On Saturday morning we killed a woman who was sniping from an hotel window in Dame street. When the RAMC brought her in, we saw she was only a girl about 20, stylishly dressed and not at all bad looking. She was armed with an automatic revolver and a Winchester repeater. Altogether we Anzacs were responsible for 27 rebels (twenty-four men and three women).

'On Saturday afternoon the colonials were given the honour of capturing Westland Row Station. We entered the Grosvenor Hotel, which faces the station, and by means of a ladder climbed over the railway arch and then over to the station. We got four there, and I had a narrow squeak. Two of us were going through the ticket office, and as soon as we entered the Sinn Feiners tried to bayonet the chap behind me. They just missed him, and caught me in the hand – just a mere scratch. Then we both got him together with our bayonets. The same night we were on duty on the roof doing two hours on and four off, and I had just taken my boots off and was going to sleep, when a ricochet bullet caught me just below the left ankle. It only went in a little over half its length. The doctor pulled it out with a pair of forceps.

'Of course by this time the town was in ruins, and bodies of soldiers, horses, civilians, and Sinn Feiners were lying about Sackville Street until Saturday. The looting that was going on was simply terrible. Small boys of 10 to 14 who were brought in and searched had cameras, watches, diamond tiepins, etc. The rebels themselves did not do much looting. Several of the chaps from Gallipoli reckon that one had a far better chance of getting off with his life there than in the Dublin riot, for the reason that these rebels were posted in twos and threes in almost every house and shop in the city. As it was, there were 700 casualties on our side, while there were only about 500 on the other.

'My chum [Nevin] left on Monday night, after the rebels were supposed to have surrendered. I waited till the next day in order to get some of my effects replaced for the ones that went up in smoke when Wynn's Hotel was burnt. The next night (Tuesday) I left the College at 6 p.m. in a motor-bicycle side-car. On our way three shots were fired at us, but no damage was done. I left Dublin at 8 p.m. on Tuesday, after doing nine days' duty, living on biscuits and water the whole time, and only having about twenty hours' sleep. At the Custom House there were about 300 refugees who had been burnt out of their homes, including two theatrical parties. All they had to eat for six days were hard biscuits and water, with tea occasionally. There was also an opera company at the police station. Among the actors was a Christchurch man named Hobbs. Of course it was a great experience, but I was not sorry when I left Dublin.'

2. Finlay McLeod (*Grey River Argus*, 22 July 1916, p. 8)

Sinn Fein Revolt. Wellington Boy's Experiences. Takes a Hand for King and Country.

Mr Finlay McLeod, well known in Wellington, has written to his attorney, Mr Aubrey Gualter, enclosing a letter from his son, Finlay, who was educated at the Terrace School in Wellington. Young Finlay was in the Dublin action against the Sinn Finn rebels, and the Commanding Officer says of him: 'On behalf of the officers and men, I wish to express our warm appreciation of Corporal McLeod's services.' Headquarters have also written to Finlay thanking him for the brave part he took in attacking the rebels.

In Finlay's letter to his mother, he says: 'I noticed a very bitter feeling against England. Soldiers were even jeered at, and the following Saturday, April 22, a man was arrested for threatening to shoot anyone in khaki. On the Monday the fun started. The Sinn Feiners marched through Dublin and captured the principal buildings, including the post office, St. Stephen's Green, in the heart of the city, and hoisting the Republic Flag. They then started to attack soldiers, and when I was walking down to the post office with an Australian we were fired on, but the fellow who fired was a bad shot. Two officers were shot just ahead of us. We then walked back and volunteered at the Dublin University Officers' Training Corps. On the way we got eleven more Colonials. We were given rifles. The Sinn Feiners had then surrounded us, and we were unable to start owing to lack of Service men, and ammunition. Only thirteen of us had seen service before. The others were raw recruits, and all told we only totalled 44. We had the Bank of Ireland to hold. During the day and evening more recruits came in and firing commenced. Tuesday, Anzac Day, was well kept up, for at 3.30 am three Sinn Feiners, as an advance party, came riding towards us, and we dropped them. Only another Australian and New Zealander were with me at this time. We were cheered by the corps, and the officers were very pleased with us. During that day [Tuesday] we killed six in one building, 26 in another and snipers here and there. We were at last reinforced by troops from England, and with them went out and captured the Weston [Westland] Row Railway Station. We were then relieved and patrolled the city, getting prisoners and doing house searching, and it was not an easy job. We had only one casualty, and it was slight. I am back again in England, feeling A1, and none the worse for the "fun" we had.'

3. Alexander Don (*Dunedin Evening Star*, 21 July 1916, p. 5)

'Dunedin Boy in Dublin.'

The following are extracts from a letter written by a New Zealand soldier to his father, who lives in Roslyn.

'I was over in Dublin at the rebellion, and in hospital there at Belfast with enteric before the "fun" started. I will tell you how I got on. On Easter Monday morning I was walking past Dublin Castle, and everything seemed all right, when a couple of shots rang out, and two Tommies, who were in front of me, fell over. I thought I must be dreaming, and went over to where they were lying, and saw that one had got it through the head and the other through the neck. Then I looked up and saw a couple of men in green uniforms and slouch hats, rifles and bandoliers, regarding me from the housetops. It was my hat that saved my life, because it seemed to puzzle them, being so very like their own, although, of course, not green. Then I went on up the street, and had a couple of shots at them from the nearest corner – I always carry my revolver. That was the first intimation that I and many others had of the rising of the Sinn Feiners, this sniping of unarmed soldiers being a sort of specialty of theirs.

'After going up the street a little way I saw more rebels walking on the [roofs of the] houses, and only for the crowd would have been shot. Then a lot of women got round me, crying and wailing for the soldiers, whom they had seen shot before. They pushed me into a place, and I got into civilian's clothes, as I didn't want to stay there all day. I then went out and saw the different places the rebels held in the town. At the Post Office I saw the Commander-in-Chief, Connelly [*sic*], standing with folded arms in a doorway. I could have shot him from the crowd, but should have got two or three into me, as rifles and green could be seen from every window.

'I was just turning round to come away when I saw two New Zealanders. They were on holiday. The rebels started shooting at them, so I told them to come along with me. We were passing Trinity College when one of the porters called us in, unlocking the gates for us. I went back for my uniform, and on returning put it on. That night we kept the rebels from taking the Royal Bank of Ireland, firing from the top of Trinity College. There were only about 30 armed men in Trinity that night, and as it occupies the whole block it took some holding, and we were right in the centre of the rebels.'

'I won't say too much about the things we did, because the whole affair was just about 10 times worse than even the people of England knew. So I suppose in New

Zealand you thought it was a very small affair. But from Monday to Thursday one could hear all the time the rattling of rifles in every part of Dublin and the boom of our artillery. I had seven hours' sleep from Easter Sunday night to the following Friday, as we were shooting from the roof the whole time and house-to-house searching. It was very dangerous work, too, and if information came to the officer in charge of the Dublin University to the effect that a sniper was on the roofs opposite, the cry was for the "Anzacs" – numbering five New Zealanders and one Australian!

'They even had the church tower opposite, and were firing from it. I took our fellows over, and we fired a volley through the tower from the back of the buildings opposite. Then we went into the church, and crept upstairs to the belfry, and found one of them dead and the other wounded. That was our job, and I left a couple of Tommies on guard while we went on another job.

'On Thursday night I saw the big crowd of rebels in the G.P.O. surrender – about 350 there were ... It was a grand sight, the whole of Sackville street being in flames, and the fire flashing on the bayonets of the guards ranged round the prisoners. I met some of the finest people I have ever met in Ireland, and the Irish people must not be judged by the "Sinn Feiners."'[1]

4. Frederick Nevin (*Liverpool Daily Post*, 2 May 1916, p. 5)

From the Daily Post and Daily Chronicle Special Correspondent.

DUELS ACROSS HOUSETOPS. REBELS' CONFESSION TO ANZAC GUARD.

The story of the fight for Trinity College, already briefly mentioned, was told me in detail to-day by one of the Anzac non-commissioned officers, who, home after a share in Gallipoli doings, was in Dublin for an Easter holiday. He and another New Zealander – a corporal – put up at the Windsor [Wynn's] Hotel, in Abbey-street, and went sightseeing.

'We heard returning from Killarney [Killiney] at midday that there had been trouble at the college,' he said; 'but we did not think seriously of it. We had a bit of [a] surprise when we got to the corner of Abbey-street and Sackville-street, for as we came to a halt the rebels deliberately fired on us from their loopholes above the post office, and a bullet went through the sleeve of a civilian a few feet off. We shifted from that point. Then we found that help was needed at Trinity College, which the rebels were likely to attack; and we went in to help the students to hold their building.

'Had the enemy come earlier it might have been easy to seize a number of rifles and 7,000 or 10,000 rounds ammunition; but Colonials had now filed in – seven Anzacs, two South Africans, and a Canadian, all on holiday – to give the students a hand. A rifle and bayonet were passed to me, and up to the roof I went. There we watched for hours. Insurgents passed, but we made no move, for we were without

1 Reprinted in the *Bendigo Advertiser*, 9 Aug. 1916, where Don's father had formerly lived. The last line of the *Advertiser*'s version read 'and the Irish people, especially in the north of Ireland, must not be judged by the "Sinn Feiners"'. It also added the word 'innocent' before 'unarmed soldiers' in the last line of the first paragraph.

orders. We had to prevent them seizing the college, and there was only one way to it. There we stuck until two o'clock Tuesday morning, watching quietly in hiding the glare of the turmoil around the rebels' quarters. Night after night we kept watch, and the hours were crowded in incident.

'Very early one morning a big crowd came up, thinking Trinity College safely closed down, and presumably an easy capture, and three men stole around by way of Grafton-street. We let them have it as they came within range. One was accounted for with four bullets in the head, a second one was wounded, and the third man got away.

BULLETS THAT TORTURE.

'We were continually being sniped at from points all around. We drew a line on them straight down the street from Trinity as far as Nelson's pillar, where we could just see them. They were aiming at us from a building close by, and, getting the range beautifully, we were soon busy replying. Then there were some men making a fuss in the upper part of a hotel, and we were obliged to send a few bullets amongst them. We had the range so accurately that one occupant on the roof was held up for ten hours – he dare not leave the cover behind which he was sheltered, and it was exciting business this protracted sniping and counter-sniping. Bullets were flying around us on every hand, striking against the roof, but by a good stroke of luck none of us was wounded. What the casualties were on the opposite roof I cannot say.

'I find that three descriptions of cartridge were used by the enemy. These were found on some of their prisoners' cases from which shot had been removed, and large pellets of lead, capable of terrible injury, substituted. Then there were bullets of a foreign type, and others big and clumsy, evidently home-made, tipped with soft lead so that they flatten on impact, and are calculated to knock the back out of a man.

BETRAYED INTO REVOLT.

'My duties did not end with the duel on the roof, where, by the way, I had a narrow escape of having my head blown off through the accidental discharge of a student's gun. I was asked to carry on at the Custom House, where I was put in charge of a guard of twelve. Three hundred rebels had surrendered in front of the Post Office, and word had been sent to Trenely [*sic*] asking us to convey prisoners from the Custom House to the Castle. But as the Castle was full our guard had to look after four rebel officers and forty or fifty other prisoners at the Custom House, where they were placed in a cellar. A rebel captain in uniform was an Irishman twenty-one years of age; we had prisoners as young as fifteen. Some of the prisoners were surprised at being involved in the revolt. They frankly said that they were brought out for manoeuvres on Easter Monday, not knowing what they were doing, and they were shoved into some building and told to fight for their lives, otherwise they would be shot. I heard, too, that civilians were put into buildings and told to fight for liberty. These men, I was distinctly assured, did not know what they had come out for, but were summarily given express instructions to fight for liberty, being informed all the time that reinforcements were coming up, although such was not the case. The rebels shot three old men in Upper Sackville-street. After my unexpected spell of military duty in the midst of holiday, I returned to find that there had been a fire at the Windsor [Wynn's] Hotel, causing the destruction of my luggage.'

5. Frederick Henry Hobbs (*Christchurch Sun*, 12 July 1916, p. 9)

The Dublin Riots. Christchurch Man's Experiences.

An old Christchurch boy, Mr FH Hobbs, who is now a member of the D'Oyly Carte Opera Company, and was in Dublin during the recent troubles, writes interestingly of his experiences to his people in this city. 'The whole thing,' he says, 'was started by some thousands of Irish volunteers of the class that is always opposed to British rule. Twenty-five thousand troops were hurried over from England and, in six days, the rebels were defeated in a thorough manner. The loss of life, in both the military and civilian ranks was enormous while the principal part of the city was reduced to ruins.

'The Sinn Feiners simply marched into the different places and took possession, turning out the rightful occupants, whom they shot if resistance was offered. I had just left the [Gaiety] theatre on Easter Monday night when I saw a party of volunteers march into the Public Gardens nearby and deliberately shoot a policeman within 50 yards of me. In a few minutes we learnt that similar incidents had happened in various parts of the city. It was not safe in the streets, and we had to wait several hours in the theatre. About four in the afternoon I was able to get to my rooms, which were situated in one of the streets where the fighting was most severe.

'The streets were crowded with people, and the lower classes looted all kinds of shops, passing our windows carrying bundles of boots, toys, clothing, food, etc. At 8 o'clock on Wednesday morning a gunboat in the river and a field gun on the other side commenced bombarding Liberty Hall. The military were being fired at from a high building behind our house. They weren't sure where the firing was coming from, so they blazed away at our windows. The only safe place was the cellar, so we went down there dragging mattresses with us. By Thursday morning, as no shopping could be done, we ran short of supplies. About midday a barricade made of paper taken from a printing warehouse, caught fire and soon all the buildings behind us were burning fiercely.'

Mr Hobbs then describes the difficulties and the narrow escapes experienced in getting to a place of safety. The whole block in which his rooms were situated was burnt down before morning. Proceeding, he says, 'We were perfectly safe within the police station, and there saw many interesting sights. By midday on Saturday the Sinn Feiners had had enough of it and gave themselves up unconditionally to the military. I met several New Zealand soldiers who had come over to Ireland on leave. When the trouble started they reported themselves, and took part in the fray. Those I saw had been posted to the top of Trinity College as sharpshooters on the lookout for snipers and, from what I heard, they did deadly work. They were up there on a fifteen hours' shift, with nothing in the way of sustenance but a couple of biscuits and a water bottle.'

6. 'A Canterbury lady' (*Christchurch Press*, 25 July 1916, p. 8)

The Sinn Fein Revolt. A Personal Narrative.

A Canterbury lady has received a letter from a relative in Ireland, giving an interesting account of the recent revolt. We are permitted to extract the following: 'And now we have just lived through a week that will stand out even if we live to be centenarians! Imagine an ordinary, peaceful 20th century sort of Easter Sunday, with church decorations and holiday-makers enjoying glorious sunshine, and loyal volunteers going out for a field day, and then on Monday came the thunderbolt that the Sinn Feiners, in huge numbers and fully armed, had seized most of the public buildings in Dublin, including the GPO, the Law Courts, the City Hall, St Patrick's Cathedral, and others, and were firing at anyone who came near them. They had also got the railway stations and cut all the telegraphic communications and the cables to England. Sinn Fein means "ourselves alone," and their volunteers wear green. I can't go through all the events of the week. *** went in to the brewery (a small part of which was held by the rebels for a day) on his bicycle (there was, of course, no other way of getting anywhere), dodging the worst streets which varied from day to day, with rifle bullets singing round, mostly from windows and roofs on the rebels' part, and from street barricades on the part of our troops. I never knew whether he was safe till he turned up, tired but triumphant, in the evening. He wanted to defend Trinity College with his OTC, but they were short of food, so couldn't accept his services. Buildings behind and in front of the brewery were held by the rebels. Two of the brewery men were shot in the streets. Most of them did not attempt to get to work at all. *** helped to fill and deliver sandbags on motor lorries in the streets. More troops arrived every day – it is said that there are now 30,000, and they were all complete with everything down to camp kitchens and chaplains!

'Wednesday, Thursday and Friday that week the booming of the guns and the rattle of the machine-guns never stopped day and night, and it seemed so queer to be playing in the garden with the children and the deadly work going on within earshot all the time. Every night the sky was lit up with the glare of huge fires – whole streets burning, and bits of burnt fabric lay on our tennis court. One wondered what was being left of Dublin, and certainly there isn't much left of the principal streets on the further side of the Liffey. Sackville Street and others are just literally like Ypres – many of the biggest buildings heaps of bricks ten feet high.

'One evening the firing came very near to us. Mr *** , in Veterans' Corps uniform, has been most useful as guide to our officers. Six of the poor Veterans were killed on their return from their field day. Also numbers of wounded soldiers out walking from the hospitals on Easter Monday. Women and children got shot accidentally in their houses, and others who had gone out, starving, to buy bread of which there was practically none: and others who had to leave their houses because they were on fire. Many of the bullets in possession of the rebels were dum-dum. But on the whole, the rebels played the game, and the Red Cross was respected.

'Our troops behaved splendidly; it was a most utterly nerve-racking experience for them, in an unknown city, an unknown brogue, with hidden snipers on roofs and round ever corner, friend and foe indistinguishable (for the rebels soon discarded their uniform) forcing their way up narrow staircases with possible death at every landing; and most of our young soldiers were very young with only a few months' training. And no rest, and little food, for four or five days and nights on end. Kingstown was the base, and every approach to it was defended. I went there every day with a military permit to buy food, which I brought back on my bicycle; and one night after seeing *** and *** off, I had to break martial law by being out after 7.30 p.m.! It was very eerie in the deserted and unlit and silent roads, with groups of khaki and gleaming bayonets challenging me at every corner. I thought I never should get past one barricade, with its row of businesslike rifles laid along the top of the sandbags, but happily I knew the part of England the soldiers came from, and eventually prevailed on them to let me climb over. They had been eight days and nights there, with only odd hours' sleep on the pavement. It was quite comic, the proclamation of the Irish Republic, if it hadn't all been so tragic, and the waste of life so pitiful.'

APPENDIX 2

Irish letters

1. Mr McDermott (*Evening Post*, Wellington, 1 May 1916, p. 7)

One 'Mr McDermott', a Trinity student, returned from the races on Easter Monday. 'We went along to Trinity College [on Tuesday], and were given rifles and cartridge belts, and assisted to maintain a watch from the windows, where, with others, we sniped at rebels with accuracy. About 11 o'clock fairly heavy fighting was heard from the direction of the Castle. We fired three rounds at the enemy, who was handicapped through having weapons inferior to ours. Throughout the day firing was maintained. We first learned that the rebels held the two newspaper offices near the Castle and a house almost next door. From 9 o'clock until 11 in the evening there was fairly brisk firing at St Stephen's Green. We despatched pickets up Dame Street, and these succeeded in clearing the rebels from the houses. This system of attacking houses with pickets was extended successfully, and largely accounted for the effective way in which the hostile forces were gradually penned in a ring. A section of troops was brought up at 8 o'clock on Wednesday morning to deal with "Liberty Hall." With a couple of small guns, shells of small calibre were pumped into the building. They did not contain high explosives, but within five minutes the building was reduced to a pitiable spectacle. Altogether forty shells struck the building, the first demolishing a green flag which floated defiantly from the roof. The noise was deafening, and the bombardment was accompanied by the ceaseless rattle of machine-gun and rifle fire. The rebels had evidently withdrawn by the back way, for they did not reply to the fire of the troops, who dashed forward with fixed bayonets and established themselves in the ruin, the whole building having crumbled under the bombardment. Upon the top of Trinity College soldiers were posted with a machine-gun in a window, and fought a duel with rebels in the houses in Sackville Street who were also armed with a machine-gun, but the latter's fire was ineffective.'

2. Mr Rentoul Brown (*Christchurch Star*, 22 June 1916, p. 3)

From our correspondent, London: Mr Rentoul Brown, TCD student, wrote in a Dublin newspaper that he entered college, carrying his college gown over his arm: 'The gates of the University are shut. The front windows are "sandbagged". One can see the muzzles of rifles protruding. I wave the gown at the gates. A porter takes notice. I am admitted. Everybody is wondering if the examination will be held. We find that the examination will take place as usual. Trinity is held by some members of the Officers' Training Corps, who happen to be in college in holiday time. Some Tommies on leave are gradually filtering in for protection. Ought I to join the garrison or stand my examination? I am a member of the OTC. I decide to try the examination. I am ready to seize a rifle if the college is attacked. Only 17 turn up to be examined; 100 might have been expected under normal conditions. The examination begins. It is difficult to fix the mind on logic, astronomy and mathematical physics. Try to fix my mind on the demand of the examiners for the battleground of the ancients. During recreation time a fusillade begins. It seems as though the rebels are storming the gates. We rush to seize rifles, and we are told that blanks are being fired to show that Trinity is manned against the insurgents … Again on Wednesday morning I made my way to the gates of the historic University. The place was now crowded with military. Only about half the students of the day before came to be examined. The firing was terrific on this day, and yet examiners were as exacting as ever in probing our knowledge. A Sinn Feiner was lying dead in one of the passages. Although the rebellion has brought ruin to many homes, people have treated the whole affair with philosophic calm. The spirit of humour has been as keen as ever before.'

APPENDIX 3

OTC letters and reports

1. Robert Tweedy, OTC cadet, to his mother, 7 May 1916, TCD MS 7533/3

After 24 hours' sleep, I feel able to write to you, and you will be glad to hear at first-hand that I am none the worse for my experience of active service. One wrote and telegraphed to you several times, but nothing could get out or in, as you know. No one seems to know how one of your wires got through. The whole thing came on us like a thunderbolt on Monday, and out here we could not guage [*sic*] the seriousness of the rising. As I could not get in on Monday night, I went down to the Dalkey Police Station to see if they wanted special constables, but all the police were in barracks and seemed to be taking matters with a light heart. They assured me that everything would be quiet in the morning, so I went home to bed, and cycled in early on Tuesday morning in mufti, riding quite unconscious of danger down one side of Stephen's Green, which was in the hands of the rebels. I was the only living thing in the street this time, and I went along slowly to get a good view of the barricades. Rifle firing from the Shelbourne Hotel in the Green, the sight of a dead horse at the corner, and a crowd more or less sheltered in Merrion Row, (which runs into Stephen's Green) gave me the first impression of danger.

There were no police or military to warn people from straying into such places, and I was to see later how idiotically contemptuous of rifle firing the crowd is until someone gets hit, and even then how quickly the effect is overpowered by morbid curiosity. I went straight to Trinity College, and found a dozen others arguing with the porter, who would not budge from his order to admit no one. Nor would he send a message to head-quarters at the front gate facing College Green, so we gave it up for the time and wandered about for a bit to see how things were looking. There were crowds of foot passengers quite orderly, and not in the least understanding the situation. Shots were being fired here and there, especially between Dublin Castle and the rebels in the Daily Express building just across the road, but the entire absence of any armed person in the streets produced a feeling of unreality, almost of deliberate drama, in the beholder. For instance, the huge breadth of Sackville Street at the GPO was spanned by a strand or two of barbed wire, and one callow youth in the uniform of the Sinn Fein (pronounce 'Shin fane') army was leaning on his rifle chatting to a knot of people while keeping the wire inviolate. The windows of the GPO were smashed, mail-bags, office furniture and miscellanea formed cover for the defenders, and some of these could be seen more or less at their ease looking down upon us, just as if they were awaiting the arrival of some royal procession. In Sackville Street there was no shooting, and the crowd laughed and talked gaily. A few shops had been looted to the last article, but it seems only those into which the rebels had forced an entry for purposes of defence. At that time the mob had not taken the initiative.

My friend and I returned to the College gates and obtained admission at about 11 am, and until the following Sunday I left it only once, and that for the purpose of guarding prisoners at the Custom House, just opposite the famous Liberty Hall, now blown to bits. The duty of the OTC reinforced by stray soldiers of all kinds – Anzacs, Canadians, AOC, South Africans, RIR, RDF, Manchesters, and others who had fled from the streets on Monday night – was to hold TCD which happens to occupy the most important strategic position in the City. When the rising occurred about midday on Monday afternoon and night there were never more than 40 to 60 armed men in the garrison. The military acumen of the rebel leaders may be judged from the fact they did not make any serious attempt to capture the position. If they had done so the rebellion might have been a much more serious matter.

During the afternoon of Tuesday, the first regiment of soldiers arrived from the Curragh and you may imagine that we cheered them as they entered the gates. From that time the College was the scene of the greatest military activity, and at one period later in the week a whole brigade with cavalry and artillery billeted and bivouacked within the walls. The actual defence of the College was left in our hands and we had a strenuous ten days of manning windows and roofs and mounting guards. A machine gun and a party of sharp-shooters on the roof did good execution down Sackville Street, and TCD may be said to have saved the banks and business premises of the most important thoroughfares of Dublin. Only one shop within range of our rifles was looted and I shall never understand how the riff-raff of the streets could brave the hail of bullets – even though most of them were fired high – in order to steal boxes and sacks full of fruit and vegetables.

The College buildings are high and formed a perfect protection from the enemy's bullets, but it was not a pleasant experience to do guard duty in the various quads, while rifle and machine gun fire was going on briskly overhead, but I got used to it in a short time. I know now what a diet of bully beef and biscuits means, for we had them three times a day almost the whole time, very rarely seeing bread or butter, and meat of the uncanned variety only once. Even jam was scarce, and after the first two days there were no potatoes. That was nothing, but we all felt the want of sleep, as the garrison was not strong enough to permit a proper system of reliefs. For five nights I slept something less than ten hours, and that of course with all clothes and equipment on. But what is that compared with one spell of duty in the driest trench at the front. If the rebels had possessed anything heavier than a machine gun we should have slept still less.

The madness of it all! But was the plan mere madness? I do not believe it. The rebels were convinced, in my opinion, that they were taking part in a great German push by sea and by land, and you will find that they had good reason for their belief. The rebels adopted defensive tactics from the beginning, and they gambled upon (a) a general rising of the populace, (b) German assistance arriving before the British could send enough men from England. They hoped that the German Navy, or the

Submarine part of it, would deal with the transports, and that the paralysis of Dublin would be followed immediately by a rebel occupation of every important town in the country.

We call them madmen now because they did not succeed, but we shall not know for a long time how mad they really were. If it were not for the wanton burning of Sackville Street, the city and the country would have suffered no more than trifling inconvenience, and a few hundred casualties, but that immense act of arson has ruined Dublin for the time. I saw the fire, and it will never fade from my memory. No photographs can reproduce the awful devastation which it wrought, nor any writing the misery which it leaves behind.

Nevertheless, this rebellion has done one good thing in that the reality of war has been brought to our doors, and I shall have more hope for Ireland from now on. Perhaps if the rebellion had flared up in the provinces before it was suppressed, the ultimate result would be happier, but in the Dublin area at least the people will turn from the pleasure of making profits out of the war to the sterner task of fighting adversity.

There is still an OTC garrison in TCD, but the business men are being relieved, and I gave up my rifle on Friday, after 9 days continuous duty. It is said that TCD saved the city, and I am proud to have been one of the garrison. Luckily the long range shooting of the rebels was poor while ours was fair to good, so that we suffered no casualties.

2. Gerald Fitzgibbon (10 Merrion Square, Dublin) to William Hume Blake, 10 May 1916, TCD MS 11107/1

Dear Billy … We are now, so far as immediate danger is concerned, over our troubles, but it will take Dublin many a long day to recover its position. The finest street in the city is a smoking heap of ruins, and for two or three blocks on either side everything is burnt out. There are shell holes in the Four Courts, the College of Surgeons and half a dozen other public buildings, and dozens of shops in uninjured streets have been broken open and looted, while hundreds of people, the number will never be ascertained, have been killed. Many bodies have been buried in the ruins, many are still being disinterred from backyards and gardens. We buried three dead in College, two soldiers and a rebel that I know of, and there were probably others, and the financial cost to this city is incalculable. I was confined to College for nearly a fortnight, and so know little of what was going on outside except what they have told me here since I came home, and so much as one could see from the College buildings.

When war broke out two years ago I joined the College OTC as I thought possibly everyone who could bear arms, however decrepit, might be required in case of invasion, and I have been drilling in College ever since. As time went on the young men got commissions and the corps had no young men except recruits and I was gradually promoted to be a platoon sergeant and instructor, and I used to drill the newest recruits in rifle exercises and squad drill, and from me and a couple more like me they went on to the regular sergeant major for further instruction.

We, like the Government, knew long ago of the Sinn Fein danger, and ever since Christmas we kept a night guard in the OTC headquarters, which are at the East end of the College Park, detached by a quarter of a mile of playing grounds from the College buildings. As we had some 300 rifles, 5000 rounds of ball [ammunition] and a quantity of medical and other stores there, we thought it very probable that a raid might be made some day by the Sinn Feiners and that a guard was necessary. We did not think the rising would take the form it did, at least not so soon; what we feared was a night raid to steal our arms. Police barracks and patrols had been dispossessed of their arms from time to time recently through the country, and rifles had been stolen from Dublin barracks.

On Easter Monday I was working in my study, when Terry Shore, who is in a private hospital here, came rushing in to say that a rebellion had broken out, that he had seen the Sinn Feiners entrenched in Stephen's Green and firing on everyone in uniform, that he heard they had taken the Castle, the Post Office, and the railway stations and that several policemen and soldiers had been killed. I got up at once and went to put on my uniform to go to College, as I knew everyone would be wanted there, and while I was changing Capt[ain] Alton called to summon me there. He and I walked down together. I am now coming to the conclusion that I was very brave to go, as I did not think it likely there would be more than half a dozen men at headquarters on an Easter Monday, with College empty and everyone out of town, but at the time I rather thought I was a fool to go, and I certainly contemplated the possibility of not coming back.

We found about a dozen collected, and at once got out rifles and ammunition and served them out, and then all Monday afternoon and night the queerest military menagerie you ever saw kept gathering round. Unarmed soldiers on the streets warned by plainclothesmen or friends to 'run for the College' were taken in at the front gate and sent down across the College Park to headquarters, where we armed them and enrolled them. We had five Anzacs, two, or perhaps three, Canadians, one from Ottawa, one from Alberta, and, I think, a Winnipeg man, three South Africans, one in a kilt, three Army Ordnance men, a Corporal of the Irish Guards, home on sick furlough, two or three Middlesex Imperial Yeomen, a couple of South Irish Horse, a couple of Dublin Fusiliers, a couple of Royal Irish Rifles, a couple of Royal Irish Lancers, one of whom had had his horse shot dead under him in Sackville Street, and half a dozen other miscellaneous details, almost all men on leave or sick furlough in Dublin, who had been fired upon – unarmed – as they were walking through the streets.

We had an anxious evening and night, as the rebels held the Railway Station beside us with a fairly strong body, and had a patrol marching up and down the line which overlooked us fifty yards off and stray sniping shots were fired at us from the roof of the houses in Westland Row, Nassau Street and Brunswick Street. We put the place in as good a state of defence as possible, and posted sentries all over the shop and so worried through the night. All night, of course, we heard firing going on in the city. Next day we packed all our stores and ammunition with the transport wagons belonging to our ASC unit, and hauled them up across the College Park into College, as the Headquarters, besides being untenable if attacked in force, were too far from the main College buildings and our numbers were far too small to hold both.

My mind is almost a blank about Monday and Tuesday, except that I, like most others, had no sleep, and was on some patrols and guards, and was working all the time. Tuesday we were in the main part of the College, with sentries all over the place. On Wednesday the troops began to arrive in College. All Tuesday afternoon they had been working towards the centre of the City where we were through wicked street fighting from house to house. The Sherwood Foresters, who were the leading battalion that came from England and approached from Kingstown, had very heavy casualties – 18 officers killed or wounded (I think 9 killed) and about 200 casualties in all. Very few troops were available from the Curragh, about 1200 I think, and they came in from the West. From College we could see the fierce firing across the head of Dame Street half a mile away, from the rebels in the City Hall and the Express Offices, and from the soldiers fighting their way from house to house up to that position. I forget what day the field guns began in the City, it was either Wednesday or Thursday.

College saved the centre of Dublin and the big banks, all of which have their head offices in or about College Green. The rebels thought we were far more numerous than we really were, and they were afraid to assault the place, which they could have had for the asking up to two o'clock on Monday, and at very small cost up to two o'clock on Tuesday. One thing that terrified them was early on Tuesday morning, just after dawn, three of their despatch riders came pelting down on bicycles from Stephen's Green, bringing despatches to the Post Office, and we had twelve or fifteen men posted in windows and on the roof in front of College. They fired on the cyclists, killed one, wounded another, and the third left his bicycle and rifle and bolted down a side street. No doubt he went back to his headquarters and told them College was stuffed with armed men. The booty collected was their bicycles, four rifles, 400 rounds of ammunition and some despatches, and of course the corp[se]. We planted him out later on to fertilise the Provost's daffodils.

From that on nothing was done to us beyond continual sniping from the roof and windows of surrounding high buildings. When we concentrated in front of College we absolutely commanded College Green, Dame Street, Westmoreland Street, Nassau Street, and Brunswick Street, so that no looting could take place in any of them, also half Grafton Street, the end where the big jewellers are. The upper half of Grafton Street, which lies round a bend and was covered from our fire, was badly looted. If the rebels had had the sense to occupy College the whole of that splendid mass of building would have had to be shelled out, as the other strongholds of the rebels were later on, the Banks would have been taken and looted, and probably College Green and Dame Street and Grafton Street would have been burnt.

The importance of College as a centre is shown by the fact that all the troops, a whole Division, which came to Dublin have bivouacked there, and it is the Headquarters of the Army of occupation. We were lucky to have held it. I doubt if we could have stuck out for twenty-four hours with the means at our disposal if we had been seriously attacked, but we were there to do our best, and the rebels were bluffed by the confident face we put on.

I haven't the satisfaction of knowing that I hit any of these Home Rule rebels. I only got shots at windows with snipers in them, and at a couple of looters. I didn't want to fire at looters, it was rebels I wanted, and the only time I ever was on a really good pitch for them, they weren't rising. One Anzac got nine, but he was a marksman, and the Anzacs were given all the eligible situations, which it must be allowed they deserved. They were an outstanding gang. I have never seen their like. The man they shot on the bicycle in the early dawn was riding fast, it was a hard shot at a downward angle from a high window. I believe they only fired four or five shots and he had two through his head, one through his right lung, and a fourth shot got and winged the second man of the party. If they hadn't concentrated so much they would have bagged all three.

If that accursed Home Rule Bill had been in force no Irish Government could have, or would have, dared to try to put down this rebellion. As it was the great body of nationalists throughout the country would probably have joined the rebels in a day or two if the English Division had not arrived with such unexpected promptitude, and dealt so faithfully with the rebels ... I hadn't my clothes or even my boots off from 12 on Easter Monday till the following Friday evening, and on the Monday after Easter I got four hours leave and went home for a bath. Till Friday we lived on bully beef and biscuit, then we generally got bread and jam at breakfast and tea.

One washed at a tap or when one could. We had to furnish sentries and guards for College all the time, even after the troops came in, and I was several times Sergeant of the Guard for 24 hours. One got no rest then, as patrols kept bringing in prisoners to be lodged in the Guard room, some of whom had to be searched, and for whom one had to give receipts, and then one had to post reliefs every two hours, and visit the sentries in between to see that they were alert, and all that sort of thing. It was a great experience but I don't want to do it again, at least unless I can get a shooting job. I have felt very bloodthirsty about these rebels since I saw the men they shot down in Stephen's Green and Haddington Road, and saw all Sackville Street in flames.

Cromwell was the only governor who ever dealt properly with Irish rebels and Providence choked him off before he had finished his work. The Government had more than ample warning months and months ago of this rising. Within the last three months these rebels had two or three practice sham fights by night in the Dublin Streets, and actually took the Castle in one of them – for practice, posting pickets, holding up traffic, throwing up barricades, and going through all the practice for the performance they carried out on Easter Monday.

It is said that ten days before the revolt the Chiefs of Police put a list of leaders to the Government and demanded the authority to arrest them and raid their different headquarters, on the ground that a rising was imminent, and that Birrell wrote 'Rubbish' on the face of the file, and turned it down. Anyway all the Police and Constabulary through Ireland suspected it, drilling was going on openly everywhere, and the Government sat by and did nothing.

I think the Germans promised them large support in men, never intending to send any – but knowing that if even an abortive rising could be fomented it would divert a large body of English troops more or less permanently to this country and to paralyse or weaken the offensive in France which was due to come off about now. The rebels had [an] abundance of ammunition, and plenty of rifles and revolvers, they had several strongly fortified holds in the City, but the field guns knocked the stuffing out of them, and now, like all Irish patriots, the prisoners who turned traitors to England are tumbling over one another in their eagerness to betray their comrades in rebellion. The Irish patriot has always been the same from the days of Elizabeth to today. Put his dupes in the cart and then sell them to save his own skin, after murdering as many unarmed people as he can get at from behind a ditch or any other sap even. And their political gang talk treason and stir up the silly sentiment of the half-educated population with 'Ireland a nation' and 'Home Rule' and 'Independence' and all the rest of it.

They had out a Proclamation on Easter Monday in which they proclaimed the support that was coming from 'our generous allies in Europe' and 'our relations in America'. There were other proclamations which I did not see, but in which I hear they announced that all was going well with the cause, that the country was surrounded by a cordon of German submarines which would prevent any English troops from coming over, and that 40,000 or 50,000 German troops had landed or were about to land to help them to throw off the hated yoke of English rule forever.

The Home Rule gang are all the same, they differ only in degree, and if this rising had had even a temporary success thousands in the country who were waiting to see how the cat jumped would have come in. It was because Ulster knew them that she was determined never to be placed at their mercy.

3. Gerald Fitzgibbon (10 Merrion Square, Dublin) to William Hume Blake, 15 May 1916, TCD MS 11107/2

I am afraid there is a tendency to over estimate very greatly, not what we did, but the way we did it. We suffered no casualties, and scarcely anything that could be rated higher than discomfort. Of course, we did not know that no attack would be made on us, and we took a big risk willingly, but the Sinn Feiners so overrated our strength that I do not think they ever seriously contemplated an assault on College. If they had come anytime after midday on Tuesday it would have been a merry fight. Before that we would have been scuppered if they had pushed the attack home with all their might.

4. Ernest Alton, 'Work of the OTC', *TCD*, 19 June 1916

Easter week proved the OTC and did not find them wanting. The anxiety of the first days was great; the physical work would have taxed the strength of a far larger body. There was very little food, less rest, and no comfort for most of the members; but they exhibited a uniform good temper, keenness and discipline, which deserves all praise. There was no shirking, every man put his back into his task. Language occasionally was a little forcible, but it was only symptomatic of cheerful alacrity. Of course, we criticised one another's efforts. Our first meal, I remember, was rather dubious; there was a lively discussion whether the contents of the dixy should be styled tea or cocoa or poison. The canteen cook was annoyed, and wanted to leave the fire for the firing line. But that little cloud was swept away, and Paddy next moment, stuttering with enthusiasm, was dishing out 'wash' and smiles. That little incident was typical. We had to do the best with the materials at hand, and the men did their best, and a bit more, and smiled as they did it.

Our commissariat was, perhaps, the least prepared to meet the crisis. But things improved immensely when our QMS appeared. He was a genial pirate – ready to commandeer anything from a bread cart to a fishing smack, and his efforts were ably seconded by our French ally in the kitchen. The kitchen staff worked like niggers to provide every man with his 'bit and a sup.' And there were two fair volunteers who were attached to the OTC, and to whom, I may assure them, the OTC are equally attached. We owe them our respect, gratitude and a general salute when they appear on our parade ground.

The powers that be decided that an election and a Term Examination should be held – as well as the College – during the week. But the outside entertainments detracted largely from the popularity of the shows in the Theatre. Even the Senior Fellows were affected, and gazed with benevolent wonder at scenes that would on other occasions have incurred their heaviest censure. Soldiers invaded the sacred grass plots, horses and mules kicked up the time-honoured cobbles, and impetuous Tommies brushed aside impatiently the most august of our academic figures. Dr G[wynne], who every son of Trinity loves and reveres, took on a new lease of life; we trembled for him as he made his way amongst the skittish mules or passed fearlessly through the ranks of the 2nd – when they were 'easing springs.'

The discipline of the Cadets would have done credit to a company of veterans. Orders were promptly and strictly obeyed. The acting CO was inclined to deplore their rigid obedience when he attempted to patrol at dawn in front of his own sentries. The NCOs spared themselves even less than their men, and few of them thought of sleep or rest during the first week. And yet they always turned out the smartest and best groomed on parade. On some other occasion it may be possible to give a detailed account of the doings of those days; at present it is necessary to confine myself to general remarks. Yet I would like to express our appreciation of the work done by the RAMC unit, who tended to friend, foe and neutral with equal sympathy and care. As regards the officers of the OTC; the writer himself knows best how well they did, how unceasingly they laboured, how loyally they conspired with every member of the Corps to cloak the shortcomings of their CO. It was a great game; we were handicapped by the absence of two of our best officers, but the team played every ounce till the whistle blew. We are at present *nostri superstites* [survivors], the majority of the old A, B and C Companies are fighting on far-flung battle lines; but I am sure that they will think that those who scored in Easter Week were not unworthy of the traditions of the Corps.

It is difficult yet to take a dispassionate survey of the events of that week. The scenes unroll themselves in memory like the mad unrealities of a nightmare. But in those days of violence the OTC held steady, and tried to do their duty quietly and with coolness. The consciousness that they did their best to protect the College and maintain order must be their sole reward: they feel little elation in a victory over their misguided countrymen, and their hearts are saddened by the ruin of Dublin and the sorrow of Ireland.

5. Ernest Alton's report in *Sinn Fein rebellion: a souvenir of presentations to the Officers' Training Corps, Trinity College Dublin* (Dublin, 1916)

I heard of the trouble when on my way to College at 2.15 o'clock on Monday, April 24th. I visited the Headquarters and saw that the guard were already on the alert. I found that the front gates of the College had been closed by order of Lieuts Waterhouse and Mullen. I rode to my house, put on my uniform, called for Sergt Fitzgibbon, and entered Lincoln Place Gate about 2.45. On our way in we found that the Sinn Feiners had seized Westland Row.

As it was expected that the enemy would attack us at once, it was decided to concentrate for the present on the OTC Headquarters; a small guard of six men was detailed for the Front gate. Our numbers about this time (3.30 p.m.) were between twenty and thirty, but in the course of the afternoon we were reinforced by odd numbers of the OTC and regulars who were unable to rejoin their units. Commissariat was a serious difficulty; but we obtained provisions for the present from the College Co-operative. We could not get in touch with the Irish Command, and it seemed impossible to obtain correct knowledge of the situation.

To some extent we were enlightened by the reports of some students who went out in plain clothes through the City. We found that there was almost no military in Dublin, and that the police had been confined to barracks.

The police in Brunswick Street sent over some regulars, three of whom we armed and placed in charge of a corporal with instructions to do their best for the Brunswick Street Police Station. By this measure it was hoped to protect in some way the North gate of the College, which was commanded from the barracks.

We succeeded in communicating by means of a despatch rider with Beggar's Bush, where we had learned that Major Harris was confined with the GRs. We could not do anything to relieve them, but we were satisfied that they could hold out. Our messenger later on in that evening was able to take a revolver to Major Harris.

In the meantime the Headquarters was placed in some sort of security. The position was anything but a desirable one from the point of view of defence. We removed windows, which we filled in with sandbags.

Firing platforms were constructed along the walls. We organised our guards, firing parties, ambulance unit, cooking, fatigue, etc, etc.

A considerable amount of desultory firing was proceeding, especially from the Nassau Street side, but evidently no serious attack was meditated for the present. When detailing posts for the night – our numbers were now forty-four – it was decided to remain at Headquarters for the present, but to strengthen the guard at the Front. We succeeded in placing scouts in one of the Westland Row houses, who kept us informed of the enemy's movements in the Railway Station. His patrols passed frequently along the railway in our rear and an attack from the railway bridge would place us at a serious disadvantage.

In the course of our patrols that evening we became convinced of the grave danger which was incurred in leaving the streets to the enemy without challenge. Dame Street especially seemed to demand protection; as large bodies of the enemy were seen marching from Stephen's Green to the North side of the City. The extraordinary recklessness of civilians, who moved about the streets till a late hour, though there was firing in all directions, was particularly conspicuous on that first evening. Some, no doubt, were active Sinn Feiners; a couple of women were seen to fire revolvers – out of sheer gaiety of heart – into the College Park.

About 7.30 our cooks provided us with a miscellaneous meal of tea, chocolates, and sandwiches. A few obtained bread, but bread was a scarce commodity with us that week. Parties had to remain at their posts all night for we had not enough men to provide relief. The circuit of the college was continually patrolled and a watch was kept on several danger points, such as the lanes in Brunswick Street. About 12.30 a.m. on Tuesday it was discovered that our telephone in College was working, and we got in touch with the Irish Command. We learned that there was not much prospect of relief for the present, but that the authorities were fully alive to the gravity of the situation.

It was decided that we would be in a stronger position and would be more useful at the Front than at the Rear of the College, so we called in some parties and under the cover of darkness proceeded to evacuate the OTC headquarters. Several tons of stores had to be removed, but the men worked like niggers. At the same time we transferred our first firing party to the roof. This change was at once operative. After one brush with a small body of the enemy, we were able to keep Dame Street and the approaches clear. From time to time the enemy was reported on roofs in the neighbourhood, but it was not difficult to clear him from any points from which he could seriously interfere with the movements of troops.

At dawn the last of our men was withdrawn from our old Headquarters. We placed a strong picket in No 40, and another in No 38; from these windows any attempt to force an entry into the Park could be checked. By occupying the two pavilions of the Front we were enabled to keep Grafton Street and Westmoreland Street open. We had in No 4 College our orderly room, with guardroom hard by. All the details and incidents of that first night will live in the memories of those who were present. The uncertainty, the suddenness of the outbreak, the lack of proper equipment and commissariat, the various incidents, tragic and comic, that seemed to fill each moment, form a phantasmagoric memory. It may have been a fluke, but I think we took the right measures that night. The circumstances were particularly alarming, as not many of our force had heard the rattle of firearms and faced bullets fired with intent to kill. But it was astonishing how quickly they adapted themselves to the novel conditions. In a few days the crash of artillery seemed a commonplace event.

On the following afternoon we were visited by the first body of regulars, who had come from the Curragh, but our duties as guards were continued even when the troops occupied the College in force on Wednesday. To detail the multifarious tasks that we had to discharge that week would be tedious. Anxiety was at an end as regards the safety of the College and the neighbourhood by Thursday, and officers, who had hitherto slept little and washed less, began again to appear more like their former selves.

After the first two days we were reinforced by members of the OTC who were now able to enter, and our duties were to some extent less anxious. On the following week Major Harris took over command. A rumour had got about that he had been killed, so we were particularly delighted to see his genial face again.

6. Major G.A. Harris, report to War Office, 'Defence of TCD by the DUOTC, during the period 25th April 1916 to 4th May 1916', WO 32/9576, National Archives, London

For some time past, owing to rumours that the Sinn Fein Organisation were trying to acquire rifles, a permanent guard of one cadet NCO and three cadets was placed on the OTC Headquarters Buildings where upwards of 300 rifles, in addition to ammunition and equipment, were stored.

On Easter Monday morning I saw the Guard duly mounted at 9 a.m. and left the Headquarters Buildings at 10.30 a.m. to go out to the Dublin Mountains to act as umpire at military exercises, which were being carried out by the Volunteer Training Corps.

According to official reports received by me, the Corporal of the Guard, Corporal Mein, received a message from the Store Keeper here, shortly after noon, that the Sinn Feiners had risen, and that there was heavy firing in the city. Corporal Mein immediately had all the College gates locked and sandbagged the windows of the Headquarters Buildings. Messages were sent out by motor cyclists to such cadets as lived in Dublin instructing them to report to OTC Headquarters immediately, and by evening upwards of 40 cadets and ex-cadets of the Corps had reported, many of them at considerable risk, as they were fired upon in passing through the streets. This number was further augmented during the night by various details, eg young officers, Colonials and soldiers of various regiments on leave in the city. A great many cadets were in the country on Easter vacation. On hearing of the trouble in Dublin they immediately set out for the city on bicycles, or on foot. Many succeeded in getting into the College in mufti, and others, who could not reach the College reported at the various barracks and military offices where they were attached for duty. The garrison of the College was divided into small bodies and posted at tactical points round the College, the boundary of which is upwards of a mile in perimeter.

The rebels were in a strong force at Westland Row Station, about thirty yards from the Headquarters Building, and also on the railway viaduct which commands the Parade Ground on one side. Although heavy sniping came from these points, and from the houses overlooking the College Park on the first two days, the rebels were prevented from entering the College grounds and buildings. A rebel prisoner subsequently explained that his party was alarmed at the sight of the sandbags, and thought the place was very much more strongly held than it really was.

By holding the College on the first and second days of the rising, the Corps fulfilled three important objects:

(1) The College was situated between two important rebel storm centres, the GPO to the north and St Stephen's Green to the south, and commanded the main avenue of communication between these points. The rebel orderlies passing to and fro between these places suffered severe casualties by the fire directed on them from the College during the first two days of the rising, and eventually all rebel communication was cut off.
(2) The holding of the College preserved for military authorities an important link in the principal line of communication, and provided a centre for offensive operations when reinforcements arrived.
(3) Looting was preventing [*sic*] in the important streets surrounding the College by the accuracy of the fire from the College walls and roofs. The Bank of Ireland is directly opposite to, and completely commanded from the College, and the rebels were prevented from making any attempt on it. Also the headquarters of other principle [*sic*] banks in Ireland are in close proximity.

On the other hand, had the rebels taken the College on the first or second days of the rising, it would have been exceedingly difficult to dislodge them, as the buildings are of a most substantial character, and heavy artillery would have been required to retake the College. In view of their great historical association the destruction of the buildings, particularly the Library, would have been a national calamity. Further, as already pointed out, had the College been taken, the Bank of Ireland would also have run considerable risk of capture.

On the evening of Tuesday 25th April, a detachment of the Leinster Regiment with two machine guns arrived, and the guns were posted in commanding positions on the College buildings. The fire from these guns greatly assisted the troops in their operations against the GPO.

On the nights of Wednesday–Thursday 26/27th April the Advanced Party of the troops from England succeeded in entering the College covered by the fire of the garrison. Having thus established themselves in the centre of the city, they were enabled to get into touch with the troops operating from the north and west, and also carry on offensive operations from a secure base.

From the Wednesday onwards the situation was well in hand, and the services of the OTC were utilised in various capacities. They acted as guides to the troops during the clearing of suspected area [*sic*]; as guards, escorts and despatch riders. These duties were often performed under fire from enemy snipers.

Six of the cadets undertook to go out in mufti to dig emplacements for the guns detailed to shell Liberty Hall, one of the chief strongholds of the rebels. This duty was performed under most trying circumstances, and when the guns went into action, the cadets acted as ammunition carriers.

During the first two days the Garrison was commanded by Capt[ain] EH Alton, DUOTC, who was ably assisted by other officers of the Corps. The Commandant, Major Tate, was in the country on leave and could not return. I was informed of the outbreak at 3 p.m. on the 24th ult and succeeded with the utmost difficulty under rebel fire, in getting into Beggars Bush Barracks, where I took command, and held the Barracks with only twelve serviceable rifles. Later, I succeeded in getting into touch with the OTC in Trinity College, by a motor-cyclist in mufti, and hearing of the state of affairs there, I reported to Irish Command Headquarters who ordered me to remain on duty at Beggars Bush Barracks.

Every available officer of the Corps reported for duty, either at the College, or at various military centres, and from the official reports I have received, all appear to have rendered excellent service.

Practically all the arms and most of the equipment of the DUOTC are intact, and little damage, except broken glass etc has been done to Headquarters.

7. John Joly, *Reminiscences and anticipations* (London, 1920), ch. 8, 'In Trinity College during the Sinn Fein rebellion' by 'One of the Garrison'

Easter Monday, the 24th of April, 1916 – not yet one fortnight old as I write – looked a day of peaceful thoughts if ever there was one. It was cool, bright weather. The Dublin hills stretched away to the south-east, a picture of immovable repose in the afternoon light.

Down the Dundrum road a band of the Veteran Volunteers – the GR's – came swinging along at a steady pace, their faces towards the City. An officer on horseback led them. As he passed us, we recognised in him Major Harris, of the Officers' Training Corps of the University of Dublin. He stopped us. 'Have you heard that the Sinn Feiners have risen in Dublin, and seized the General Post Office and Stephen's Green, and shot several of the police?' The Veterans passed on their way to the City, leaving us bewildered. Some of them were to meet their death within an hour of that instant.

Peace indeed! Rather madness and bloodshed this fine holiday afternoon. To a change so outstanding the mind at first refuses to adapt itself. The blessed isolation from the horrors of invasion, for which we daily give thanks, suddenly replaced by that worst of all forms of strife – civil war. For the danger of the Sinn Fein is known to all in Ireland save, apparently, to the authorities. It is not only a danger in itself, but it possesses all the potential danger of the spark amidst the gunpowder. And now at last it is at hand, and to each one comes the same thought – to seek his duty and to do it. To him who has not the great obligation of defence of wife and family during the unknown dangers of the coming night the cause of law and order and of the institutions which he holds dearest may appeal for all he can give. In the minds of each one of us the same question is being debated, and the claims upon him weighed one against the other. And to each the littleness of few years of life speaks with the same quieting voice.

I was in Trinity College by four o'clock. I had already been in the City that same morning visiting a sick friend. There were then no signs of the fatal events proceeding elsewhere. The Post Office was actually being seized at the time I was sitting by my friend's bedside. But now how different! Carriage traffic had almost ceased, and crowds hurried, partly in terror, partly in curiosity, about the streets. An occasional shot was heard. But it soon became evident that the Rebels were virtually in possession of the city.

I left Trinity cautiously by one of the side gates of which I possessed a key. I was anxious to ascertain, if possible, the magnitude of the movement and to get some idea of the numbers engaged in it. I visited the General Post Office, the central building in Sackville Street. It was a wreck. Glass littered deeply the path and pavement in front of it. Armed men stood behind its shattered windows. Useless barricades had been piled up within – mail-bags, evidently filled with letters, to keep out bullets! Chairs and tables through which bullets would pass almost as easily! And, peering out from their defences, the unhappy warriors threatened with their rifles the scared crowd which alternately approached and ran away. At one window a mere boy was still knocking out the glass with the butt of his rifle. Above the building floated a huge green banner with the inscription in white letters, 'Irish Republic.' Truly Der Tag had come! But oh, how pitiful! A fantastic chimera, and death the sure and certain wage!

The Rebels were moving about freely in the streets. All seemed armed with rifles. The police had entirely disappeared. They had done all they could, and some had offered their lives in a vain endeavour to save the City. St Stephen's Green, which I next visited, was closed. A sort of barrier had been placed within the large gate facing the foot of Grafton Street. Behind it stood, with set face and in Sinn Fein uniform, an armed man. He held his rifle at the ready. But neither military nor police contested his supremacy. A couple of lads of seventeen or eighteen years of age lay on the grass near by. They, too, were armed and equipped with rifle and bandolier. A man in a small crowd remarked to me on the juvenile appearance of these Sinn Feiners. What, indeed, could they know of right and wrong? What could they do to save themselves even if they knew the truth? It was a pitiful sight. One formidable-looking man of maturer years lay stretched in the most approved attitude, with rifle immovably directed towards Grafton Street. I estimated that if the distribution of men around the Green was everywhere such as it was at this point, 400 or 500 men might be within. One comforting inference could be drawn. No German officer was responsible for such strategy. For no officer in his senses would shut his men in an enclosure commanded by tall buildings on every side, from any one of which almost every corner of the Green could be reached. And as it turned out, this was just what the Sinn Feiners found to their cost a few days later.

I returned to the College but little wiser than I had left it. From the first the gates had been closed, and no unknown person was allowed to enter. What force was within? I had come in almost direct from the meeting with Major Harris, and as he must moderate his pace to that of his men of foot, and as I was on a bicycle, it seemed unlikely that even by this time he could have returned. Inquiry confirmed this view. At the Headquarters of the Officers' Training Corps I heard that several officers in khaki had been fired on, and it was believed to be doubtful if Major Harris would ever reach the College. In point of fact he never did. Approaching the town, the Veterans divided into two parties. One of these was under command of Major Harris. The other, under command of Mr Browning, was ambushed and badly cut up by the Rebel fire. The survivors of both parties were finally driven to take refuge in Beggar's Bush Barracks, then in a state of siege, and into which they only penetrated by climbing over a back wall. The 'GR's' had gone on their route-march, as was their wont, totally unprovided with weapons of defence.

Thus it happened that Trinity College seemed almost without defenders. Major Tate, the CO, was unfortunately away. But Captain Alton, of the OTC, Lieutenant Luce, of the Royal Irish Rifles, who was home from the front on sick leave; and Lieutenant Waterhouse, were fortunately at hand. A few boys in khaki were about. There was no doubt of the seriousness of the position. Help from military or police was not to be expected for some time – possibly for some days. That the College had not already been captured was most inexplicable. It was obviously the most central and commanding position in the city. There was the additional attraction of the military stores of the OTC depot. In this were kept some hundreds of service rifles and many thousands of rounds of ammunition. The loot of the buildings would supply many requirements of those in possession. And once captured, nothing but the wholesale destruction of buildings, containing the most precious heirlooms of the ancient University, would suffice to dislodge the enemy. I visited the Provost. He faced the position with which he had been so suddenly confronted with calmness. Then I left for home by the Lincoln Place Gate, having first received promise of a rifle when I returned. It was highly probable that no daylight attack would now be made, so there was ample time for a bicycle ride to the suburbs to inform my small household of my intention to remain in the College during coming events.

It was about six o'clock by the time I got back to the College. The ride in proved an anxious one. I had rather thoughtlessly put on a Swedish leather jacket which bore somewhat the appearance of a uniform. I had a pistol in my pocket. Several groups of the enemy seemed on the point of challenging me. It was evident I had made myself an object of suspicion, and capture was the best I could hope if I was stopped and searched. But at length I got back to Lincoln Place Gate and was admitted. A message had been got through to Beggar's Bush Barracks, and we knew that help from that quarter was no longer possible. By great good luck eight Anzacs, who had been on leave in the city, had taken harbourage in the College. The total number of defenders amounted to forty-four.

Sentries had, of course, already been posted at the gates, and others were stationed at important points of observation. After my arrival I spent some time on the roof of the Physical Laboratory, with a view to its utilisation as a point of observation during hours of daylight. Then came orders to sandbag the back windows of the OTC Headquarters. This was laborious work, but the younger men made light of it; filling the bags below and carrying them up the stairs. After this a little time was left me in which to practise the use of the service rifle. The pattern was new to me, but in half an hour, and under the instruction of one of the Cadets, I was sufficiently familiar with it to feel confidence that I could fire and refill with fair rapidity. To rank as a good shot with a rifle to which one was unaccustomed, under conditions when probably the sights could not be seen, was, of course, out of the question. But on the other hand, there was the comforting reflection that if attacked the fighting must necessarily be at close quarters and accurate shooting would not be required. Evidently under such circumstances the principal matter was to master the purely mechanical conditions of quick loading and handling. With these comforting thoughts I practised myself upon the rifle till I felt at home with it. I was also so fortunate as to get a dozen cartridges for my pistol, for which I had but one cartridge on entering the College.

The geography of the College ground requires some description for the benefit of those unacquainted with Dublin. The grounds of Trinity College cover about 35 acres, and form a roughly quadrangular area having a width of about 900 feet and a length of about 2,000 feet. The area is surrounded by the most important thoroughfares of Dublin. The quadrilateral extends its greatest length in, approximately, a west to east direction. The principal buildings of the College – the magnificent Library, the Examination Hall, the Dining Hall, the Provost's House, the School of Engineering (building beloved by Ruskin), as well as the fine Belfry and the living-rooms of the students and of the staff – lie in the western half. The splendid frontal buildings of the College, with their exquisite pavilions, command a city view unsurpassed by any in the United Kingdom, the broad thoroughfares of Westmoreland Street, Dame Street, and Grafton Street converging to the spacious pavement fronting the façade of the College.

At the eastern end of the Park are placed the modern buildings housing the various Schools of Science, many of which have been recently built by the Chancellor of the University, Viscount Iveagh. The Headquarters of the OTC are placed along the extreme eastern boundary of the College grounds, and thus lie outside, as it were, the group of the Science Schools. Between the group of buildings lying to the west end and that lying to the east end of the Park there intervenes an open space devoted to the recreation of the students in normal times. Just now the existence of this area constitutes an added difficulty in the defence of the College. And it is an aggravation of the difficulties that telephonic connection between the west and east ends of the Park does not exist. For the City Exchange is closed to us, and this was the normal means of communication. Even to a novice this evil was at once apparent, and I thought of searching the Physical Laboratory for a telephone, which might be installed as a field telephone, but I feared that the requisite leads would certainly fail us. This want involved a serious degree of isolation of the main points of defence of the College.

The difficulties of the defence were obvious even to an unskilled observer. The railings and walls which bound the south and north sides of the Park are scalable at any point. The wall on the northern boundary is skirted by a lane, which may be in the enemy's hands. It is, moreover, commanded by the rear of the houses on Brunswick

Street, which also he may hold. The railings separating the south boundary of the Park from Nassau Street are by no means unscalable. So much for the College Park.

As for the practice-grounds of the OTC, in which my first sentry duties lay, on the east side they are separated from a lane by a high wall surmounted by barbed wire. But this would not be a serious obstacle, and the lane is open at both ends to the entry of the Rebels. Moreover, the houses of Westland Row from their rear overlook almost the entire grounds from this eastern side. If they harboured the enemy and he knew how to shoot, it would render existence difficult for the garrison. The north end of the OTC grounds is further overlooked by the high embankment of the Loop Line from Westland Row Terminus. And there was ocular evidence that the Sinn Feiners held the railway and patrolled the embankment. Under such conditions we began our watch of the College on the night of Easter Monday. This estimate of our difficulties must be read as that of one unacquainted with the art of war, and who had no share in planning the defensive steps actually taken.

My beat extended from the small side door leading into the Chemical Laboratory (and so into the College Park) to the large gate opening near the main Lincoln Place entrance of the College Park. The inner gate, which limited my beat, had for better security been barricaded with a military waggon. Without, the couple of sentries watching the Lincoln Place Gate could be observed and were within hail. It was part of my duties to keep in touch with these sentries, and to convey to Headquarters any alarm they might transmit to me. I had also to keep under observation the wall separating this part of the grounds from the lane, and to observe the rear of the houses overlooking the grounds.

Night now slowly closed in. The City without was plainly in a state of chaos. Shots rang out every now and again. Distant shouts and challenges were heard. Sometimes a more rapid succession of shots suggested more serious fighting. Slowly the precincts around became indistinct. Impending dangers, unknown disasters, seemed to fill the gloom. Was this indeed to be, perhaps, the last night of our ancient University? The question is no mere extravagance of the imagination. For so much of the very existence of so venerable a foundation is bound up with its century-old buildings, with its literary and artistic treasures, that sack and conflagration in a single night might obliterate practically all but its memory from the earth. So might perish Ireland's most priceless treasure – the University of Berkeley, Goldsmith, Burke, Hamilton, and Lecky.

A sentry must not indulge in imaginings. I endeavoured to banish gloomy forebodings from my mind and to school my attention entirely into the immediate present. The thought of what might or might not happen, either to my College or to dear ones passing the night exposed, perhaps, to serious dangers, I drove from my mind. And, indeed, there was enough to claim immediate attention. There was constant coming and going through the now dark passage leading from the side door into the Park. Each individual must be challenged and recognised. In intervening moments the walls and buildings opposite must be watched. There were now only the City lights without, reflected from the cloudy sky, to shed any light in the space around me. A cause of uneasiness soon became apparent. Two adjoining windows just overlooking my beat, I discovered, had been recently opened. No lights were within. If the enemy was in possession of these windows, not 60 yards away, he might cover me at his leisure, and having disposed of me, then pick off anyone entering through the side door. He could from his position shoot right into the latter, and it was possible he had enough light to do so. But for these evils there was no remedy. The strict order given to all sentries and patrols was, 'No firing till attacked.' And, of course, even if an individual did show himself at the open windows, he might be only a curious observer. And presently I became aware that the hypothetical individual had become a reality. Someone was within – a man, apparently, with white shirt-sleeves. I strained my eyes to discover what he was doing, and when I did so he drew back and vanished into the darkness within. Obviously he held the whip hand, and there was nothing for it but to trust to luck.

Slowly the hours passed. I kept this post for four hours, during the latter half of which time I had the company of a second sentry. Then I was relieved; and as my dinner had consisted of a single sandwich, I was glad to look for something to eat at Headquarters. It was cold enough to make a hot drink very desirable.

Bright lights are not permissible at Headquarters. In the kitchen only a feeble lamp dispels the gloom and reveals the incessant but quiet bustle which prevails. Cadets in their great-coats are pushing in and out. The sounds of eating and drinking are mingled with questions and opinions as to what is happening. There is an atmosphere of expectancy which is not allowed, save inferentially, to reveal the anxiety which all most certainly feel. The talk is all in a low tone, as if the Sinn Feiner was listening without. It is reported that the Castle has been captured by the Rebels, and is strongly held. The office of the *Daily Express*, and both Guinness' brewery and Jacob's biscuit factory are believed to have also been taken. There are but few military in the city, and they can barely hold their barracks. It appears, then, that our own chances depend entirely on the speed with which troops can be brought up from the Curragh or from Belfast. Some think that the capture of the General Post Office means that telegraphic communication with England is cut, and that assistance from the other side of the Channel must consequently be long delayed. It is certain that the railway termini, or some of them, have been taken by the Rebels. Of this we have good evidence. Rebels have been seen patrolling the embankment overlooking our little territory. I myself, riding past the previous evening – it is now past midnight – saw heaps of barrels thrown over the high walls of Harcourt Street terminus, apparently with a view to making barricades in the street beneath. What might the object of all this be? There was only one answer: to delay the arrival of troops in the City. These matters are discussed. The Anzacs listen; they say but little. They are magnificent of physique and lithe of figure. How keen of eye and what unerring shots they were we soon came to know.

On the fire a huge pot holds water for making cocoa and for washing plates. There is bully beef and bread, and there is a sack full of apples. You dip your cup – someone else has just been drinking out of it – into the hot water; you shake a little cocoa powder into it, and you drink when the beverage is cool enough. Nearly everyone smokes, and few smoke anything but cigarettes. I am offered so many that I feel as if we were back in those apostolic days when men had all things in common.

I have just prepared a cup of cocoa and got some bully beef. The word 'alarm' is said in a low voice at the door, and the speaker hurries off. Almost immediately we are without in the cool night air – listening.

A violent fusillade can be heard in the direction of the front gate of the College. The immediate alarm, however, is said to have come from our men posted on one of the Westland Row houses. They had been given a signal lantern – red for danger, white for safety. It now seemed certain that the apprehended attack was about to be delivered. Concerted attacks at several points were probable. But at this stage it was impossible to say at what point our defence might first have to be directed. With rifles on cock we stood for about a quarter of an hour awaiting orders. The City lights reflected from the clouds dimly showed us the walls, but no foe appeared. Our patrols were out, and it was probable that the first call to action would come in the form of a shot fired at an invading enemy. But no further alarm came. The distant firing was directed not against the College. And the attack was not on us.

The guard was to be relieved immediately. The selected men, of which I was one, marched off. We went round the Park relieving sentries. Finally, I was given a post of observation over the lane-way without the eastern boundary-wall of the OTC grounds already referred to. This lane can be observed for a considerable distance up and down through chinks in a great rolling door opening into it. It was an irksome duty, for the chinks must be carefully investigated at each turn of one's beat. Without, the lane remains silent and empty, as seen by the light of an electric lamp which burns at one end of it.

All things come to an end. Grey dawn slowly breaks. Objects insensibly become more and more distinguishable. At about 3.30 o'clock I am relieved, and return to Headquarters. Those off duty are lying down on the floor of a large storeroom almost in darkness, for the light of dawn is as yet but feeble. Alongside forms lying prone, with rolled-up coats for pillows and one blanket serving as mattress and covering, sleep comes soon. But before yielding to oblivion I could not help brief thoughts on matters psychological. I had lately been worrying a good deal about various things, and often dreaded, rather than courted, a comfortable bed. I was now a more contented individual than I had been for weeks. And it may be, I thought, that this is just the reason why so many return healthy and cheerful from the Front. The life of action is perhaps, after all, the happiest. I have been making a grand mistake all along. That boyish instinct for the Navy was perhaps the truest wisdom. But now it is too late a day. This present episode can only be a late farewell to what might have been. But let me sleep while I can. There is only a feeble flicker of candle-light in the room, and one of the shrouded warriors snores soporifically. I am off –

'Turn out! We are going to evacuate this bally place, and all the stores are to be removed.' Alas! I had been but fifteen minutes asleep! But it is a wise decision. The quadrangles of the College we might indeed hold for some time. This open and almost defenceless courtyard must, in the event of an attack, simply become a shambles. Shots, mostly revolver shots, fired from Nassau Street into the College Park, as reported by patrols, warned us what to expect.

The sandbags are brought down from the windows, for they will be wanted elsewhere; the rifles are carried off on field stretchers, and, along with the ammunition, are transported to the quadrangles. Finally, every article which might prove of use to the enemy, such as clothes, provisions, blankets, culinary vessels, china, etc, is heaped upon one of the great military wagons in the yard and dragged away to the Front Square of the College by a train of men. Someone suggests leaving a few dummy men in the windows. The idea is obviously good. A few caps are judiciously arranged on props in partial concealment, the building is locked up, and we evacuate our fort with such a brilliant exemption from casualties as marked the retreat from Gallipoli.

Daylight has now fully come, and the more concentrated garrison is to be distributed in various coigns of vantage in the quadrangles. One of the great windows on the stairs ascending to the Regent House is assigned to me, in company with Sergeant-Major B–.

These front windows of the College command a view which extends the whole length of Dame Street. In the farthest distance is visible the corner-house, the office of the *Daily Express*, which is held by the Rebels. Opposite to it is the City Hall, which may be regarded as an out-lying part of the Castle premises. In the foreground is the wide pavement, having the Bank of Ireland on the right and beyond it the Royal Bank. To the left the buildings form a curved façade, which flows into Grafton Street. Here are some of the finest offices in Dublin. Grattan's statue and the equestrian statue of King William of Orange stand in the midst of the pavement. These regions are now empty. Neither friend nor foe appears – the former because not strong enough to march the streets, and the latter because of the rifle fire from the College.

The Anzacs had been above on the roof of the College since an early hour. Owing to the strict order received from the Irish Command not to fire until attacked, many chances of 'potting' Rebels had been missed. But later in the morning this order had been withdrawn. Already before daylight a despatch-rider of the enemy had been brought down by the fire of the Anzacs. It was wonderful shooting. He was one of three who were riding past on bicycles. Four shots were fired. Three found their mark in the head of the unfortunate victim. Another of the riders was wounded and escaped on foot. The third abandoned his bicycle and also escaped. The shooting was done by the uncertain light of the electric lamps, and at a high angle downwards from a lofty building. The body was brought in.

Later I saw him. In no irreverent spirit I lifted the face-cloth. He looked quite young; one might almost call him a boy. The handsome waxen face was on one side concealed in blood. Poor boy! What crime was his? That of listening to the insane wickedness and folly preached by those older and who ought to be wiser than he. And was not he, after all, but one of those who carry to its logical conclusion the long crusade against English rule which for generations has kept peace from Irish hearts? More honest than many of his teachers, he has been led into crime and now pays the penalty. It is true, if truth exists at all, that this life cut short and the rancour and bitterness with which it was filled are as much the handiwork of the 'constitutional' agitator as of many who are doomed to summary execution for this night's work. When will England appreciate the Irish temperament? When will our rulers learn that these rash and foolish sons of the Empire require quiet and resolute government, sane education, and protection from the fanatic and the agitator, to whose poison they are at present exposed from their earliest years?

Tuesday, the 25th of April, was now a new day. The events of the past night seemed folded away, as if but a troubled dream. What would the new day bring forth? When might help be expected? With advancing day the numbers in the streets increased. It was evident that the public even yet had not realised the dangers of the streets. Shots from roofs and windows did not seem to deter the curious from risking his life. Not a few were aimed from the roof and windows of the College at snipers lurking in surrounding buildings. One window in the top storey of a large insurance office was an object of special suspicion. A man and woman had shown themselves at it more than once. They had been seen to fire into the streets beneath. The shooting from the College was undeniably good. The window was turned away at a sharp angle from the College, and was distant about a hundred yards. Nevertheless, spurts of lime and powdered stone were sent flying from its embrasure at every shot. Whoever was within was certainly very foolhardy or very stupid. To look forth even for the fraction of a second under such conditions was courting death.

There can be no doubt that the accurate fire maintained from the College was an important factor in the salvation of the City. The Bank of Ireland (formerly the Irish House of Parliament) was otherwise unprotected, but no hostile being could have approached its doors. Its whole front was in view of the College. The sentries, which in ordinary times never cease to guard its doors, were absent, but the building was safe. An attempt was, in fact, made to take possession of its roof, but it was frustrated. The many important and stately buildings – banks, insurance offices, business premises – of Dame Street and Grafton Street were protected from the Rebel or from the looter in the same manner. The whole length of Westmoreland Street was kept clear by the College rifles; and even the strongholds of the enemy in Sackville Street were assailed from the northern end of the College. Regarding the position as a whole, the grounds and buildings of Trinity College filled the function of a loyal nucleus, dividing the forces of the Rebels and keeping open to the troops some of the principal thoroughfares of the City.

After being relieved, I joined the Anzacs on the roof. They were undoubtedly men fashioned for the enjoyment of danger. And certainly it would be harder to find nicer comrades. Alas for the thousands of these fine soldiers who have left their bones on Gallipoli!

Breakfast was at length to be had in the College kitchen. Thither we repaired according as we got off duty. There was bully beef, with bread and tea, administered by the amazed but indefatigable French cook. Those who were silly enough to criticise the menu had something more to grumble about later on. The fact was, we were in a state of siege, and no preparations had been made even for the small garrison requiring support.

Later in the day troops began to come into the City. They had, in fact, been marched direct from the Curragh to Kingsbridge. Others came from Belfast. Within the College it was, of course, impossible to find out what was happening without. But every hour, as the day wore on, the sounds of firing in the City increased in volume. Troops of khaki-clad men, too, occasionally passed the College. For us the situation was evidently more hopeful. The Rebels would now hardly be in a position to undertake fresh conquests; they must hold their own if they could. Moreover, our garrison had somewhat increased in numbers. Partly the additions were refugee soldiers sent over by the Dublin Metropolitan Police, whose newly erected premises stand facing the Brunswick Street entrance to the College. Partly our recruits were OTC men who had made their way in mufti to the help of their College.

The great event of Tuesday was the recapture of the *Daily Express* offices by the military. We were at the time in ignorance of what was actually happening; for we were possessed with the idea that the Sinn Feiners held the Castle. When, therefore, we saw at the head of Dame Street men in successive waves rush across the street from the City Hall towards the *Express* offices, we thought they represented the enemy in process of expulsion from the Castle. As a matter of fact the waves of men were composed of the troops. From our position in front of the College we could see that a terrific fire was being directed against the *Daily Express* building; plaster and powdered brick were flying in showers from its façade. This fire was to cover the advance of our soldiers. But in spite of this we saw, more than once, one of the running figures pitch forward and fall. It was expensive tactics; and later a better method of dealing with the Rebel strongholds was found when the artillery came into the City. The fight seemed to last a considerable time – about an hour at its greatest intensity – before the firing began to wane. Not till later did we learn that the final phase of the struggle took place, under deadly conditions for the soldiers, in the narrow passages of the newspaper office. But they were not to be withheld, and the Rebels were ultimately bombed out or captured.

This event took place on the afternoon of Tuesday. Shortly after a small body of troops entered at the front gate of the College – a welcome sight. But it was not certain if they were to remain for the night.

In the course of the afternoon it became necessary, in view of certain operations to be undertaken by the Regulars, to ascertain if Butt Bridge, which spans the Liffey near the notorious Liberty Hall, was occupied or not. The necessary scouting was assigned to me. Two of our OTC cadets in mufti were to accompany me. We agreed that it was best not to remain together. I accordingly went by Tara Street, and my colleagues proceeded by Hawkins Street. My route being the shorter, I reached the bridge first. It was unoccupied. Being anxious to ascertain if Liberty Hall was occupied and in a state of defence, I crossed the bridge and traversed the pavement in front of the Hall. The building looked empty, but I noticed that some of the windows of the basement had been broken out. This, of course, might betoken the presence of inhabitants, and suggested sniping. As I could not turn back in front of the building, I walked past it, and turned when near the railway arches, crossing the street lower down. It was unwisely done. I had probably been seen from the Hall, for as I again passed in front of it two rifle shots were fired in rapid succession from one of the lower windows. I saw the smoke, so there was no doubt whence the shots came. If the intention was to hit me it was quite extraordinary they did not succeed, seeing that only some 30 or 40 yards intervened, and I was walking slowly. Two men just behind me, who seemed the only other pedestrians present, took to flight and ran across the bridge. This course I did not imitate, for I reasoned that as the bridge was commanded right across from the windows of Liberty Hall, flight might have the actual effect of drawing the fire of the Rebels. No more shots were fired, and I met my OTC supports on the bridge.

On the ensuing night [Tuesday], in spite of our better position, no precaution appeared to be relaxed by Captain Alton. My own duties lay at the railings and gate in the New Square, near No 40. This house is at the end of the bay, and overlooks the entire central area of the Park. The railings beneath it commands [*sic*] a view reaching across to Nassau Street. Here I passed two very cold hours peering across the lawn. I was to shoot anyone seen beyond the railings: none of our men were to quit the quadrangles.

When relieved, my brother-sentry and I sought repose on the boards of the first floor of No 40. But things were not so bad as they looked. Some mattresses were available, and I got half of one on which to sleep. My companion, however, deprived for so long a time of the pleasures of the cigarette, must have a preliminary smoke. He fell asleep with the weed unfinished. I was again unfortunate, for I had hardly dropped asleep when I was, by a mistake, summoned to duty. This time my business was to watch from the open window of the room in which we were. It was unpleasant work, for a very cold wind blew straight in, and, of course, there was no way of sheltering from it. Hour after hour passed. There was darkness within the room by express orders; even the dying fire had been screened from view of the window. Strange revolution of circumstances! Many an hour I had sat in this very room along with that kindest and most courteous of men, the late Dr Benjamin Williamson. His gentle spirit would, indeed, have viewed his old apartment with wonder – the academic furniture all gone, and the floor closely covered with sleeping soldiers. Danger and strife where, for years without number, the only contests were those of wit against wit, and the only victories those which the mathematician claims when the refractory problem yields to investigation. Less than a year ago I was here with him.

Towards morning [Wed.], as the objects in the Park were becoming distinguishable in the strengthening daylight, I became aware that a party of five or six men were stealing from the trees at the remote side of the Park. I was on the point of firing. Indeed, it was while sighting that it seemed to me they were in khaki. This might be a ruse, and I confess to some moments of agonising indecision. I hastily roused a brother-sentry who had fallen into a state of – well, mental abstraction, and asked him to use his eyes. He agreed with me that the invaders of the Park were in khaki. They were going eastwards, away from the residential part of the College, and had apparently entered from the Fellows' Garden. Their movements confirmed me in the idea that they were our own men; for they seemed to be avoiding detection, not from my side, but from the Nassau Street side of the Park. They were, to all appearance, inspecting the railings bordering that side of the grounds, and taking cover behind the shrubs which grow along this border. Presently they passed behind the pavilion at the east end of the cricket-ground, and a moment afterwards I heard a rifle-shot fired from near by, followed by a second shot. The sentries in No 38 had evidently opened fire. This was serious. The next moment there was a party running towards us. Even then I was not quite sure of my ground. I threw the window further open and shouted, 'Who are you?' The leading runner waved and called to us to cover them against fire from the railway. I now recognised one of our officers. It appeared that his party had really a narrow escape from a danger to which actors in this sort of warfare are peculiarly liable. The bullets which went near to hitting them were, in point of fact, from our own boys – and they made tolerably good shooting. A very small misunderstanding may give rise to such incidents. It is certain that similar incidents were not uncommon in Dublin in the days which followed. The sharpshooters had acted strictly on injunctions; but I suppose, with the evidence before me, my failure to do so was excusable.

I spent the rest of the night on this duty. When Wednesday the 26th of April at length came, I was glad to get away from that window. There was now no bread in the College and no sugar, and the hardness of the ship's biscuits was something of scientific interest. But for all that I have never had a more delightful breakfast than I had that morning. The kitchen was filled with men trying to eat the biscuits. The interesting historical narratives of current events made it difficult to remember the duty of reporting oneself. I was again stationed at one of the front windows of the College.

There were adventurous people to be seen in the streets as the day got older. The impelling force of curiosity would appear to rank with the strongest passions of mankind. Here were bullets flying about, death lurking at every corner, and yet troops of foolish people running about the street. There had been looting already in some of the shops, and in the midst of the broad pavement in front of the College a small ragged boy was rejoicing in a toy motor car which was certainly value for three or four guineas. It was rather small for him, but he managed to sit in it and to pedal himself round Grattan's statue. Bullets were nothing to him. For the nonce he was one of the fortunate ones, and a lordly toy was his to play with. In after-years this trivial sport will stand for the Great Rebellion in his memory. So it is with us all, if only we could see our actions and thoughts in the light of history.

Troops were now coming into the College in large numbers. It was arranged, with the consent of the Provost, that the military in Dublin should take up Headquarters in the College. There was no doubt as to the mutual benefits to be derived from the arrangement. The weather had held out, and in the Park fresh young grass was found for the horses. The Examination Hall, the Engineering School, and part of the Dining Hall, were thrown open to the men. Owing to the absence of students, a very large number of chambers could be placed at the disposal of officers as well as of the rank and file. These rooms were all in part furnished, and contained good sleeping accommodation. But in truth the Tommies off duty had little to do with rooms. They lay about and slept in the open all day, rejoicing in the sward of the College courts and in the brilliant sunshine. The senior officers enjoyed the hospitality of the Provost.

The immediate safety of the College was now assured. Our escape from utter destruction had indeed been marvellous. I heard the view commonly expressed among the officers that had the Sinn Feiners taken possession of the College buildings in force, nothing but shell-fire would have dislodged them. Having regard to the great strength of the place, no other course but one which must probably involve the ruin of the buildings would be justifiable. Nor would any policy of starvation have availed to save the priceless treasures of the College from the same fate which befell every public building in Dublin into which the Sinn Feiner entered. With the Library, enriched at the voluntary expense of soldiers, the most precious heirlooms of ancient Irish civilisation would perish; with the exquisite School of Engineering, the most beautiful structure of the kind in the world would disappear; with the Provost's House, a treasury of art would vanish.

Early on Wednesday Liberty Hall received its quietus. Two 18-pounders and the guns of HMS *Helga* brought up the Liffey, were used to demolish it. The noise was tremendous. To the general din was added the spitting of a machine-gun placed high on the tower of the Fire Brigade Station. When next I saw Liberty Hall its empty shell alone remained. Every floor had been blown out of it. It was stated that none of the Rebels had remained to face the attack. A few weeks ago I saw armed men keeping guard within this building to keep out the police: and this was known to, and suffered by, the authorities. It was known to, and noticed in, the Press. But nothing was done.

Early in the day I went on duty at the Brunswick Street gate. This is the main entrance and exit for troops and others communicating with the east and north sides of the City. I soon found myself busy. A sentry was, of course, given to me. I was to deny or grant admission or exit according to circumstance. Every precaution had to be taken. The smaller door was opened only in face of fixed bayonet and after preliminary parley as to who was without. There appeared to be one evident oversight in the military precautions at this point. The large business premises of Messrs McKenzie & Co overlook this entrance and command it, more especially from the inner side. The building was apparently deserted. But if the enemy by any means gained access to it the gate would obviously be untenable. As we were still none too strong, and the numbers and intentions of the Rebels were unknown, it seemed prudent to occupy the building. Accordingly thirteen Regulars were put into it later in the afternoon. Its occupation continued until the Rebellion was substantially put down.

Casualties began to come in. No 15, a house in the College quadrangle known as Botany Bay and near the Brunswick Street gate, had been fitted up as an emergency hospital. It proved to be the greatest value, not only for dealing with wounds, but for administering to the ailments of the soldiers within. The treatment of sore feet, for instance, was continually proceeding. A staff of Red Cross volunteers and members of the RAMC were available day and night.

At one o'clock on Wednesday night, or rather on Thursday morning, I got off duty. The orders were that after midnight no one was to be allowed in or out. The custody of the gate became, therefore, a matter of sentry duty. I resigned it accordingly to the sentry and a night porter of the College – a trustworthy man who had formerly served in the Army.

I now looked for a place of repose. I had not had a total of two hours' sleep since Sunday night. Moreover, I was going lame from keeping on my boots for so long a time. This was the most imperative of my troubles. First I sought sleeping accommodation in No 40. But the room was already full, and there were neither blankets nor mattresses for anyone. The fire was by order not lighted, and [an] open window and door permitted a cold wind to blow upon the unprotected sleepers. From these forbidding conditions I recoiled; and being too tired and footsore to go much farther, I retired to one of the laboratories near by, and, spreading a College gown on the floor, slept till morning. I awoke so stiff from the effects of my hard bed that it took me about ten minutes to rise to a sitting attitude.

We had now reached Thursday, the 27th of April. The quadrangles presented an extraordinary appearance. Some 4,000 troops were stationed in the College. Horses tied to the chains which enclosed the grass plots gave the place the appearance of a vast open-air stable or horse fair. Men stood in ranks or sprawled on the pavements or on the doorsteps – anywhere – sometimes closely packed and fast asleep in every conceivable attitude. Many of them had put in a hard night's work. A large number were of the Sherwood Foresters and of the South Staffordshire Territorials. Many of these men were very young, and most of them had but recently joined the Colours. Looking now at their sleeping forms and tired faces, one must remember that the work of rounding up and hunting down the Rebels is not only arduous, it is in the highest degree dangerous. Not a few of the officers and men who had been through these nocturnal and diurnal operations told me that they would prefer being at the Front. At the Front, they said, you know the direction from which you may expect a bullet. Here the enemy is all round you. He lurks in dark passages and among chimney-stacks, and when at last you think you have hunted him down, you find yourself in possession of a peaceful citizen who gives some plausible reason for his presence. That these young fellows should be wearied after their night of perilous and strenuous exertion was not to be wondered at.

On this day a dead soldier was brought in. He found burial in the Fellows' Garden, service being said by the Army Chaplain. This was not the only internment within the College grounds. Later, another soldier – whose grave is now inscribed 'Private A Smith, 2373, 10th Cavalry Res Regt, killed 29th April 1916' – was buried in the College Park. The boy despatch-rider was laid to rest at an earlier date.

Then a little boy was brought in on a stretcher. He had been shot through the hand on Monday, and there was fear that the wound had become septic. The father accompanied him, but even in these circumstances was not admitted to the quadrangles. He told me that none of the family had tasted food since Monday night. The child looked very ill – too ill to cry or to complain – and on hearing this I left the man in charge of the sentry and made my way into No 15 to suggest the application of internal as well as external remedies. Hot tea was given to the little patient. There was rapid revival. He thanked us in a voice which never rose above a whisper. The manners of these little Irish children are sometimes lovely, and this child had all the confiding and appealing way about him which constitutes their special charm.

And it was quite true. The people were starving. Food supplies had early been exhausted or the shops had been closed. Wages had ceased, for there were no employers and no work to do. But wages would not have helped; there was nothing to buy. Relief of the starving was begun by the officers of the OTC. Later, on the Thursday, the Military Authorities humanely and wisely took the problem in hand. Stores were commandeered and warehouses opened, and the food distributed to the starving families. I heard that the people were so grateful they would do anything for the soldiers.

But I was yet to see a more terrible tragedy. There was the sound of the ambulance bell without. The van was admitted. It seems that the horse had been shot and a riding-horse substituted, and they had difficulty in getting the van farther than the College. Accordingly they sought first-aid at our Red Cross station.

A woman was lifted out. The stretcher dripped with her blood. A glance showed that death was not far from her. It was a face without hope. A shocking wound was hers. Shot through the lower part of her abdomen, the infernal bullet used by the Sinn Feiners had done work which must surely be fatal. They tried to plug the wound. A little later she was brought on to hospital, where she died.

This woman had done no wrong. She was probably seeking food for her six little children when death met her. There will be no one to sing her sorrows in modulated verse. The guilty 'Countess' may possibly one day evoke the strains of the bard. But this woman's anguish of farewell to her little children will be absorbed unnoticed – save by these poor words – in that great total of human sorrow which the mind cannot evaluate or even conceive.

Two 18-pounder field guns were now in the College. Today they were used to break up an enemy stronghold. The Sinn Feiners had seized and fortified a fishing-tackle and ammunition shop overlooking Carlisle Bridge. From this they maintained a fusillade upon everyone within reach. The 18-pounders were brought out into Brunswick Street and anchored to the pavement by lifting some of the setts. They were trained on Kelly's shop (the stronghold referred to), the shells traversing the length of D'Olier Street. Eleven shells were put into the brick walls of the premises. What the effects were within we could form no conception, but great holes were torn in the walls. The shells (shrapnel), we afterwards heard, penetrated into the adjoining house beyond and damaged a valuable photographic stock. The story that these field-guns were brought to the top of the College is, of course, absurd. They could be neither maintained on, nor fired from, a foundation of slates and rafters, nor would it be a simple matter to hoist them up.

Fires were now raging in the City. With the approach of night the flames lit the sky. In the lurid heavens the planet Venus shone with extraordinary brilliancy.

As the struggle between the Military and the Rebels became more and more a series of isolated combats, the streets grew ever more dangerous. Even at my post at the gate bullets were constantly singing overhead. Whence they came it was impossible to find out. The only risk here, however, was from a ricochet. A case of an 18-pounder shrapnel shell, emanating from an unknown source, fell in the Provost's garden. All this Thursday night firing continued, sometimes breaking out in one direction, sometimes in another. The vicious rattle of maxims, and the tap, tap, tap of some quick-firer – wickedest sound of all – mingled every now and again with the crash of bombs, filled the night with a sense of horror and danger. The streets were in many places barricaded and no one was permitted to pass. Indeed, only the Military were now to be seen on the streets. Even the police, if a message had to come to the College, crossed the street at the double.

An hour past midnight on Thursday I left the gate in charge of the night watchman and the sentry and retired to rest on a sofa in the Fellows' Common Room. This was a most luxurious indulgence.

Conditions suggesting famine reigned in the College on Friday. And but for the plucky exertions of a messenger from the Junior Army and Navy Stores in D'Olier Street, even the Fellows' table might have been reduced to the ship's biscuits and bully beef which constituted the universal ration elsewhere. But the soldiers had known worse times and did not grumble. The lack of cigarettes alone disturbed Tommy's equanimity. There was a tobacconist nearly opposite my gate. This, being near the DMP Office, felt, I suppose, under special protection, and opened today. On this becoming known, a deputation reached me from some of the Tommies to the effect that I would confer a great favour on them if I would buy then 10 ounces of cigarettes. They entrusted me with a one-pound note. I was pleased with this mission, for as janitor I discharged very unpopular duties. There was no conceivable excuse they did not urge to get out of barracks, and I pitilessly listened to none of them. One poor lad who had escaped – by another gate, I hope – was carried in on a shutter – drunk! Tommy is a forgiving creature. I got the cigarettes, and returned absolved and popular.

If you want to study human nature – that human nature which constitutes your fellow-countrymen – mix with Tommies. There is no shade of affectation about them. 'It is every one for himself in the Army,' said one of them to me. And this is true of the lesser things. But Tommy hates really unfair dealing, and if selfishness leads to it he condemns it. He has a tender heart. I have seen a big man relieve of rifle and kit a footsore youngster on the march. And of his fine deeds in the field all know. Of course there are black sheep, but even the black sheep is, I suspect, not so black as he is painted. A handy article will be 'pinched' by the black sheep. But he looks at things from a standpoint at which the theft is insidiously refracted into the joke. It is not the less wrong. But in any case we may forgive the few unrighteous for the sake of the many righteous. Moreover, I hold the theory that, essentially, the humbler classes are more honest than the educated part of the community. This theory is founded on observation, and I think it applies to the Army as it does to the rest of society. And then you must think of the things Tommy has to suffer – hunger and cold and danger.

Just realise what he has done for the terrified citizens of Dublin. After my few days with him I like him very much indeed.

Perhaps the most taking feature of Tommy is his childishness. 'Have you got aw lead, Guv'nor?' 'A what?' 'Aw lead.' 'He means a pencil,' says a neighbouring interpreter. Well, I had not got the desired article, but I had a pen, which I lent him. A letter was being written, for a makeshift postal service had just been established. He showed it to me with evident pride. It began, 'Dear Mother, I write these from here hoping they will find you as they leave me in the pink …' After all, this is no divulgence of confidence. I give no names. I was consulted as to the address. Having assured him as to the perfect nature of the writing, I was asked by a young fellow near by to 'vet' a letter of a more sentimental character. With stiff and difficult fingers, but with no shyness whatever, he was writing to 'Dear Sweetheart'. Every other line began with this address. The whole thing was the perfectly naïve pleasure of the child showing his accomplishments. It is impossible not to feel drawn to these fine men. Human nature is naturally beautiful to us, just as are the other phenomena of Nature. It is only when it is sullied by sins against the peace and goodwill of social life that it becomes ugly.

I fear the rule that the sentry is not to speak was occasionally broken by me – who ought to know better – when in the dead of night we watched the gate together. I heard then the simple narrative of how home and occupation had been left for service of King and Country. Some were anxious as to what might be happening in their absence. But there was no boasting, no display of sacrifice, never a word of regret. They had only done what a brave man should do.

Several instances occurred which well showed the effrontery of the enemy. He was evidently anxious to know what was going on within the College. More especially he was probably anxious to ascertain the military force within. On the Thursday two men thrust themselves in among a body of soldiers entering at the small door under my charge. They were, of course, instantly seized. One shammed a deadly enmity to the other man; refused to stand near him, and, declaring that he was himself an old soldier who wished to help us, accused the other individual of every wickedness. A bottle of whisky was found on this voluble person. The other man declared he had never before set eyes on his accuser. I put a stop to the dispute by placing them each in one of the deep doorways of Botany Bay, under a guard. I was anxious that they should not see what was going on. The departure of the guns at this moment called me away. When I returned I found the two prisoners had been taken to Headquarters in the Front Square. Later, I heard they had been allowed to leave the College. They had probably ascertained everything they came to find out. Annoying as the incident was, it was impossible not to feel that the cool courage of these visitors deserved the success it met with.

It was, I think, on the Thursday that a strange demand was made on the hospitality of the College. An operatic company, of well-known excellence, unaware of the extraordinary conditions prevailing in the City of Dublin, had reached the City on Wednesday. They found all the hotels closed and no possibility of getting accommodation. Eighteen members of the company took refuge with the Police. The

Police sent across to my gate to know if hospitality – mere housing within the College – could be extended to them. Under the conditions, to grant this request was clearly impossible. Accordingly the stranded actresses and actors had to abide in the premises of the DM Police.

Then a change came over that house of retribution. Strains of clever song and sounds of pleasant laughter reached my gate, mingled with the crack of distant rifles and the crash of bombs. Cheerful faces peered from door and window. Inexorable duty brought me across to the DMP barracks that afternoon. The scene within was worthy of Gilbert and Sullivan at their best. The gigantic uniformed Inspectors – grey of hair and upright of bearing – beamed with parental indulgence upon the graceful forms which tripped down the stone stairs or laughed and sung in groups in the hall. Among all the experiences of a week of novelties this was not the least novel. It may safely be predicted that such a scene of mingled gaiety and tragedy will never again visit the halls of that building. The trite saying that laughter and tears are near together seemed exemplified. I was carrying on a conversation with one of the huge Inspectors. It was about the battle of Tallaght in 1867 – the last Irish Rebellion. I was surprised to find that the Inspector was unacquainted with some of the most interesting facts of that extraordinary contest. I told him of how a dozen of the Constabulary captured some hundreds of armed Rebels, and to keep them from running away had cut their braces – a clever ruse which might well be matter of instruction to a police force, and which, I hear, has been used at the Front in the case of German prisoners. But no, he had never heard of it, and was in great delight at the idea. Nor had he any reluctance in imparting it to the assembled company. 'Mister Finnigan, Mister Finnigan,' he shouted to a distant Inspector, just as gigantic as himself, and just as paternal of countenance, 'do you hear what – says? How they kept the Rebels from running away? They cut their braces. Ho, ho, ho!' Then followed shrieks of laughter from giddy youth.

There were some strange happenings, also, within the College. There two cases of sudden lunacy: one among our own OTC; the other case was that of a Sinn Fein prisoner. Lieutenant X [Gilbert Waterhouse] – gave us a horrifying account of the treatment dealt out to the latter, who was violent. 'It took four of us to hold him down. We tied his hands behind his back and we tied his feet together. Then we laid him on a table and wound ropes round him and the table. Finally we wrapped a blanket round his head.' 'I suppose,' said one of the Fellows of the College, whose remarks are generally worth listening to – 'I suppose you call that "First Aid."' The strangest part of the story was the effects on the prisoner. He was left in the mummified state for six hours. At the end of that time he was found to be quite sane except with regard to his political convictions.

A feature of these curious times was the prevalence of extraordinary rumours as to what was going on in the world outside. The tendency to imagine the worst was consistently manifested in these reports. Verdun had fallen; there had been a great naval battle disastrous to British supremacy; there had been a landing of Germans on the East Coast of England. With such items of news we were regaled, and on the most conclusive evidence. Nor were events nearer home more favourably reported. The number of risings in the Irish counties and the strength of the Rebels were alike exaggerated. All this did not conduce to our peace of mind. Fortunately, the immediate surroundings were too engrossing to permit us to reflect on the calamities which appeared to be crowding upon Great Britain during our temporary sequestration from the newspapers.

For, in point of fact, all postal connection with the outer world was cut off. Such local papers as appeared at first contained only the Military Proclamations. These were brought in by the soldiers, and proved disappointing reading. In the City the first (and last) number of the extraordinary *Irish War News* had appeared on Tuesday morning, a small and very seditious sheet, price one penny, and headed, 'Vol I, No I.' It contained the proclamation of the Rebel leaders.

On Friday the Military appear to have finally disposed of the Rebels in the General Post Office. It was only carried through by the all but complete destruction and burning of the building, the outer walls alone remaining. Fires were now increasing in number on the north side of the river. It was related that looting was going on on a most disgraceful scale. Shops of all sorts were broken open and the goods freely distributed to the citizens of the Irish Republic. Men stripped off their old clothes and dressed themselves anew in the open streets, donning fashionable suits. Women selected jewels for their personal adornment, and rich and rare were the gems they wore on toil-stained fingers and grimy wrist. Watches were carried off heaped in aprons. Toys were given to the young. Fruit and champagne and other expensive luxuries were freely partaken of. The wines were in some cases retailed for a few pence the bottle. Bookshops only were immune from attack. It is related that some officers captured by the Rebels on Monday were conveyed by the enemy to a tobacconist's shop, and with true Irish hospitality were treated to the best cigars, the owner of the shop having fled.

I myself engaged in looting operations. Barbed wire was required by the Military Authorities. As there should have been plenty of it in McKenzie's stores near the gate, I suggested a raid on these premises. But, in spite of a fairly complete search, none of the desired wire was to be found. We could only conclude that either the enemy had been before us or the owners had secreted it. All uncivilised organisms are thieves. A proclivity so natural must be attended in its gratification with pleasurable sensations. I can vouch for the very enjoyable nature of looting operations.

On this Friday night I ventured on a cycle ride out to my house. The desire for a bath and a change had become a mania. I got a pass, and although strongly urged not to go, I traversed the dark streets in safety. Within the City all lights had been extinguished. Only an occasional shot or the challenge of a sentry showed that the City was inhabited. I carried a bicycle lamp as I most feared the attentions of our own men, who might well conclude that I was an enemy despatch-rider. I was frequently challenged. I confess I was glad when I got into the lighted area outside the canal. I returned to the College early the ensuing morning. The streets were in a most dangerous state, and few ventured abroad. House-top fighting was specially lively in the neighbourhood of Upper and Lower Mount Street. I had to call on a relative living in the former street. Bullets had been fired through her window, but, contrasted with many of the inhabitants of Dublin, she had but little annoyance.

Saturday the 29th was to be my last day at the gate. There were now available many better fitted for such a duty. I was given leave for Sunday. In the streets Saturday was marked by a certain liveliness. Prisoners were coming in or passing in batches all day. A poor and pitiable lot they looked. Surrenders were taking place all over the City: surrenders accepted on unconditional terms only. The leaders were now in the hands of the authorities, and the Sinn Fein Rebellion was in a fair way to be a thing of the past, and to take its place in Irish history as one of the many insane rebellions which constitute its principal episodes.

Late that night I accompanied Captain Alton to the top of the lookout tower of the Fire Brigade Station. The view northward was sublime and terrible. Acres of flame and red-hot buildings stretched across the middle distance. The lurid light, reflected on rolling clouds of smoke, rose and fell as roof and walls toppled over. Fresh fires appeared to be springing into existence at a point to the north-east, and it really looked as if we were witnessing the wholesale destruction by the devouring flames of the entire northern side of the City. The night was still or the damage had been far greater than it was. The Brigade was said to be overwhelmed with the magnitude of the work assigned to it – as well it might be; but undoubtedly it did valuable service. And its work was in some cases done under the fire of the Rebels. Two and a half million pounds' worth of property were destroyed during the rising.

And from this tower, looking over unhappy Dublin, stretching like a map beneath us, we seem to be reviewing the whole miserable story: the growth of lawlessness, dating back to days of cattle-driving and boycotting. To the landlords every evil was to be traced. Settle the land question and you would have a peaceful and prosperous Ireland. Well, the landlords are gone and now you have rebellion. The long, pernicious Aberdeen regime, year by year bringing authority more and more into contempt; the laxity towards the Larkinite movement; the folding of the hands, no matter what might be done in Liberty Hall. 'We serve neither King nor Kaiser, but Ireland,' stood for months writ across the face of that house of sedition; but still all was well. Then we have the pressure of Home Rule, leading to the arming of the North. Next comes the arming of the South. Finally arises the usual rift between the 'constitutional' and the unconstitutional. All these long series of ominous events mishandled, or not handled at all, by a helpless Government.

Hundreds of the untimely dead lie beneath us in the stricken city. Upon hundreds of others the shades of death are even now closing. The ruined, unhappy leaders are there – now at length seeing all their own mischance. The pitiful dupes who took their word for the future of the 'Irish Republic'; and now only look forward to death or penal servitude! Others, just as guilty, lurking in hourly fear of detection! The orphaned children crying for mother or father! Ruined lives and ruined business! All this and far, far more make up the tragedy at our feet.

And the future? Nothing can be more gloomy save the miserable present. Does anyone believe that this is indeed the end of madness in this unhappy land? A bloody and desperate war to claim for its victims all we have most brave and most loyal. And when that is past our wretched domestic politics all over again, with the certainty that sacrifices for King and Empire will count for nothing. Is this sea of lambent flames, this harvest of death, a hopeful augury for the future of self-governing Ireland? Who will be found to educate my fellow-countrymen to that self-control which accepts the victory in the Senate as the final verdict? Who will be found wise and strong enough to waken them from the phantasmagoria of vain and foolish dreams to the sober light of day? Be very sure that till that measure of self-mastery is attained, and till that awakening is accomplished, this is not the end of violence. Today you deal with the Sinn Fein; tomorrow you deal with – Whom?

Truly our future is as lurid as those rolling clouds which, rising around us into the night, dissipate in space the hard-won wealth of the loyal citizens of Dublin.

Dramatis personae

ALTON, ERNEST HENRY (1873–1952), a Westmeath-born academic, was a brilliant classical scholar, debater, and rugby player. His impressive performance during Easter Week earned him a Military Cross. Despite his journalistic experience, Alton's two published reports (see Appendix 3) skirt around the brutal details of the week's events, adopting almost a '*Boy's Own*' approach. He became a member of Dáil Éireann (1922–37), a senator (1938–43), vice provost of Trinity (1941–2) and provost (1942–52). In 1951 he supervised the publication of the first complete photographic facsimile of the Book of Kells. Married in 1915, his brother-in-law was J.E. Healy, editor of the *Irish Times* (1907–34).

BRENNAN-WHITMORE, WILLIAM JAMES (1886–1977), a Wexford-born journalist, who was aide to Joseph Plunkett in the GPO during the Rising, then in charge of a squad that occupied the Imperial Hotel. He engaged in a prolonged sniping duel with Fred Nevin, whom he later encountered when imprisoned at the Custom House. He misidentified Nevin as 'the Aussie sergeant' in his vivid account of Easter Week, *Dublin burning: the Easter Rising from behind the barricades* (Dublin, 2013).

CONNOLLY, JAMES (1868–1916), as commandant general of the Dublin forces, ran military operations from the GPO, dictating a stream of orders to be typed up by his indefatigable secretary Winifred Carney. His belated decision to order an attack on Trinity was reversed after a gun battle in the early hours of Tuesday, 26 April. It was fire from artillery based at Trinity College, rather than from the gunboat *Helga*, that caused most damage to the ITGWU's headquarters at Liberty Hall.

DE VALERA, EAMON (1882–1975). No rebel force was harder hit by Eoin MacNeill's countermand than de Valera's 3rd Battalion, with only 130 of its nominal strength of 500 turning out on Easter Monday. Had it been otherwise, he may have solved his garrison's acute shortage of arms and ammunition by ordering a raid on Trinity's OTC armoury. None of the many critics of de Valera's performance as commandant during the Rising mention his failure to take this opportunity.

DON, ALEXANDER WILLIAM (1895–1954). Little is known of Don's activities immediately after returning to New Zealand, but in 1929 he opened Hadlow Preparatory School for Boys in the isolated backblocks of the Wairarapa. 'The Boss' ran his school on military lines, regaling the pupils with popular wartime songs, displaying his uniform and medals on Anzac Day, and recounting how he had helped to quell the Irish rebellion. Much of his profile contributed to *Who's who in New Zealand* (1952) raised questions of accuracy, and his career ended tragically when he committed suicide after being arrested and charged with the indecent assault of a pupil.

FITZGIBBON, GERALD (1866–1942) was born in Dublin and educated at Trinity College. A fierce unionist, he soon overcame his objections to the new Free State and accepted appointment to the supreme court (1924–38). He had represented the University of Dublin as unionist MP (1921) and independent TD (1922–3). Fitzgibbon's letters to his Canadian brother-in-law provide a lively account of the Irish Revolution, telling how unwillingly he was 'dragged ... into the maelstrom of Irish politics'.[1]

GARLAND, JOHN GODWIN (1894–1960), on returning to New Zealand, went back to work with the New Zealand Dairy Association. After marrying in 1920 he settled on Auckland's suburban North Shore. He also resumed his Orange activities, responding in 1924 to a circular appeal from the Loyalist Association of Ireland 'for funds to support the thousands of orphans who have been left destitute through the murder of their parents' during the Irish Revolution. There is a fair chance that Garland himself was responsible for a few of these deaths.

GLEN, JAMES A. (1896–?), a native of Newtown Cunningham, County Donegal, was a Trinity College graduate and a former member of its OTC. Aged 22 at the time of the Rising, he was a second lieutenant in the Royal Field Artillery and on leave in Dublin. In his account composed over fifty years later, he stated that 'a determined [rebel] attack during the first night might well have been successful'.[2] Glen was yet another Irishman guilty of describing New Zealanders as Australians.

HARRIS, GEORGE ARTHUR (1879–1935) was a 36-year-old civil servant from Killashee, County Longford. A Trinity College graduate, he acted as adjutant and second-in-command of the OTC, which he had helped to found in 1910. Despite spending the whole of Easter Week under siege in Beggar's Bush Barracks, Harris was given credit by General Sir John Maxwell for the alleged exploits of his corps, being awarded a DSO in January 1917.

HOBBS, FREDERICK HENRY (1874–1942), born in Christchurch, New Zealand, was the son of a former mayor of that city. After training as a concert singer, he joined the D'Oyly Carte Opera Company in 1914, performing as a baritone in numerous roles in Gilbert and Sullivan operas. He became stage manager for D'Oyly Carte in 1923 and its business manager from 1927 until his death. His compensation claim for losses during the Rising (deemed to be 'exaggerated') included a set of golf clubs, bag, and balls.[3]

1 Fitzgibbon to Blake, 1 July 1921, TCD, MS 11107/30. **2** Glen, 'TCD: Easter Week 1916', TCD, MS 4456. **3** Property Losses (Ireland) Committee record, PLIC/1/1469, National Archives, Dublin.

JOLY, JOHN (1857–1933) was born in County Offaly, and studied classics, modern literature and engineering at TCD, becoming a world-renowned geologist and physicist. He invented a system of colour photography in 1897, the same year as he wrote a pioneering paper on the nature and origin of Martian canals. Forty years after his death, a crater on Mars was named after him. His vivid account of the Rising from inside Trinity College is a relatively unknown classic.

KEOGH, GERALD ANTHONY (1894–1916), a 22-year-old former Fianna member, was the youngest of four brothers 'out' in Easter Week on the rebel side (another soldier brother had been killed in France). As a pupil at St Enda's school he had played the role of a warrior in a school pageant, 'The boy deeds of Cúchulainn', in 1909. Seven years later he played the drama out in real life.

LUCE, ARTHUR ASTON (1882–1977) was born in Gloucester, England. A Trinity College graduate and fellow, he became a distinguished philosopher and clergyman and fought on the Western Front as a lieutenant in the Royal Irish Rifles (1915–18). He was awarded the Military Cross for his part in the defence of TCD during the Rising. He spent most of his life within the college community, serving as Trinity's vice provost from 1946 to 1951. After tutoring a youthful Samuel Beckett, Luce wrote that his pupil's future prospects were 'quite dismal'.[4]

MacDONAGH, THOMAS STANISLAUS (1878–1916), who was commandant of the Dublin Brigade's 2nd Battalion, decided not to risk the heavy losses he (wrongly) believed an attack on Trinity College would involve. He chose instead to take over the vast complex of Jacob's Biscuit Factory, an easily isolated post that became 'as much a liability to the Volunteers as to the British'.[5] He had earlier considered ordering twenty of his 150-strong force to occupy Trinity's commanding West Front buildings. Had he done so the course of Easter Week may well have taken a very different turn. It is worth noting that in 1913 MacDonagh had applied (unsuccessfully) for the vacant chair of English literature at Trinity College.

McHUGH, MICHAEL JOHN (1893–1955) was the sole Australian in the Anzac squad. Son of Irish Catholic immigrants, the Queenslander's background helps to explain why (like Fred Nevin) he chose not to write or speak about his Dublin experiences. He worked for the railways as a fettler until his death aged 61.

McLEOD, FINLAY HUGH (1895–1985) was born and grew up in New Zealand, but moved with his family to Sydney during his final year at school. He enlisted in Wellington with the New Zealand Field Engineers, while his elder brother Donald joined the Australian Imperial Force. McLeod probably went over to Dublin with Michael McHugh, who is the 'Australian' he mentions in his letter home. The two men

4 *DIB*, v, p. 592. 5 Norstedt, *Thomas MacDonagh*, p. 133.

were photographed together (with Private Edward Waring) at the conclusion of hostilities. McLeod was married in 1917 and lived later in England and Malaya. He died in Australia aged 90.

MAHAFFY, ELIZABETH ('ELSIE') (1869–1926), the elder of Provost Mahaffy's daughters, is remembered for her lengthy diary kept during the Rising. Written while living at the Provost's House, it reflects the reactionary views of her father and the British military officers with whom she mixed. She is contemptuous of all rebels, most politicians (especially Liberals) and the Irish administration (Augustine Birrell above all), yet also captures many fascinating details and revealing incidents of Easter Week. In her eyes, Captain Bowen-Colthurst was 'one of the best young men I have met', while his victim Francis Sheehy-Skeffington was 'a poisonous microbe whose writings were a source of danger to the community'.[6]

MAHAFFY, JOHN PENTLAND (1839–1919) found himself reduced to the unusual role of spectator during Easter Week, while the battle raged in his city and around his university. He played host to the British military and was an apologist for their actions. Not noted for his sensitivity to Irish nationalist sentiment, Mahaffy dismissed the Rising as an attempt to 'put a lot of fanatics and criminals into all the positions of emolument now held by loyal persons'.[7] His elder daughter noted ruefully that this would have included Patrick Pearse as 'prospective Provost of Trinity College and future master of our house'.[8]

MAXWELL, JOHN GRENFELL (1859–1929) was only second choice for the position of military governor of post-Rising Ireland, his rival General Sir Ian Hamilton being deemed unacceptable after his poor performance during the Gallipoli campaign. Maxwell had opposed this particular adventure, stating 'I am all for leaving the Gallipoli peninsula severely alone.' He retained a warm admiration for what he saw of Anzac soldiery in 1914–15.

MEIN, CHARLES (1898–1967) was born in Scotland but grew up in Dublin. The 18-year-old cadet-sergeant and his three comrades were all that stood in the way of a possible rebel attack on the OTC armoury in the critical first hours of the Rising. A year later he landed in France as a commissioned officer in the Royal Scots (Lothian Regiment). He survived the war and died in York.

NEVIN, FREDERICK LESLIE (1895–1953), after returning to New Zealand, worked as a salesman for the Farmers Trading Company, a department chain store in Christchurch. In December 1917 he went down to the port of Lyttelton to see the *Marama* return from its third commission. After helping to disembark the wounded

6 Elsie Mahaffy diary, p. 97, TCD, MS 2074. 7 *Times* (London), 16 May 1916. 8 Elsie Mahaffy diary, p. 42, TCD, MS 2074.

soldiers, he took a photograph of his old ship, for which offence against the war regulations he was subsequently convicted and fined five shillings. Nevin married in 1928 and had three children, none of whom were aware of his wartime exploits in Dublin. He died in Christchurch aged 58.

TATE, ROBERT WILLIAM (1872–1952) was commanding officer of the OTC from its foundation in 1910 to its demise in 1922. Born in Leitrim, the son of a Church of Ireland rector, and educated at St John's College, Cambridge, he was elected a fellow of TCD in 1908, where he was professor of Italian. He was on holiday in the north of Ireland when the Rising began and could not get back to Dublin for a week. Nevertheless, he received a cup and an inscribed sword, followed in 1920 by the award of the KBE for ten years' service with the OTC.

THORNTON, FRANK JOSEPH (1891–1965), who was born in Drogheda, brought 67 of his Volunteer Company over from Liverpool (and 50 from Bootle) to join the rebellion, including his brothers Hugh and Paddy and sister Nora. He was based at North Frederick Street and regarded his group as part of the Kimmage garrison. During Easter Week he fought under the name of Drennan and was sentenced to twenty years' penal servitude. He later worked as a Volunteer organizer, then as part of Michael Collins' intelligence organization. He was badly wounded in a Republican ambush near Clonmel in August 1922.

WARING, EDWARD (1892–1918) is the only one of the five New Zealanders not known to have recorded his account of the defence of Trinity College. His death so soon after returning to New Zealand robbed him of the chance to do so, but family tradition kept the memory alive. In 1966, perhaps prompted by the 50th anniversary of the Easter Rising, Waring's nephew wrote to the New Zealand Ministry of Defence seeking confirmation of his uncle's involvement. The ministry replied that Waring's military file contained no indication as to where he had spent his period of leave at Easter 1916. (This was also true of the other four New Zealanders.)

WATERHOUSE, GILBERT (1888–1977), a 28-year-old Yorkshireman, was educated at the universities of Cambridge and Berlin. After a spell lecturing at Leipzig University, he became professor of German at TCD in 1915. According to his biographer, his vitriolic attitude towards Germany during the First World War included advocating the study of its language and literature as a means of indoctrinating students with hatred for its people. In 1933 he was appointed to the chair of German at Queen's University Belfast. Waterhouse died in 1977 aged 89.

Bibliography

1. PRIMARY SOURCES

AUSTRALIA

National Archives of Australia, Canberra

Military file of Michael John McHugh (1985), B2455

CANADA

Canadian Military Archives, Ottawa

Personal records of the Canadian Expeditionary Force:
Howard Cassidy (454045), Accession 1992–3/166, Box 1568–9
George Webb (447766), RG 150, Accession 1992–3/166, Box 10177–44

IRELAND

Digital Repository of Ireland

Herbert Fitzgerald's 'Diary of events in Ireland during the Sinn Fein insurrection'

Military Archives, Dublin

Bureau of Military History Witness Statements:

WS 6 (Liam Ó Briain)
WS 152 (A.P. Agnew)
WS 165 (Luke Kennedy)
WS 186 (Thomas J. Doyle)
WS 194 (Domhnall O Buachalla)
WS 249 (Frank Henderson)
WS 263 (Thomas Slater)
WS 307 (Thomas MacCarthy)
WS 327 (Patrick Egan)
WS 348 (E. Gerrard)
WS 361 (Peadar Bracken)
WS 399 (Mary Josephine Mulcahy)
WS 409 (Valentine Jackson)
WS 481 (Simon Donnelly)
WS 487 (Joseph O'Connor)
WS 510 (Frank Thornton)
WS 511 (Michael Lynch)
WS 535 (James Francis Hughes)
WS 615 (Frank Thornton)
WS 655 (Nora Thornton)
WS 660 (Tom Leahy)
WS 694 (Feargus de Burca)
WS 724 (Desmond Ryan)
WS 822 (W.J. Stapleton)
WS 1019 (Alfred Bucknill
WS 1071 (George Chester Duggan)
WS 1280 (Eamon Broy)
WS 1670 (Seamus Kavanagh)
WS 1686 (Ruadhri Henderson)
WS 1770 (Kevin O'Shiel)

Military Service Pensions Collection:

MSP24SP1276 (Andrew O'Neill)
MSP24SP1302 (Frank Thornton)
MSP24SP5682 (Alexander Thompson)
MSP24SP6296 (John J. Murphy)
MSP24SP9813 (John Edward Bracken)
MSP24SP11634 (Daniel Colgan)
MSP24SP12028 (John Bracken senior)
MSP34REF194 (George A. Lyons)
MSP34REF830 (Patrick McBride)
MSP34REF1217 (Thomas Joseph Kelly)
MSP34REF1776 (Michael John Lennon)
MSP34REF10234 (Richard Pearle)
MSP34REF41334 (Gilbert Lynch)
MSP34REF42907 (Michael Meagher)
MSP34REF46260 (Patrick Meagher)
MSP34REF46955 (Laurence Moore)

National Archives of Ireland, Dublin

Property Losses (Ireland) Committee record, PLIC/1/1469

National Library of Ireland, Dublin

Diarmid Coffey papers, MS 21193/2
Joseph O'Connor papers, MS 13735

Trinity College Dublin, Department of Manuscripts

MS 2074
MS 2309
MS 2313
MS 2783
MS 4456
MS 4873
MS 4874
MS 7533/3
MS 9820
MS 11107
MS 11571
MS 7533/3
MS 10066/192
MUN/V/5
MUN/V/6

University College Dublin Archives

De Valera papers

Representative Church Body Library, Dublin

St Andrew's Church (Dublin) vestry minute book, 1916–17

NEW ZEALAND

Archives New Zealand, Wellington

Lieutenant-Colonel Percy Cook's reports to GOC, AD1 887 39/182

New Zealand Defence Force, personnel archives:
A.W. Don (2/1745)
J.G. Garland (1/636), (3/1315)
Finlay McLeod (4/666)
F.L. Nevin (3/1347)
Edward Waring (12/1523)

Auckland War Memorial Museum
Maunganuian, 1:1 (28 June 1915)

Loyal Orange Order Archives, Auckland
City of Auckland (No. 1) Lodge minute book (1922)

SOUTH AFRICA
Department of Defence Archives, Pretoria, South Africa
Military files of:
George Russell (7624)
Blackburn Charlton (9343)
George Moffitt (9435)
Eric King (9380)
George Gibson (9405)

UNITED KINGDOM
National Archives, London
Report on 'Defence of TCD by the DU OTC', WO 32/9576
William Wylie papers, PRO 30/89/2

2. NEWSPAPERS AND PERIODICALS

An tÓglách
Auckland Star
Ballymena Observer
Belfast Evening Telegraph
Belfast News-Letter
Blackwood's Magazine
Church of Ireland Gazette
Daily Express (Dublin)
Daily Mail (Dublin)
Dublin Evening Mail
Evening Star (Dunedin)
Freeman's Journal (Dublin)
Grey River Argus (Greymouth)
Hermathena
History Ireland
Irish Examiner
Irish Independent
Irish Times
Irish Volunteer
Liverpool Daily Post
New Zealand Herald
New Zealand Tablet
Northern Whig (Belfast)
Otago Daily Times
Sun (Christchurch)
Sunday Press (Dublin)
Sydney Morning Herald
TCD: A College Miscellany
The Times (London)
Volunteers (Auckland)

3. SECONDARY SOURCES

Arrington, L., *Revolutionary lives: Constance and Casimir Markievicz* (Princeton, 2016).
Augusteijn, J., *Patrick Pearse: the making of a revolutionary* (London, 2010).
Arthur, G., *General Sir John Maxwell* (London, 1932).
Bailey, K.C., *A history of Trinity College Dublin, 1892–1945* (Dublin, 1947).

Baker, P., *King and country call: New Zealand, conscription and the Great War* (Auckland, 1988).
Barnes, F., *New Zealand's London: a colony and its metropolis* (Auckland, 2012).
Bartlett, T. and Jeffery, K. (eds), *A military history of Ireland* (Cambridge, 1996).
Bassett, M., *Sir Joseph Ward* (Auckland, 1993).
Belich, J., *Replenishing the Earth: the settler revolution and the rise of the Anglo-World, 1783–1939* (Oxford, 2009).
Bennett, D., *The silver collection, Trinity College Dublin* (Dublin, 1988).
Bowman, T., *Irish regiments in the Great War* (Manchester, 2003).
Boyle, P., *Trinity College Dublin: the provosts, 1592–1927* (Dublin, 2015).
Brennan-Whitmore, W.J., *Dublin burning: the Easter Rising from behind the barricades* (Dublin, 2013).
Brown, T., *Ireland: a social and cultural history, 1922–2002* (London, 2004).
Brown, T., *The Irish Times* (London, 2015).
Bryant-Haigh, J., 'The military occupation of German Samoa, 1914–19', *Volunteers*, 40:2 (Nov. 2014), pp 9–15.
Buchan, J., *The history of the South African forces in France* (London, 1920).
Buckner, P. and Douglas Francis, R. (eds), *Rediscovering the British world* (Calgary, 2005).
Bunbury, T., *Easter dawn: the 1916 Rising* (Cork, 2015).
Burke, T., 'Fancy the Royal Irish captured Moore Street: attitudes to the Easter Rising of Irish soldiers serving in the British army in Dublin', *Irish Sword*, 28:112 (2012), pp 187–207.
Burton, O., *The silent division: New Zealanders at the front, 1914–1919* (Sydney, 1935).
Caulfield, M., *The Easter Rebellion* (Dublin, 1995).
Connell, J.E.A., *Dublin in rebellion: a directory, 1913–1923* (Dublin, 2006).
Connell, J.E.A., *Where's where in Dublin* (Dublin, 2006).
Connell, J.E.A., *Who's who in the Dublin Rising, 1916* (Dublin, 2015).
Coogan, T.P., *Michael Collins* (London, 1990).
Crawley, R. and LoCicero, M. (eds), *Gallipoli: new perspectives on the Mediterranean Expeditionary Force* (Warwick, 2018).
Crowe, C. (ed.), *Guide to the Military Service (1916–1923) Pensions Collection, Dublin* (Dublin, 2012).
Cuimhneachán, 1916–1966: a record of Ireland's commemoration of the 1916 rising (Dublin, 1966).
Daly, M.E. and O'Callaghan, M. (eds), *1916 in 1966: commemorating the Easter Rising* (Dublin, 2007).
Darwin, J., *The empire project: the rise and fall of the British world-system, 1830–1970* (Cambridge, 2009).
Davis, R.P., *Irish issues in New Zealand politics, 1868–1922* (Dunedin, 1974).
Delaney, D.E., *The imperial army project: Britain and the land forces of the dominions and India, 1902–1945* (Oxford, 2017).
Denman, T., *A lonely grave: the life and death of William Redmond* (Dublin, 1995).
de Paor, L., *On the Easter Proclamation and other declarations* (Dublin, 1997).

Dickson, D., *Dublin: the making of a capital city* (London, 2014).
Doherty, G. and Keogh, D. (eds), *1916: the long revolution* (Cork, 2007).
Dooley, T.P., *Irishmen or English soldiers?* (Liverpool, 1995).
Dooney, L., 'Trinity College and the war' in D. Fitzpatrick (ed.), *Ireland and the First World War* (Dublin, 1986), pp 38–46.
Dudley Edwards, O., *Eamon de Valera* (Cardiff, 1987).
Dudley Edwards, O. and Pyle, F. (eds), *1916: the Easter Rising* (London, 1978).
Dudley Edwards, R., *James Connolly* (Dublin, 1998).
Dudley Edwards, R., *Patrick Pearse: the triumph of failure* (Dublin, 1977).
Duff, C., *No angel's wing* (London, 1947).
Duff, C., *Six days to shake an empire* (London, 1966).
Duggan, J.P., *A history of the Irish army* (Dublin, 1991).
Dunleavy, G.W., *Douglas Hyde* (London, 1974).
Dunlop, D., *1916 and beyond the Pale* (Croydon, 2016).
Eley, G. and Suny, R.G. (eds), *Becoming national: a reader* (Oxford, 1996).
Elliott, J.S., 'The New Zealand hospital ships' in H.T.B. Drew (ed.), *The war effort of New Zealand* (Auckland, 1924), pp 127–37.
Falls, C., 'Maxwell, 1916, and Britain at war' in F.X. Martin (ed.), *Leaders and men of the Easter Rising: Dublin 1916* (London, 1967), pp 203–14.
Ferriter, D., *Judging Dev: a reassessment of the life and legacy of Eamon de Valera* (Dublin, 2007).
Ferriter, D., *The transformation of Ireland, 1900–2000* (London, 2004).
Fitzgerald, D., *Desmond's Rising* (Dublin, 2006).
Fitzpatrick, D., 'Eamon de Valera at Trinity College', *Hermathena: a Trinity College Dublin Review*, 133 (1982), pp 7–14.
Fitzpatrick, D., 'Historians and the commemoration of Irish conflicts, 1912–23' in John Horne and Edward Madigan (eds), *Towards commemoration: Ireland in war and revolution, 1912–1923* (Dublin, 2013), pp 126–33.
Fitzpatrick, D., 'Home front and everyday life' in John Horne (ed.), *Our war: Ireland and the Great War* (Dublin, 2008), pp 131–42.
Fitzpatrick, D., 'Imperial loyalties: Irishmen, Anzacs, and the conflict of empires at Gallipoli', *Irish Sword*, 30:121 (2016), pp 305–31.
Fitzpatrick, D., 'Instant history: 1912, 1916, 1918' in Richard S. Grayson and Fearghal McGarry (eds), *Remembering 1916: the Easter Rising, the Somme and the politics of memory in Ireland* (Cambridge, 2016), pp 65–85.
Fitzpatrick, D., 'Militarism in Ireland, 1900–1922' in Thomas Bartlett and Keith Jeffery (eds), *A military history of Ireland* (Cambridge, 1996), pp 379–406.
Fitzpatrick, D., *The two Irelands, 1912–1939* (Oxford, 1998).
Fitzpatrick, G., 'A sideshow in Dublin', *Wartime*, 14 (2001), pp 48–9.
Fitzpatrick, G., *Trinity College and Irish society, 1914–1922* (Dublin, 1992).
Foster, R.F., *Modern Ireland, 1600–1972* (London, 1989).
Foster, R.F., *Vivid faces: the revolutionary generation in Ireland, 1890–1923* (London, 2015).

Fox, P., *Trinity College Library Dublin: a history* (Cambridge, 2014).

Fox, R.M., *The history of the Irish Citizen Army* (Dublin, 1943).

Foy, M. and Barton, B., *The Easter Rising* (Stroud, 2000).

Garton, S., 'The dominions, Ireland, and India' in Robert Gerwarth and Erez Manela (eds), *Empires at war, 1911–1923* (Oxford, 2014), pp 152–77.

Gibbon, M., *Inglorious soldier* (London, 1968).

Gibney, J., *A history of the Easter Rising in 50 objects* (Cork, 2016).

Gibney, J. (ed.), *Dublin City Council and the 1916 Rising* (Dublin, 2016).

Godley, A., *Life of an Irish soldier* (London, 1939).

Godson, L. and Bruck, J. (eds), *Making 1916: material and visual culture of the Easter Rising* (Liverpool, 2015).

Graff-McCrae, R., *Remembering and forgetting 1916* (Dublin, 2010).

Grayson, R.S., *Dublin's great wars: the First World War, the Easter Rising and the Irish Revolution* (Cambridge, 2018).

Grayson, R.S. and McGarry, F. (eds), *Remembering 1916: the Easter Rising, the Somme and the politics of memory in Ireland* (Cambridge, 2016).

Gregory, A. and Pašeta, S. (eds), *Ireland and the Great War* (Manchester, 2002).

Griffith, L.M., *Stones of Dublin: a history of Dublin in ten buildings* (Cork, 2014).

Gwynn, D., *The life of John Redmond* (London, 1932).

Hally, P.J., 'The Easter 1916 Rising in Dublin: the military aspects', part I, *Irish Sword*, 7:29 (1966), pp 313–26; part II, 8:30 (1968), pp 48–57.

Hamilton Norway, Mrs M.L., *The Sinn Fein rebellion as I saw it* (London, 1916).

Haverty, A., *Constance Markievicz* (Dublin, 2016).

Hayes-McCoy, G.A., 'A military history of the 1916 Rising' in Kevin B Nowlan (ed.), *The making of 1916: studies in the history of the Rising* (Dublin, 1969), pp 255–338.

Heuston, J.M., *Headquarters Battalion Easter Week* (Dublin, 1966).

Higgins, R., *Transforming 1916: meaning, memory and the fiftieth anniversary of the Easter Rising* (Cork, 2012).

Hogan, J.F., *Irish Catholics and Trinity College* (Dublin, 1906).

Holland, C.H. (ed.), *Trinity College Dublin and the idea of a university* (Dublin, 1991).

Horne, J. and Kramer, A., *German atrocities, 1914: a history of denial* (New Haven, 2001).

Horne, J. (ed.), *Our war: Ireland and the Great War* (Dublin, 2008).

Horne, J. and Madigan, E. (eds), *Towards commemoration: Ireland in war and revolution, 1912–1923* (Dublin, 2013).

Inglis, B., *Roger Casement* (New York, 1973).

Irish, T., 'Trinity College Dublin: an imperial university in war and revolution, 1914–1921' in Marie-Eve Chagnon and Tomás Irish (eds), *The academic world in the era of the Great War* (Basingstoke, 2018), pp 119–39.

Irish, T., *Trinity in war and revolution, 1912–1923* (Dublin, 2015).

Jackson, A., *Ireland, 1798–1998* (Oxford, 1999).

Jackson, A., 'Irish unionists and the empire, 1880–1920: classes and masses' in Keith Jeffery (ed.), *'An Irish empire'? Aspects of Ireland and the British empire* (Manchester, 1996), pp 123–48.

Jeffery, K., *1916. A global history* (London, 2016).

Jeffery, K. (ed.), *'An Irish empire'? Aspects of Ireland and the British empire* (Manchester, 1996).

Jeffery, K., 'Gallipoli and Ireland' in Jenny Macleod (ed.), *Gallipoli: making history* (London, 2004).

Jeffery, K., *Ireland and the Great War* (Cambridge, 2000).

Jeffery, K., *The GPO and the Easter Rising* (Dublin, 2006).

Jeffery, K., 'The Irish military tradition and the British empire' in Keith Jeffery (ed.), *'An Irish empire'? Aspects of Ireland and the British empire* (Manchester, 1996), pp 94–122.

Jenkins, R., *Asquith* (London, 1967).

Johnson, N.C., *Ireland, the Great War and the geography of remembrance* (Cambridge, 2003).

Joly, J., *Reminiscences and anticipations* (London, 1920).

Jones, F.P., *History of the Sinn Fein movement and the Irish rebellion of 1916* (New York, 1919).

Keane, H., 'Anzac defender of Trinity College Dublin 1916', *Volunteers*, 42:1 (July 2016), pp 60–2.

Keane, H., 'New Zealanders in the 1916 Irish rebellion', *Volunteers*, 40:1 (July 2014), pp 44–52.

Kenna, S., *Thomas MacDonagh* (Dublin, 2014).

Keogh, R.M., 'Well dressed and from a respectable street', *History Ireland*, 17:2 (2009), pp 32–3.

Kiberd, K., '1916: the idea and the action' in Kathleen Devine (ed.), *Modern Irish writers and the wars* (Gerrards Cross, 1999).

Kildea, J., *Anzacs and Ireland* (Sydney, 2007).

Kildea, J., 'Called to arms: Australian soldiers in the Easter Rising', *Journal of the Australian War Memorial*, 39 (Oct. 2003).

Kildea, J., '"We personally had no quarrel with the rioters": Anzacs in Dublin during the Easter Rising 1916', paper given at the conference 'The 1916 Rising: Australasian Perspectives', University of Melbourne, 7–8 Apr. 2016.

Killingray, D., 'The war in Africa' in John Horne (ed.), *A companion to World War I* (London, 2012), pp 112–26.

Kinloch, T., *Godley: the man behind the myth* (Dunedin, 2018).

Kirkpatrick, D., 'A Coleraine student witnesses the 1916 Easter Rising', *North Irish Roots*, 28:1 (2017), pp 29–31.

Lecane, P., *Beneath a Turkish sky: the Royal Dublin Fusiliers and the assault on Gallipoli* (Dublin, 2015).

Lee, J.J., *Ireland, 1912–1985* (Cambridge, 1989).

Leonard, J., 'The reactions of Irish officers in the British army to the Easter Rising of 1916' in H. Cecil and P.H. Liddle (eds), *Facing Armageddon: the First World War experienced* (London, 1996), pp 256–68.

Levenson, S., *James Connolly* (London, 1973).

Liverpool, Earl of, *The voyages of his majesty's hospital ships 'Marama' and 'Maheno'*, vol. 2 (Auckland, 1917).

Loughlin, J., *The British monarchy and Ireland* (Cambridge, 2007).

Loveridge, S., *Calls to arms: New Zealand society and commitment to the Great War* (Wellington, 2014).

Luce, J.V., *Trinity College Dublin: the first 400 years* (Dublin, 1992).

Lynch, D., *The IRB and the 1916 insurrection* (Cork, 1957).

Lyons, F.S.L. (ed.), *Bicentenary essays: Bank of Ireland, 1783–1983* (Dublin, 1983).

Lyons, F.S.L., *Culture and anarchy in Ireland, 1890–1939* (Oxford, 1979).

Lyons, F.S.L., *Ireland since the Famine* (London, 1982).

Lyons, F.S.L., 'The minority problem in the 26 counties' in Francis MacManus (ed.), *The years of the great test, 1926–39* (Cork, 1967), pp 92–103.

Lyons, G.A., 'Occupation of Ringsend area in 1916', *An tÓglách*, 4:13–16 (10, 17, 21 Apr. 1926).

Lytton, Sir H., 'Innocent bysinger' in Roger McHugh (ed.), *Dublin 1916* (London, 1976), pp 145–57.

Lytton, H., *The secrets of a Savoyard* (London, 1922).

Lytton, Sir H., *Wandering minstrel* (London, 1933).

McCarthy, M., *Ireland's 1916 Rising* (London, 2012).

McDowell, R.B. and Webb, D.A., *Trinity College Dublin, 1592–1952: an academic history* (Cambridge, 1982).

McGarry, F., '"A land beyond the wave": transnational perspectives on Easter 1916' in Niall Whelehan (ed.), *Transnational perspectives on modern Irish history* (London, 2014), pp 165–88.

McGarry, F., *The Rising: Ireland: Easter 1916* (Oxford, 2010).

McGibbon, I. (ed.), *The Oxford companion to New Zealand military history* (Oxford, 2000).

McGibbon, I., *The path to Gallipoli: defending New Zealand, 1840–1915* (Wellington, 1991).

McGreevy, R., *Wherever the firing line extends: Ireland and the Western Front* (Dublin, 2016).

McGuire, J. and Quinn, J. (eds), *Dictionary of Irish biography*, vols 1–7 (Cambridge, 2009).

McHugh, R. (ed.), *Dublin 1916: an illustrated anthology* (London, 1976).

McLean, G., *The governors: New Zealand's governors and governors-general* (Dunedin, 2006).

McLean, G., *The white ships: New Zealand's First World War hospital ships* (Wellington, 2013).

McMahon, D., 'Ireland, the empire, and the commonwealth' in Kevin Kenny (ed.), *Ireland and the British empire* (Oxford, 2004), pp 182–219.
Martin, F.X., '1916: myth, fact, and mystery', *Studia Hibernica*, 7 (1967), pp 7–126.
Martin, F.X. (ed.), *The Easter Rising: 1916 and University College Dublin* (Dublin, 1966).
Martin, F.X. (ed.), *Leaders and men of the Easter Rising: Dublin 1916* (London, 1967).
Martin, F.X. and Byrne, F.J. (eds), *The scholar revolutionary: Eoin MacNeill, 1967–1945 and the making of the new Ireland* (Shannon, 1973).
Maume, P., *The long gestation: Irish nationalist life, 1891–1918* (Dublin, 1999).
Maxwell, General Sir J., 'Introduction' to C.G. Powles, *The New Zealanders in Sinai and Palestine* (Auckland, 1922), pp vii–xi.
Mitcham, J.C., *Race and imperial defence in the British world, 1870–1914* (Cambridge, 2016).
Molyneux, D. and Kelly, D., *When the clock struck in 1916: close-quarter combat in the Easter Rising* (Cork, 2015).
Mulvagh, C., *Irish days, Indian memories* (Sallins, 2016).
Mulvagh, C., *The Irish Parliamentary Party at Westminster, 1900–18* (Manchester, 2016).
Murphy, J.H., *Abject loyalty: nationalism and monarchy in Ireland during the reign of Queen Victoria* (Cork, 2001).
Naughton, L., *Markievicz: a most outrageous rebel* (Newbridge, 2016).
Nevin, D., *James Connolly* (Dublin, 2005).
Ní Dhonnchadha, M. and Dorgan, T. (eds), *Revising the Rising* (Derry, 1991).
Norman, E.J., *Hadlow, 1929–1979* (Masterton, 1979).
Norstedt, J., *Thomas MacDonagh: a critical biography* (Charlottesville, 1980).
Nowlan, Kevin B. (ed.), *The making of 1916: studies in the history of the Rising* (Dublin, 1969).
O'Brien, C.C. (ed.), *The shaping of modern Ireland* (London, 1960).
O'Brien, M., *The Irish Times* (Dublin, 2008).
O'Brien, P., *Havoc: the Auxiliaries in Ireland's War of Independence* (Cork, 2017).
Ó Broin, L., *Dublin Castle and the 1916 Rising* (New York, 1971).
Ó Broin, L., *The chief secretary: Augustine Birrell in Ireland* (London, 1969).
Ó Broin, L., *William Wylie and the Irish Revolution* (Dublin, 1989).
O Donoghue, B., *Activities wise and otherwise: the career of Sir Henry Augustus Robinson, 1898–1922* (Sallins, 2015).
O'Donoghue, F., 'Plans for the 1916 Rising', *University Review*, 3 (Mar. 1963), pp 3–21.
O'Farrell, P., *Who's who in the Irish War of Independence, 1916–1921* (Dublin, 1980).
O'Higgins, B., *The soldier's story of Easter Week* (Dublin, 1925).
O'Malley, E., *On another man's wound* (Dublin, 1979).
O'Sullivan, B., 'New Zealand and the peaked felt hat', *Volunteers*, 39:2 (2017), pp 72–9.
Pašeta, S., *Before the revolution: nationalism, social change and Ireland's Catholic elite, 1879–1922* (Cork, 1999).

Pašeta, S. (ed.), *Uncertain futures: essays about the Irish past for Roy Foster* (Oxford, 2016).
Phillips, W.A., *The revolution in Ireland, 1906–1923* (London, 1923).
Price, S., *A mind of his own: the childhood of Hugh Price* (Wellington, 2012).
Pugsley, C. and Ferrall, C. (eds), *Remembering Gallipoli* (Wellington, 2015).
Pugsley, C., *The Anzac experience: New Zealand, Australia and empire in the First World War* (Auckland, 2004).
Reid, C., *The lost Ireland of Stephen Gwynn* (Manchester, 2011).
Reilly, L., 'Frank Thornton: a Drogheda man's contribution to the 1916 Rising' in Brendan Matthews (ed.), *Reflections on the 1916 Rising* (Drogheda, 2016).
Renan, E., 'What is a nation?' in Geoff Eley and Ronald Grigor Suny (eds), *Becoming nation: a reader* (Oxford, 1996), pp 41–55.
Richardson, N., *According to their lights: stories of Irishmen in the British army, Easter 1916* (Cork, 2015).
Robbins, F., *Under the Starry Plough* (Dublin, 1977).
Rogers, A., *With them through Hell: New Zealand medical services in the First World War* (Auckland, 2018).
Ryan, J., 'In the GPO: the medical unit' in F.X. Martin (ed.), *The Easter Rising 1916 and University College Dublin* (Dublin, 1966), pp 83–90.
Sagarra, E., *Kevin O'Shiel, Tyrone nationalist and Irish state-builder* (Dublin, 2013).
Sandford, S., *Neither unionist nor nationalist: the 10th (Irish) Division in the Great War* (Sallins, 2015).
Sexton, B., *Ireland and the crown, 1922–1936* (Dublin, 1989).
Sinn Fein rebellion handbook (Dublin, 1916); republished as *1916 Rebellion handbook* (Dublin, 1998).
Sisson, E., *Pearse's patriots: St Enda's and the cult of boyhood* (Cork, 2004).
Smith, S.J., *The Samoa (NZ) Expeditionary Force, 1914–1915* (Wellington, 1924).
Stanford, W.B. and McDowell, R.B., *Mahaffy: a biography of an Anglo-Irishman* (London, 1971).
Starkie, W., *Scholars and gypsies: an autobiography* (London, 1963).
Stephens, J., *The insurrection in Dublin* (Gerrards Cross, 1978).
Stowers, R., *Bloody Gallipoli* (Wellington, 2005).
Stowers, R., *Heroes of Gallipoli* (Christchurch, 2015).
Sweetman, R., *Bishop in the dock: the sedition trial of James Liston in New Zealand* (Dublin, 2007).
Sweetman, R., 'Beery Bill the Orangeman: another look at William Ferguson Massey' in James Watson and Lachy Paterson (eds), *A great New Zealand prime minister? Reappraising William Ferguson Massey* (Dunedin, 2011), pp 77–86.
Sweetman, R., 'New Zealand Catholicism, war, politics and the Irish issue, 1912–1922' (PhD, University of Cambridge, 1990).
Sweetman, R., 'Who fears to speak of Easter Week? Antipodean Irish Catholic responses to the 1916 Rising' in Ruan O'Donnell (ed.), *The impact of the 1916 Rising: among the nations* (Dublin, 2008), pp 71–90.
Taaffe, M., *Those days are gone away* (London, 1959).

Taylor, J.W., *Guilty but insane: J.C. Bowen-Colthurst: villain or victim?* (Cork, 2016).

Tierney, M., *Eoin MacNeill: scholar and man of action, 1867–1945* (Oxford, 1980).

Tolerton, J., *An awfully big adventure: New Zealand World War One veterans tell their stories* (Auckland, 2013).

Townend, P.A., *The road to home rule: anti-imperialism and the Irish national movement* (Madison, 2016).

Townshend, C., *Easter 1916: the Irish rebellion* (London, 2006).

Townshend, C., *Political violence in Ireland* (Oxford, 1983).

Trinity and the Rising (Dublin, 2015).

Wallace, S., *War and the image of Germany: British academics, 1914–1918* (Edinburgh, 1988).

Wells, W.B. and Marlowe, N., *A history of the Irish rebellion of 1916* (Dublin, 1916).

West, T., *The bold collegians: the development of sport in Trinity College, Dublin* (Dublin, 1991).

White, L.W. and Quinn, J. (eds), *1916: portraits and lives* (Dublin, 2015).

Willoughby, R., *A military history of the University of Dublin and its Officers Training Corps, 1910–1922* (Limerick, 1989).

Wren, J., *The GPO Garrison Easter Week 1916* (Dublin, 2015).

Wright, M., *Shattered glory: the New Zealand experience at Gallipoli and the Western Front* (London, 2010).

Yeates, P., *A city in wartime: Dublin 1914–18* (Dublin, 2012).

Index

Numbers in italics refer to plates.

Adelaide (South Australia) 62
Aden 62
Africa 77; west 61n38
Afrikaners 55
air raids 67
Albany (Western Australia) 62
Alberta (Canada) 112
Alexandria (Egypt) 62–4
Alton, Ernest Henry 'Tubby' (OTC Captain) 24–5, 27, 36, 39–40, 40n21, 40n24, 41n30, 43–4, 47, 49, 52, 74, 77, 81, 83, 112, 115–17, 121, 123, 131, 140, 142, *7*
ambulances 23, 43, 74, 117, 135; field 62; Indian 92
ambushes 45, 123, 146
ammunition 80n31, 91, 91n68, 103, 105, 112–13, 115, 124, 128
Anglo-Irish Treaty (1921) 28, 82–3
animals 41, 52–3, 75, 99, 109, 112, 116, 132, 134–5
Anzac Cove 64, 91, *22*; *see also* Gallipoli
Anzac Day 67, 92, 100, 142
Anzacs (Australian and New Zealand Army Corps) 64; *see also* soldiers
Apia (Samoa) 61
armoury, Royal College of Surgeons 38, 38n14; OTC 39–40, 43, 47, 76–7, 80, 82, 119, 123, 128, 142, 145
army:
  Australian Imperial Force 63–5, 144
  Australian and New Zealand Army Corps 64
  British 53, 82, 82n2, 113, 132; Mediterranean Expeditionary Force 64
  regiments, British: 9th (Scottish) Division 83; Army Ordnance Corps 110, 112; Manchester Regiment 110; Middlesex Imperial Yeomanry 112; Royal Army Medical Corps 73, 99, 116, 133; Royal Field Artillery 143; Royal Scots (Lothian Regiment) 145; Sherwood Foresters (Nottinghamshire and Derbyshire Regiment) 53, 113, 134
  regiments, Irish 82, 82n2, 87; 10th Cavalry Reserve Regiment 134; 10th (Irish) Division 42, 64; 16th (Irish) Division 88; Connaught Rangers 82n2; Irish Guards 92, 112; Leinster Regiment 51, 82n2, 120; Royal Dublin Fusiliers 41–2, 68, 82n2, 92, 98, 110, 112; Royal Irish Fusiliers 68n63; Royal Irish Lancers 112; Royal Irish Rifles 39, 82n2, 92, 110, 112, 123, 144; Royal Munster Fusiliers 41, 82n2; South Irish Horse 82n2, 112; *see also* Irish Command; Officers' Training Corps; Volunteer Training Corps
  territorial, British 64; New Zealand 37n5, 60; South Staffordshire Territorials 53, 53n111, 134
  Canadian: 18th Battalion 83; 56th Battalion 56

army: *(continued)*
German, absence of 89, 122
Indian 63, 92
New Zealand 36, 57, 57n8, 59–60, 63–5; Samoan Expeditionary Force 59–61, 98
regiments: 3rd (Auckland) Regiment 61; 6th Hauraki Company, Auckland Battalion 63; NZ Field Artillery 65, 85; NZ Field Engineers 64, 85, 144; NZ Medical Corps 37, 61–2; NZ Mounted Field Ambulance 62; Trentham Rifle Brigade 61
Ottoman 63, 65, 91
South African: 1st South African Infantry Brigade 56; 3rd South African Division 26n36; 3rd and 4th Regiments 56, 53n114; Cape Town Highlanders 56; Transvaal Scottish 56
artillery 52, 52n105, 77–8, 91, 101, 104–5, 107, 113, 115, 118, 120–1, 130, 133, 135–6, 142
Asquith, Herbert H. 23, 23n14–15, 24, 25n28, 77, 89, *2*, *5*
assault, indecent 143
Atatürk, Mustafa Kemal 65
Athlone (Westmeath) 52
Auckland (NZ) 63, 67, 85–6, 98; Auckland Grammar School 60, 98; North Shore 143
Auckland Weekly News 12, 21, 22
Australia 55, 57, 60n33, 62, 65, 85, 94, 102n1, 144–5
Austria-Hungary 92
Automobile Association, Irish 84
Auxiliaries 27, 27–8n44
Averill, Alfred W., Anglican archbishop of New Zealand 59
Awapuni camp (NZ) 62
awards: *see* honours; medals

Bank of Ireland 24, 30–1, 45–6, 48, 50n95, 51, 100, 120, 128–9, *28*; rebel attack on 50–1, 101, 129
banks 24, 49, 110, 113, 120, 129
barracks 31, 39, 43; military 112, 119; police 112, 117; Beggar's Bush 39, 43, 43n44, 72, 117, 121, 123, 143; Portobello 43, 86; Richmond 23, *5*
barricades 104–6, 109, 114, 122, 125–6, 136
Barton, Brian 34n36
Bassett, Corporal Cyril 64n51
battlecruisers 58
Beckett, Samuel, dismal prospects of 144
beef, bully: *see* food, army
Beggar's Bush: *see* barracks
Belfast 101, 126, 130, 146
Belich, James (historian) 55, 58n22
Bendigo (Victoria) 102n1
Berkeley, George, bishop of Cloyne 125
Berlin, Friedrich Wilhelm University 146
Birmingham 64–5
Birrell, Augustine 25n28, 77, 114, 145
biscuits, ship's: *see* food, army
Black and Tans 86
blacksmiths 67
Blackwood's Magazine 40
Blake, William Hume 111, 115
Boland's Bakery 44–5, 73, 73n90, 78
bombardment 17, 22, 24, 61, 78, 91, 101, 104–5, 107, 118, 130, 142; aerial 67
Book of Kells 142
booksellers 64
Bootle (Lancashire) 146
Boulogne 84
Bowen-Colthurst, Captain J.C. 88, 88n42, 145
Bracken, John (senior) 72n83
Bracken, John Edward 72n83
Brennan-Whitmore, Captain William James 48–9, 70; *Dublin burning: the Easter Rising from behind the barricades* (1961) 142
brewery, Guinness 44, 105, 126
bridges: Butt 130–1; Carlisle 135; Loop Line 76; Mount Street 52, 80; O'Connell 37, 47, 52, 78; Westland Row railway 76, 118
Britishness, concept of 55–6, 58–9, 94n87

Brockenhurst (Hampshire), NZ General Hospital 84
Brown, Rentoul 107
Brown, Terence 28n46
Browning, F.H. 39n18, 123
Buller, General Sir Redvers H. 33
bullets, dumdum 91, 91n68, 103, 105; *see also* ammunition
Bureau of Military History 18–19, 46, 48, 51
burials, at TCD 111, 113, 134
Burke, Edmund 125
Burton, Ormond 64, 66
business premises, near TCD 24, 110, 113, 129, 133
Butt, Isaac 93

cadets, army officer 85; Dublin University OTC 40, 42, 52–3, 76, 82, 116, 119, 124, 126, 130–1, 138; New Zealand school 60, 98; *see also* Officers' Training Corps
Cairo 64
Calgary (Alberta) 56
Cambridge University 146; Peterhouse 12; St John's College 146
Campbell, James, Baron Glenavy 27, 34
camps, army: Awapuni 62; Codford 66, 85; Curragh 44n60, 45, 110, 113, 118, 126, 130; Étaples 85; Grey Towers 66; Limburg 94n87; Shorncliffe 57; Zeitoun 64
Canada 55–7, 83, 94, 143; French Canadians 55
Canterbury (NZ) 60, 104
Cape Town 56
Carisbrook Castle (ship) 64
Carney, Winifred 142
Carson, Sir Edward 34, 94
Casement, Sir Roger 92, 94n87
Cassidy, Howard Francis 56, 83
casualties: *see* civilians; soldiers
Catholicism 33, 58; Catholics 32, 67, 86, 94n87, 144
celebrations, St Patrick's Day 33
Central Powers 92
ceremonies, awards 24, 87, *4*
Ceylon 62, 64
chaplains, army 105, 134
Charlton, Blackburn 53n114, 56, 83
Childers, Erskine H. 93
children 132, 139, 143; wounded 105, 134–5
Christchurch (NZ) 57, 62, 67, 70, 98, 104, 107, 143, 145
Chunuk Bair (Gallipoli) 63, 65, 64n51
Church Army 66
Church of Ireland 33, 146
churches: St Andrew's 71, 99, 102
cigarettes 42, 127, 131, 136
City Hall (Dame Street) 45, 51, 69n66, 105, 113, 128, 130
civil servants 143
civilians: attitudes towards Anzacs 87; attitudes towards soldiers 68; deaths of 53n111, 74, 88, 90–1, 105, 135, 143; injured 90–1, 105, 134–5; recklessness of 91, 118, 129, 132
Clare, County 94
classics 142
clergymen 57, 59, 59n23, 144, 146
Clonmel (County Tipperary) 146
clubs, social 42
Codford (Wiltshire), military depot 66, 85
College Restaurant (College Street) 45
College of Surgeons: *see* Royal College
Collins, Michael 146
Colombo (Sri Lanka) 62
commissariat, OTC 116–17
communications 43, 45, 118, 120, 124; postal 137, 139; telegraphic 105, 126
Connolly, James 22–3, 30–1, 37, 45–6, 46n65, 47, 74–5, 80, 80n31, 101, 142
conscription 57
Cook, Lieutenant-Colonel Percy 62
cooks 85, 118; French 92, 116, 129
Corrigan, Eileen M. 51n100
Cosgrave, Liam 81
Cosgrave, William 28
Cowan, Colonel H.V. 50
Crawford, George 38

cricketers 39n18
crime 143; *see also* looting
Cromwell, Oliver 114
Cumann na mBan 46n63
cups, commemorative 24–6, 26n36, 82n1, 85–7, 146, *4*, *27*
Curragh camp 44n60, 45, 110, 113, 118, 126, 130
Custom House 49, 69–70, 74, 79, 100, 103, 110, 142
cyclists 105–6, 109, 119, 122–3, 139; rebel 49, 113–14, 128

Dáil Éireann 82–3, 142
Daily Express building (Parliament Street) 51, 73, 107, 109, 113, 126, 128, 130
Daily Mail 50
Dalby's lodging house (Eden Quay) 70n75
Dalkey (Dublin) 109
Daly, Ned 78
Dardanelles: *see* Gallipoli
Davis, Private George 68n65, 86n26
Davis, Thomas 31
deaths: civilians 53n111, 74, 88, 90–1, 105, 135, 143; rebels 73, 75, 108, 113; soldiers 83, 134
decorations, military 83, 142–4
defence, imperial 60; policy 58
Delville Wood, battle (1916) 83, 92
despatch riders 87n30, 113–14, 120, 128
de Valera, Eamon 28, 32, 34n36, 45, 72–3, 76, 79, 80, 80n31, 81, 83, 142
diarrhoea 66
Dickson, David (historian) 17, 24, 87
Dillon, John 90–1
disease 36, 56–7, 61, 64–6, 83–5, 101; among medical staff 84–5n15
Dockrell, Sir Maurice E. 24, 26
dominions 55, 93–4; personification of *12*; *see also* individual countries
Don, Alexander (senior) 101, 102n1
Don, Corporal Alexander William 36–7, 47–8, 59–60, 63–5, 67–9, 71–2, 75, 84–6, 91, 101, 142–3, *25*, *26*, *27*
Don, Amelia *25*
Don family *25*
Donegal, County 143
Donovan, Philip 47
D'Oyly Carte Opera Company 70–1, 84, 104, 137–8, 143; *see also* Hobbs
Drennan, Frank: *see* Thornton
Drogheda (County Louth) 146
Dublin, damage to 17, 19, 22–4, 74–5, 77–8, 84, 99, 104, 107, 111, 117, 133, 139–40; *see also* Trinity College
  city streets: Abbey 24, 37, 68, 70, 102, *15*; Brunswick 44n56, 112–13, 117–18, 124–5, 130, 135; College 25, 37, 47; College Green 23, 27, 30–1, 43, 45, 47, 109, 113, *13*, *28*; Crown Alley 45; D'Olier 135; Dame 44n60, 47–9, 51, 68, 73–4, 99, 107, 113, 118, 124, 128–30; Dundrum Road 40, 121; Eden Quay 70, 70n75; Fleet 45, 46, 51; Frederick 146; George's 69n66; Grafton 47–9, 99, 103, 113, 118, 122, 124, 128–9, *28*; Great Brunswick (now Pearse) 43n47, 72, 76, 79; Haddington Road 88, 114; Harcourt 27–8n44; Hawkins 130; Henry 24; Kildare 44n60; King 53n111; Merrion Row 109; Merrion Square 26n31, 48n73, 111, 115; Moore 79n22; Mount 26n31, 53, 139; Nassau 43, 44n56, 44n60, 47, 112–13, 125, 128, 131–2; Sackville (now O'Connell) 19, 24, 33, 37, 39, 47–8, 51, 68, 75, 78n21, 88, 98–9, 102–3, 105, 107, 109–12, 114, 122, 129; St Andrew's 71; St Stephen's Green 18, 35, 37, 39, 44, 44n55, 47, 48n73, 49, 69, 88–9, 99–100, 104, 107, 109, 112–14, 118, 120–2; Tara 74, 52, 130; Westland Row 44n56, 72, 99, 112, 117, 125, 127; Westmoreland 44–5, 47–8, 113, 118, 124, 129, *29*
Dublin Bay 44

Dublin Bread Company building 48, 70
Dublin Brigade: *see* rebel forces
Dublin Castle 23n15, 27, 30–1, 36, 44–5, 48, 51, 101, 103, 107, 109, 112, 114, 126, 128, 130
Dublin Mountains 119
Dublin University 23n10; *see* Trinity College
Dudley Edwards, Owen (historian) 90
Duff, Charles 87
Dunedin (NZ) 64, 67, 101
dysentery 61, 66

Easter Rising 17–24, 36–40, 42–54, 68–80, 87–95, 98–141
Edgbaston (Birmingham), 1st Southern General Hospital 64–5
Egypt 36, 62–5, 84, 92, 92n76
election, general (1918) 82
empire, British 55, 63, 86, 92; Irish part in 21, 83, 93–4
England 36, 57, 59, 61, 64–7, 84–5, 113, 126, 138, 144–6
enteric fever (typhoid) 64–6, 101
entertainments, troops 66
Ervine, St John 47n67, 48n73
Étaples (Pas-de-Calais), camp 85
examinations 51n100, 82, 107–8, 116

Fanning, Ronan (historian) 50–1n96
Farmers Trading Company 145
Fianna Fáil 28, 144
Finnigan (Dublin Metropolitan Police inspector) 138
Finns 53n113
fire brigade station (Great Brunswick and Tara Streets) 74, 133, 140
firearms 38–40, 43n44, 49, 51–2, 60, 73–4, 91, 99, 101–2, 107, 110, 112–13, 115, 117, 119, 121, 123–4, 128, *14*
fires 19, 70, 74–5, 84, 100, 104–5, 111, 114, 135, 139–40
first aid 62, 135, 138
Fitzgerald, Desmond 21n1, 44
Fitzgibbon, Gerald (OTC sergeant) 26, 40, 40n24, 42, 47–8n73, 49, 52, 73n89, 77, 83, 88, 111, 115, 117, 143
Fitzpatrick, David (historian) 17, 19–20
flags: imperial 23, 33, 59, *21*, *29*; Irish republican 100, 107, 122; New Zealand 59; Red Cross 90; white, of surrender 79n22
Folkestone (Kent) 57
food, army 65–7, 69, 104, 110, 114, 116–18, 126–7, 129, 132, 136; shortages 104–5, 132, 134–6
football, rugby 39n18, 142
Four Courts 78, 105, 111
Foy, Michael 34n36
France 84–5, 92, 115, 144–5
Freeman's Journal 92
Fulham (London) 65
funding, state, of university 81

Gaiety Theatre (South King Street) 70, 104
Gallipoli 36, 37n5, 41–2, 59–60, 63–4, 64n51, 65–6, 85, 91–2, 92n71, 94, 94n84, 102, 128–9, 145, *22*
Garland, Corporal John Godwin 37, 41n30, 48–9, 59–63, 63n44, 67–75, 84–6, 89, 91, 98, 143, *8*, *15*, *20*
Garland, Harriet (née Threader) 61
Garland, Thomas Henry 61, 98
General Post Office (Sackville Street) 18, 22, 31, 37, 41, 45–9, 53, 68, 75, 78, 78n21, 79, 89, 99–103, 105, 109, 112–13, 120–2, 126, 139, 142, *18*
geologists 144
George V, king 55
Germany 92, 94n87; assistance to rebels 89, 89n48, 91, 110–11, 115; hostility towards 146
Gerrard, Captain Edward 88n38
Gibson, George 56, 83
Glen, Lieutenant James A. 38, 52, 77, 143
Glenavy, James Campbell, Baron 27, 34
Gloucester 144
Gneisenau, SMS 61
Godley, Major-General Alexander 60
Goldsmith, Oliver 125
golfers 143
Gonne, Maud 33

gonorrhoea 56–7
'Gorgeous Wrecks': *see* Volunteer Training Corps
governors, colonial 59, 59n23
Grant, Bob 68n65
Grattan, Henry 31; statue 69, 128, 132
'Greater Britishness' 58–9
Greece 64–5, 67
Grey River Argus (NZ newspaper) 100
Grey Towers, Hornchurch (Essex) 36, 64–6, 64, 84
Grimes, John J., Catholic bishop of Christchurch (NZ) 57
grocers 61
Grosvenor Hotel (Westland Row) 72, 99
Gualter, Aubrey 100
Guest, Alice, Viscountess Wimborne *2*
Guinness, Edward, Viscount Iveagh 124
Guinness' brewery 44, 105, 126
gunboats 104, 133, 142
Gurkhas 64
Gwynne, Robin 76n2, 116

Hadlow Preparatory School for Boys (NZ) 86, 86n25, 142
Hague Convention (1899) 91n68
Ham, William 63
Hamilton, Sir William Rowan 125
Hamilton, Lieutenant-General Sir Ian 60, 64, 92, 145
Harris, George Arthur (OTC major) 23–4, 39–40, 43, 43n44, 50n95, 117, 119, 121–3, 143
hats, slouch 37n5, 68, 71–2, 99, 101, *14*, *26*
Hayes-McCoy, G.A. (historian) 46, 80
health, mental 83–4, 138
Healy, J.E. 142
Helga, HMY 133, 142
Henderson, Frank 34n36
history, political uses of 95n89
Hobbs, Frederick Henry 70, 73n89, 84, 100, 104, 143
Holyhead (Anglesey) 67
home rule 21, 34, 83, 93–4, 114–15, 140
honours: Order of the British Empire 146; *see also* medals
Hornchurch (Essex), Grey Towers convalescent hospital 36, 64–6, 64, 84
Horne, John (historian) 17
horses 41, 52–3, 75, 99, 109, 112, 116, 132, 134–5
hospitals 74, 112, 135; Sir Patrick Dun's (Grand Canal Street) 25
  emergency 133; Dublin Castle 31
  military 36, 56, 62, 64–6, 84–5, 95, 101; 1st Southern General Hospital, Edgbaston 64–5; Grey Towers convalescent hospital, Hornchurch 36, 64–6, 64, 84; Imtarfa Military Hospital, Malta 65; New Zealand War Contingent Hospital, Walton-on-Thames 64, 85; Royal Victoria Hospital, Netley 64
  ships 62–3, 67, 73, 84, 84n15, 85, 145–6, *20*
Howth (County Dublin) 91
Hulluch, battle (1916) 88
hurling 28n47
Hyde, Douglas 31

illness: *see* disease
Imperial Hotel (Sackville Street) 48, 142
imperialism 58–9, 83; opposition to 93
imprisonment, rebels 146
Imtarfa Military Hospital, Mtarfa (Malta) 65
Inchicore (Dublin) 23, *5*
independence, Irish 28, 115; *see also* home rule
India 55; Indians 23
industrial disputes 89
influenza 65, 85
injuries: civilians 90–1, 105, 134–5; soldiers 65, 83, 85, 99
insanity 138
intelligence gathering 44, 77, 109, 122, 130–1; rebel 35, 46n63, 137, 146
invasion: rumours 138; threat 89
Irish Brigade (Sir Roger Casement's) 92, 94n87
Irish Citizen Army 18, 37, 71–2, 74, 76, 76n2, 90

Irish Command 117–18, 121, 128
Irish Free State 79, 83
Irish Parliamentary Party 23
Irish Republican Army 27–8n44, 34, 46n63, 78n21
Irish Republican Brotherhood 21, 55, *15*
Irish Rugby Football Union 39n18
Irish Times 41–2, 44, 70n75, 86, 89, 91–2, 142
Irish Volunteers 19, 22, 34–5, 39, 44n55, 45, 48, 67n59, 68, 72, 74, 79, 90–1, 104, 146
Irish War News 139
Irish, Tomás (historian) 19, 27, 28–9n51–2, 47, 54, 77n6
Irish Transport and General Workers Union 142; *see also* Liberty Hall
Iveagh, Edward Guinness, Viscount 124

Jackson, Alvin (historian) 93
Jackson, Valentine 26n31
Jacob's Biscuit Factory (Bishop Street) 44, 78, 126, 144
Jeffery, Keith (historian) 92
Joly, John 19–20, 30, 40–1, 44, 44n60, 45, 47, 49, 51, 53, 53n111, 69, 70–1, 74–7, 77n8, 78, 82–3, 89, 91–2, 94, 121, 144, *6*
journalists 142
Jubilee, Diamond (1897) 33
judges 83
Junior Army and Navy Stores (D'Olier Street) 136

Kelly, Thomas Joseph 72n83
Kelly & Son, M., fishing tackle manufacturer and gunpowder office (Sackville Street and Bachelors Walk) 135
Keogh, Gerald Anthony 49, 74, 87n30, 144, *23*
Kiberd, Declan 31
Kildea, Jeff (historian) 54, 73
Killashee (County Longford) 143
Killiney Hill Park (Dublin) 98, 102
kilts 56
Kimmage (Dublin) 146
Kinahan, Private (South African soldier) 26n36, 57n7
King, Eric 56, 83
King's Inns (Henrietta Street) 23
Kingsmill Moore, T.C. 27
Kingstown (now Dún Laoghaire) 105, 113
Kitchener, Field Marshal Horatio H., Earl 60, 77–8
knighthoods 146
Kruger, Paul 33

labour disturbances 38, 89n45, 140
labourers 65
Ladysmith, relief of (1900) 33
Lahiff, Police Constable Michael 69
landlordism 140
languages: German 146; Italian 146
Larkinite movement (1907–14) 140
Le Havre 84
Leader (newspaper) 33
leave, army 15, 36, 39–40, 56, 67, 85, 88, 98, 104, 107, 112, 119, 121, 123, 140, 143, 146
Lecky, William (historian) 125
lectures 32, 46, 86
Leipzig University 146
Leitrim, County 146
Lemnos (Greece) 64–5
Liberty Hall 52, 78, 104, 107, 110, 120, 130–1, 133, 140, 142
Limburg an der Lahn (Hesse), prisoner of war camp 94n87
Limerick 83
Linwood (Christchurch) 62
literature, English 144; German 146
Liverpool 45, 146
Liverpool Daily Post 70, 102
Lodge, Viceregal, Phoenix Park 23, 45n59
London 59, 61, 65, 67
Longford, County 143
looting 24, 49–50, 69, 99–100, 104, 109–11, 113–14, 120, 129, 132, 139
Louth, County 146
Louvain (Belgium) 24; University library 78, 78n19
Loveridge, Steven (historian) 57

Lowe, Brigadier-General William H.M. 78
loyalism 83; imperial 58–9, 93
Loyalist Association of Ireland 143
Luce, Arthur Aston (OTC lieutenant) 27n37, 28, 39, 49, 83, 87, 123, 144
Lynn, Kathleen 69
Lyons, F.S.L. (historian) 17
Lyons, George A. 72, 72n83
Lyttelton (NZ) 145–6
Lytton, Sir Henry 70

machine guns 40, 51–2, 105, 107, 110, 120, 133, 136
machinists 67
MacDonagh, Thomas Stanislaus 31, 34–5, 35n38, 59, 79–80, 144
MacNeill, Eoin 22, 28, 31n14, 34, 34n38, 47, 79, 142
McArthur, Geoff 87n28
McBride, John 94
McBride, Patrick 72n83
McCarthy, Kevin 87, 87n28
McConnell, Albert J. 28, 81
McDermott (TCD student) 107
McDermott, Sean 23
McDowell, R.B. (historian) 17, 25, 30
McGibbon, Ian (historian) 58
McHugh, Michael John 48, 63–6, 87, 144–5, *13*, *14*
McHugh, Willie 65
McKee, Dick 34n36
McKenzie & Sons, Thomas, hardware and seed merchants (Great Brunswick Street) 133
McLeod, Donald 144
McLeod, Finlay (senior) 100
McLeod, Lance Corporal Finlay Hugh 38, 48, 59–60, 60n33, 63–4, 64n51, 66–8, 69, 72–3, 85, 91–2, 100, 144–5, *13*, *14*
Magazine Fort, Phoenix Park 45
Mahaffy, Elizabeth ('Elsie') 22n8, 23n15, 34n38, 44n54, 46n67, 47, 52–3, 73n90, 77, 77n7, 79, 91, 145
Mahaffy, John Pentland 24, 30, 32–3, 83, 90, 123, 132–3, 145, *2*, *3*
Maheno, HMHS 62
Malaya 145
Mallin, Michael 76
Malta 64–5
Mansion House (Dawson Street) 33
manufacturers, baking powder 61
Marama, HMHS 62–3, 67, 73, 84, 84n15, 85, 145–6, *20*
Markievicz, Constance, Countess 68–9, 69n66, 74, 98, 135
marksmanship 48–9, 114; *see also* snipers
Marshall, Joseph 38, 38n15, 82
Marshall, Robert (historian) 79n21
martial law 106
Massey, William 57
Masterton (NZ) 86n25
Maunganui, HMNZT 65
Maxwell, General Sir John Grenfell 22–3, 45, 52, 77–9, 63, 84–5, 90–1, 143, 145, *2*, *3*
Meagher, Michael 72n83
Meagher, Patrick 72n83
mechanics, motor 64, 67
medals 142–4; Distinguished Service Order 143; Military Cross 83, 142, 144; Victoria Cross 64n51
medical: orderlies 84, 88–9; supplies 112; New Zealand Medical Corps 37, 61; Royal Army Medical Corps 73, 99, 116, 133
Mediterranean Sea 62–3
Mein, Charles (OTC sergeant) 39, 119, 145
Messines, battle (1917) 85, 94
Methodists 61, 67
militarism 59, 78, 90
military exercises 119; sham fights 114
Military Service Act, NZ (1916) 57
Ministry of Defence, NZ 146
Moffitt, George 56, 83
Moody, T.W. (historian) 17
Moore, Laurence 72n83
Mount Eden (Auckland) 61
Mtarfa (Malta), Imtarfa Military Hospital 65
Mudros (Lemnos) 64–5
mules 52, 116

Mullen, Lieutenant 117
munitions workers 89
Murphy, John J. (Sean) 72n83
museums: Auckland War Memorial 61
music 138; *see also* opera troupes

Nathan, Sir Matthew 22, 90
nationalism 115; constitutional 93–4, 140; cultural 33; Irish 93–4, 94n84
navy, German 110–11; German East Asia Squadron 61; Royal Navy 58; Royal Naval Reserve 92
Nelson's Pillar (Sackville Street) 103, *18*
Netley (Hampshire), Royal Victoria Hospital 64
neuritis 64–5
Nevin, Sergeant Frederick Leslie 37, 48–9, 59–60, 62–3, 67–70, 84–6, 89, 98, 100, 102, 142, 144–6, *15*, *20*; father 85
Newfoundland 58n17, 92n71
newspapers, lack of 139; New Zealand 50; *see also* individual titles
Newtown Cunningham (County Donegal) 143
New Zealand 57–60, 60n33, 61–2, 64, 85, 94, 142–5; links with United Kingdom 55, 57–8, 58n22, 59; Irish in 86; *see also* army; soldiers
New Zealand Dairy Association 61, 143
New Zealand Herald (newspaper) 57
New Zealand, HMS 58
Norway, Arthur 48, 49n82
nurses, military 85n15, *25*

O Buachalla, Domhnall 48
O'Connell, Daniel 93
O'Connor, Joseph 34n36
Offaly, County 144
Officers' Training Corps, Dublin University 22–6, 26–7n37, 26n31, 27, 34, 38, 42, 43n44, 54, 78n21, 82, 85–7, 89, 98, 100, 105, 107–11, 115–17, 119–21, 125, 130, 135, 138, 143, 146, *2*, *3*; Service Corps 112–13; Royal College of Surgeons 23; *see also* cadets
O'Grady, Con 88
O'Halpin, Eunan (historian) 19, 34
O'Malley, Ernie 71, 76–7, 94
O'Neill, Andrew 72n83
Ontario 56
opera troupes 70–1, 84, 100, 104, 137–8, 143
O'Rahilly, Michael Joseph (The O'Rahilly) 94
Orange Order 86, 143
orderlies, medical 37, 61–2, 84–5, 88–9; *see also* Nevin and Garland; nurses 85n15, 25
orphans 143
O'Shiel, Kevin 32
Otago (NZ) 64
Ottawa (Ontario) 112

Pacific, South 60–1
Paddy (cook) 116
Palmerston North (NZ) 62
pandemic, influenza (1918–19) 85
Papeete (Tahiti) 61
parliament 93; members of 34, 83, 94, 143
parliament house, former Irish: *see* Bank of Ireland
patriotism, imperial 93–4; Irish 90, 115
patrols 69, 73n92, 101, 112–14, 116, 118, 126–8
pay, army 66–7
Peace Day (19 July 1919) *29*
Pearle, Richard 72n83
Pearse, Patrick 22, 31–2, 37n5, 44, 59, 69n69, 75, 79, 79n22, 87, 90–1, 145
pensions, army disability 85
petitions 34
philosophers 144
Phoenix Park (Dublin) 23, 45, 45n59
photography, colour 144; illegal 146
physicists 144
pickets 107, 114, 118; *see also* patrols; sentries
pikes 38, 76
planets: Mars, Joly Crater 144; Venus 135
plate, silver 82n1

Plunkett, Joseph 34, 142
Plunkett, William C., 4th Baron, archbishop of Dublin 59n23
Plunkett, William Lee, 5th Baron 59, 59n23
pneumonia 85
poisoning, rumoured 91
Police, Dublin Metropolitan 38, 38n15, 43, 48, 70–1, 109, 117, 122–3, 130, 133, 136; Royal Irish Constabulary 38n15
police stations: Great Brunswick Street 70–1, 104, 117, 130, 136–8; Dalkey 109
policemen 121, 138; shooting of 69, 104, 121
policing 114; military, colonial methods of 77–8
politicians, Irish-born dominion 57
porters, TCD 25, 37–8, 47, 76, 101, 107, 109, 134, *19*; Bank of Ireland 50
Portobello Barracks (Rathmines) 43, 86
post office: *see* General Post Office; communications
Potchefstroom (South Africa) 56
Prendergast, Patrick 29
Presbyterians 67
prime ministers: *see* Asquith; de Valera; Massey; Seddon
printing works 70n75
prisoners of war, Fenian (1867) 138; German 138; Irish in Germany 94n87; rebel 23, 69–70, 75, 101–3, 110, 114–15, 119–20, 138, 140, 142
proclamations, Irish republic (1916) 22, 28, 75, 90, 92, 94, 106, 115, 139; military 77, 139; official 44
processions, St Patrick's Day 33
property losses 103; compensation 84, 143; Property Losses (Ireland) Committee 84
Protestantism 32–4, 83
provosts, TCD: *see* Alton; Mahaffy; McConnell; Prendergast
publishers 64

Queen's Theatre (Great Brunswick Street) 43n47, 76
Queen's University of Belfast 146
Queensland (Australia) 65, 144
Quinn, Sean (John) 72, 72n83, 73

raiding parties 46, 71–2, 99, 102, 131, 139
railways 43, 45; embankment 72, 119, 125–6, 131, *16*; workers 62, 144
  bridges: Loop Line 76, Westland Row 76, 118
  stations 105; Kingsbridge (now Heuston) 130; Westland Row (now Pearse) 43, 45, 72–4, 72n83, 73n84, 74, 79–80, 99, 101, 112, 118–19, 125; Harcourt Street 126
Ranelagh (Dublin) 59, 144
Rathmines (Dublin) 43
rebels 122; betrayal of 115; bravery of 90; deaths of 99, 114, 128; executions of 22; German assistance to 89; mobilization 22, 79–80; motivation 50, 89–90; preparations 35, 114; public sympathy for 88; strategy 78–80, 89, 110–11, 122; surrender of 75, 79n22, 102–4; women 73–4, 129; *see also* prisoners
rebel forces:
  Irish Citizen Army 18, 37, 71–2, 74, 76, 76n2, 90
  Irish Volunteers 19, 22, 34–5, 39, 44n55, 45, 48, 67n59, 68, 72, 74, 79, 90–1, 104, 146
    Dublin Brigade 34n36; 1st Battalion 78; 2nd Battalion 80, 144; 3rd Battalion 34n36, 72, 72n83, 73n84, 76, 80, 80n31, 142; Liverpool Volunteer Company 146
rebellion, Fenian (1867) 138
'recolonization' thesis 58n22
Red Cross 23, 23n15, 62, 68, 85, 89, 90, 98, 105, 133, 135
Redmond, John 23, 31n14, 89, 89n48, 91, 93–4, 94n84

Redmond, William 94
regiments: *see* army
religious services, commemorative 67
Renan, Joseph Ernest (philosopher) 95
republic, Irish: *see* proclamation
reviews, military 22–4, *2*
revolvers 37–8, 43n44, 73–5, 99, 101, 115, 117–18, 128
rheumatic fever 85
Rhodesia, Southern (now Zimbabwe) 56
Richardson, Neil (historian) 53
Richmond Barracks (Inchicore) 23, *5*
rifles 91, 101–2, 107, 115, 119, 121, 123–4, 128, *14*; Lee–Enfield 60, 91; Mauser 91; Winchester repeating 99
riots, student 33; Dublin lock-out (1913) 38, 89n45
rising: *see* Easter
Roberts, General Frederick S. 33
Royal Bank of Ireland building (College Green) 101, 128
Royal College of Surgeons 38n14, 111; armoury 38, 38n14; Officers' Training Corps 23
Royal Dublin Society 44
rugby football 39n18, 142
rumours 44, 64, 79, 89, 119, 138–9
Ruskin, John 124
Russell, George 56–7, 83
Russia 92
Ryan, James 49, 79n22
Ryan, Min 49–50
Ryan, Phyllis 49

sailors, Swedish 53
St Andrew's Church of Ireland church (St Andrew's Street) 71, 99, 102
St Enda's School (Ranelagh) 59, 144
St John, order of 23
St Patrick's Cathedral, Dublin 105
St Patrick's Day parade 33
St Stephen's Green: *see* Dublin city streets
salesmen 145
Salonika 67
Samoa, Western (German) 59–62, *21*
Sari Bair range (Gallipoli) 63
Scharnhorst, SMS 61
schools 60n33, 86, 86n25, 100, 142
Scotland 145
scouting parties 117–18, 130–1; *see also* raiding parties
sea power 58; *see also* navy
searches, of houses 69, 101–2; of prisoners 69, 100, 114
Sedd el Bahr (Gallipoli) 41, 91–2
Seddon, Richard J. 55, 59
sentries 39, 43, 47, 50, 53, 69, 73n92, 76, 112–14, 116, 123, 125–7, 129, 131–7, 139–40, *19*
servants, college 25, 37–8, 47, 76, 82, 101, 107, 109, 134, *19*
sham fights, rebels 114
sharpshooters 70, 104, 110, 113, 128, 132; *see also* snipers
Sheehy-Skeffington, Francis, 'a poisonous microbe' 145
Sheffield Independent 14
Shelbourne Hotel (St Stephen's Green) 44n60, 45, 109
shell shock 83–4
ships, hospital 62–3, 67, 73, 84, 84n15, 85, 145–6, *20*; gunboats 104, 133, 142; troopships 63, 65; warships 58
shops, M. Kelly & Son (Sackville Street) 135; Great Brunswick Street tobacconist's 136, 139; department stores 145; *see also* banks; business premises
Shore, Terry 112
Shorncliffe camp (Kent) 57
Sikhs 64
singers 138, 143
Sinn Féin 27, 82–3, 98–9, 121
Slater, Thomas 34
Smith, Private A. 134
smoking 127, 131; *see also* cigarettes
snipers 38, 43, 44n56, 47–9, 64n51, 65, 67–8, 70–4, 78, 85, 88–91, 98–105, 107, 109–10, 112–14, 118–20, 128–9, 131, 135, 142; female 99, 73–4, 129

soldiers, camaraderie of 136; civilian antagonism towards 68, 100; dead 134; shooting at 36–7, 40–1, 44n56, 68, 68n65, 84, 88, 98, 100–1, 112, 123; wounded 84, 113; *see also* rebel forces
- Anzac 18, 26, 26n36, 40–1, 41n30, 47–51, 53, 64, 69, 72, 75, 88, 91–2, 94, 102, 110, 112, 114, 123, 128–9, 145, *22*; physical magnificence of 53, 53n112, 60, 126
- Australian 18–19, 41, 48, 54, 64, 67, 68n65, 86n26, 87, 98, 144, *14*; of Irish descent 144
- British 52–3, 53n111, 64, 72, 92, 101–2, 105–7, 110, 114, 116, 118–20, 123, 130, 133–4, 136–7, 144–5, *10*, *11*, *19*
- Canadian 38, 41, 53n114, 56, 92, 92n71, 98, 102, 110, 112
- colonial and dominion 26n36, 41, 47–50, 52, 92, 119; British-born 56–7; Irish-born 56
- French 64
- German 44, 115
- Indian 64
- Irish, in British army 41–2, 68, 68n63, 87–8, 94, 94n84, 94n87; *see also* Officers' Training Corps; Volunteer Training Corps
- Newfoundland 92n71
- New Zealand 18–19, 36–8, 41, 47–8, 59, 62–4, 64n51, 67, 86, 86n26, 89, 94–5, 98, 100–2, 104, 146, *13*, *14*, *21*, *25*, *26*; Irish-born 62–3; of English descent 63; NZ War Contingent Association 66
- South African 26n36, 38, 41, 53n114, 56–7, 57n7, 83, 98, 102, 110, 112
- Sri Lankan 64

Soldiers' Central Club (College Street) 25, 37, 68, 98
Somme, battle (1916) 84, 92
songs 71, 86–7, 138, 142
South Africa 55–7, 59, 83
Southampton 62, 64, 67, 70, 84
sports 28n47, 39n18, 66, 142–3
Stanford, William B. (classicist) 25
Starkie, Walter 42–3, 77
stations: *see* railways
statues 69, 128, 132
Stephens, James 44, 44n55, 48
steward, TCD 38, 82
Stokes, Lily 41n30
strategy, German 115; rebel 78–80, 89, 110–11, 122
students 32–4, 41–2, 76–6, 117; Indian 23; New Zealand 17
submarines, German 44, 111, 115
subsidies, naval 58
Suez (Egypt) 36, 62; Canal 63, 92
suicide 143
supreme court, Irish Free State 143
surrender, of rebels 75, 79n22, 102–4
Suvla Bay (Gallipoli) 42, 64, 92
Swedes 53, 53n113
swords, presentation 24, 146
Sydney (NSW) 144; Grammar School 60n33

Taafe, Michael 40, 76, 78–9
Tahiti 61
Tallaght, battle (1867) 138
Tannam, Liam 53n113
Tate, Robert William (OTC major) 24, 39, 121, 123, 146, *4*
TCD: A College Miscellany (magazine) 18, 21, 26, 31–2, 42, 82, 115–17
teachers 86
telephones 43, 64n51, 118, 124; telephone exchange, Crown Alley 45
Terrace School, Wellington (NZ) 100
territorial force: *see* army
'The boy deeds of Cúchulainn' (pageant) 144
theatrical troupes 100; *see also* opera troupes
theft: *see* looting
theology 33
Thornton, Captain Frank Joseph 45–6, 46n63, 47, 50, 70, 73, 80, 146, *24*
Thornton, Hugh 146

Thornton, Nora 46n63, 146
Thornton, Paddy 146
Threader, Harriet (later Garland) 61
The Times 90
Tipperary, County 146
tobacconists 136, 139
Togoland 61n38
Tone, Theobald Wolfe 31
Toronto 83
Townend, Paul (historian) 93
Townshend, Charles (historian) 30, 51, 78
trade, imperial 58
training, compulsory military 60; physical 60
Transvaal (South Africa) 56
Treaty, Anglo-Irish (1921) 28, 82–3
trench fever 83
Trinity College 17–20, 22–9, 30–5, 37–40, 42–54, 69–74, 76–83, 88–9, 104–5, 107–38, 140; board 22, 25, 34, 82; bursar, intransigence of 17; conjectured destruction of 19, 78–9; defensibility of 43, 76–7, 80, 124–5; rebel attack on 45–7, 50–1, 76–9, 108, 115, 142, 144; relationship with state 28–9, 34, 81; *see also* porters; provosts; steward
buildings: belfry (campanile) 124; Botany Bay 133, 137; chapel 77n11; Chemical Laboratory 125; Dining Hall 52, 124, 132; Engineering School 52, 132; Examination Hall 52, 124, 132; Fellows' Common Room 136; Front Building 91, 99, 113, 124; Front (Parliament) Square 89, 128, 137, *10*; guard room 114, 118; gymnasium 40; kitchen 129, 132; laboratories 134; library 28, 76, 78, 120, 124, 133; New Square 39, 131; orderly room 118; OTC headquarters 38–40, 40n21, 43, 45, 76, 82, 88, 112–13, 117–19, 123–7, *16*; Physical Laboratory 123–4; Provost's House 24, 38, 41n30, 52, 124, 133, 145; Regent House 128; School of Engineering 124, 133; Science Schools 124; west front 45, 47–9, 51, 69, 88, 144, *29*
gates 27n37, 119, 122, 140; Brunswick Street 74, 133; Front 29, 37–8, 43, 49, 76, 109–10, 117, *19*, *28*; Lincoln Place 38, 52, 76, 117, 123, 125; North 117
grounds: College Park 22, 40, 43, 52, 74, 112–13, 118–19, 124–5, 127–8, 131–2, *2*, *3*; cricket pavilion 132; Fellows' Garden 79, 132; OTC parade ground 43, 116, 119, 127; provost's garden 26, 113, 136; *see also* burials
troopships 63, 65
tropical diseases 61
Turkey 41–2, 63–4, 91–2; *see also* Gallipoli
Tweedy, Robert 26, 40n24; 51, 109
typhoid 36, 61, 64–6, 84, 101

Ulster 57, 83, 140
uniforms 36–7, 37n5, 39n18, 56, 57n7, 68, 71–2, 99, 105, *26*; rebel 91, 101, 105; *see also* hats
unionism 32, 34; Ulster 93
unionists 23, 83, 143
unions, trade 142
United Arts Club (Upper Fitzwilliam Street) 48n73
university, Dublin: *see* Trinity College; Catholic University of Ireland 33
United States 115

venereal disease 56–7, 83
Verdun, battle (1916) 138
Viceregal Lodge, Phoenix Park 23, 45n59
Vimy Ridge, battle (1917) 92
Volunteer Training Corps ('Gorgeous Wrecks') 39, 39n18, 40, 43, 88, 105, 117, 119, 121, 123; Irish Association of 23; Dependents' Fund 25

Volunteers: *see* Irish Volunteers; rebel forces
volunteering, army 56, 57n8, 58–9, 94; motivation for 59, 90

Wairarapa (NZ) 142
Walsh, Paddy 35
Walton-on-Thames (Surrey) 64, 85
war, civil 146; threat of 93–4; second Anglo-Boer War (1899–1902) 59–60
Ward, Sir Joseph G. 57–8
warfare, rules of 91, 91n68, 105; urban 89, 92, 122, 136
Waring, Private Edward 38, 48, 59–60, 63–7, 85–6, 145–6, *13*, *14*
warships 58; *see also* gunboats
Waterhouse, Gilbert (OTC lieutenant) 39–40, 49, 58, 117, 123, 138, 146
weapons 38, 120; *see also* artillery; machine guns; revolvers; rifles
Webb, David A. (botanist) 30
Webb, George Alfred 53n114, 56, 83
Wellington (NZ) 36, 60n33, 61–2, 64–5, 67, 85, 100, 144, *20*
Westland Row: *see* bridges; Dublin city streets; railways
Westmeath, County 52, 142
Westminster Abbey 67
Wexford, County 142
Whitcombe and Tombs (booksellers and publishers) 64
Who's who in New Zealand (1952) 143
Wicklow, County 63
William III, king, statue 128
Williamson, Benjamin 131
Willoughby, Roger 54
Wilmot, William 38
Wimborne, Alice Guest, Viscountess *2*
Winnipeg (Manitoba) 112
wire, barbed 139; *see also* barricades
women 73–4, 101, 116, 118, 139, 145–6; injured 90–1, 105; killed 99, 135; 'separation' (soldiers' wives) 87
Woods, Molly 48n73
Wylie, William 52, 78n21
Wynn's Hotel (Lower Abbey Street) 37, 70, 70n75, 84, 100, 102–3, *15*

Young Men's Christian Association 66
York 145; Yorkshire 146
Ypres (Belgium), Dublin likened to 105

Zeitoun (Egypt), camp 64
zeppelin raids 67